Computers
and
Family Therapy

Computers
and
Family Therapy

Charles R. Figley
Editor

The Haworth Press
New York

Computers and Family Therapy has also been published as *Journal of Psychotherapy & the Family,* Volume 1, Numbers 1/2, Spring/Summer 1985.

The Haworth Press, Inc., 28 East 22 Street, New York, NY 10010

Library of Congress Cataloging in Publication Data
Main entry under title:

Computers and family therapy.

Has also been published as Journal of psychotherapy & the family, volume 1, numbers 1/2, spring/summer 1985''—T.p. verso.
Includes bibliographies.
1. Family psychotherapy—Data processing.
I. Figley, Charles R., 1944- .
RC488.5.C66   1985   616.89'156'02854   85-956
ISBN 0-86656-375-X
ISBN 0-86656-408-X (pbk.)

Computers and Family Therapy

Journal of Psychotherapy & the Family
Volume 1, Numbers 1/2

CONTENTS

Foreword

The *Journal of Psychotherapy & the Family* was formed in 1983 to provide a comprehensive set of reference material focusing on the family for the general practitioner of psychotherapy. Other professional journals focusing either on family or psychotherapy topics adopt the more traditional structure: a balance of research, theory, and clinical articles on widely different topics. Psychotherapists rarely read these journals. Their needs are both practical and focused. They have little time to wade through scholarly journals to help them deal with various clinical challenges. Moreover, those who do not identify themselves as family therapists rarely read either family therapy journals or books; most of the concepts and theories of family therapy are alien to them.

The *Journal* is a bold and unique venture: to provide knowledge about family topics, issues, problems, and effective psychotherapeutic methods which are relevant and useful to practicing psychotherapists world-wide. In addition, however, it is our plan to publish a journal which is innovative, scholarly, accurate, on the cutting edge of clinical intervention, and oriented to the future. Each issue is published simultaneously in hardback for sale in bookstores and through book clubs and mail order requests.

Each issue/book and its editor(s) are selected by the Editor-in-Chief. This is done in consultation with the four-member Editorial Council (my colleagues here at Purdue: Wallace Denton, John Constantine, Fred Piercy, and Doug Sprenkle) and members of the *Journal*'s Editorial Board, an internationally known group of scholars and clinicians in the areas of psychotherapy and family. This elite group was listed earlier. The *Journal* and its books are refereed, since each one published is carefully screened by the Board to insure the highest quality possible.

Computers and Family Therapy is especially important since it is the *Journal*'s inaugural issue. Moreover, it is the first journal issue and book of its kind on this topic. The purpose of this fine collection is to provide a comprehensive overview of the interface between family therapy and the technology of the information age, especially computers.

Any new enterprise, especially a journal, is dependent on those who wish it to exist and flourish. We welcome your reactions to this collection and others which follow. We are now planning for future collections which also interface psychotherapy and the family and we need your guidance.

Charles R. Figley, PhD
Editor

Preface

The idea of assembling a collection of papers focusing computers emerged when the editor bought a Compaq computer. I became convinced that computer technology was an important innovation with revolutionary importance to both families and psychotherapy.

This collection represents the first attempt to bring together what is known about the interface among computers, psychotherapy, and the family client in a single work. Those who have contributed their work, represent the latest and best thinking in this area.

The collection begins with a comprehensive introduction and ends with an epilogue of the future. We would first like to recognize those who made this collection possible.

I am grateful to the *Journal of Psychotherapy & the Family*'s Editorial Board for their fine assistance. We are especially indebted to Drs. Carol M. Anderson, Dennis A. Bagarozzi, Thomas E. Clark, Stanley Cohen, Bernard Guerney, Jr., Arnold S. Gurman, Kenneth V. Hardy, Alan J. Hovestadt, Bradford P. Keeney, David Kniskern, Arnold A. Lazarus, William C. Nichols, David H. Olson, Richard C. Schwartz, Carlos E. Sluzki, Cheryl L. Storm, Karen S. Wampler, and Robert S. Weiss. Our excellent clerical staff, Beckey Harshman and Jean Grieves, and graduate assistants, Shirley Ann Segel, David Duerden, and Connie Wiemann were quite helpful. Our colleagues, too, were both helpful and encouraging: Wallace Denton, Head of the Marriage and Family Therapy Program in Purdue University's Department of Child Development and Family Studies, Robert A. Lewis, Department Head, and Norma Compton, Dean, School of Consumer and Family Sciences.

Finally, I would like to acknowledge the important contributions of John A. Constantine who wrote the Epilogue and served as my in-house consultant throughout this project. John knows much more than I do about this topic and I am sure will become a major pioneer in the development and utilization of computer technology in service to families and family professionals.

Charles R. Figley
W. Lafayette, Indiana

Computers
and
Family Therapy

Computers and Family Therapy:
An Introduction

Charles R. Figley

You who will read this collection are a special breed of psychotherapists. Special because you are interested in the growing importance and utility of computer technology. At the same time you are well aware of others who are openly hostile about the growing role of computers today. These skeptics are especially negative about the future of computers in psychotherapy practice.

Gary L. Pinkerton, who conducted one of the first scientific surveys of attitudes toward computers among human service professionals, and colleague, Paul R. Raffoul, recently offered a typical scenario:

> You are a clinician in a group practice that includes a psychiatrist, two psychologists, and an office manager. Being aware of current trends, you recommend to your colleagues that the group consider the use of microcomputers to assist in maintaining case records, help with word processing, operate a clinic billing system, and be used for client interviews, testing, and psychological evaluation. In the staff meeting you called to discuss this, you are surprised when confronted with strong resistance to the idea. The officer manager says that the current manual billing system works fine and that a computer would only make it more impersonal. The psychiatrist and psychologists ask about the use of the microcomputer for evaluation purposes and wonder how the office manager will be able to perform the task (assuming that since the computer is "office equipment," she will be in charge). When you try to explain that everyone in the office would be expected to be able to use the computer, you encounter even more questions and resistance. The psychiatrist says that he hasn't got time to learn anything else. One psychologist comments that his values won't allow him to be involved in a practice that uses a machine to do what humans should do. The other psychologist is interested, but comments, under his breath, that if he

Charles R. Figley, Ph.D., is Professor of Family Therapy/Studies, Department of Child Development and Family Studies, Purdue University and Director of the Traumatic Stress Research Program, Family Research Institute, 525 Russell St., W. Lafayette, Indiana 47906.

had wanted to learn about computers he wouldn't have become a psychologist. (1984, p. 62)

Though this situation may represent a more extreme case than the typical psychotherapy clinic, resistance to computers—irrespective of increasing use and decreasing cost—is still quite common (Pinkerton & Raffoul, 1982).

Yet, regardless of enthusiasm for its use in psychotherapy, even today computers impact nearly every facet of our life, including the intimate environment of our home. As Roland Wakefield notes in the first paper of this collection, not only is the family exposed to computer technology, it is becoming more autonomous and powerful as a result of it. With the home computer family members are able to earn income, do their banking, read the news, shop for goods, play games, and be educated. They are even able to receive psychotherapy, of sorts, through innovative computer programs, in the privacy of their own home.

PURPOSE

What are the implications for this new information technology for psychotherapy and the family client? The purpose of the collection is to provide a comprehensive overview of the interface among psychotherapy, the computer, and the family. In this introductory section we will note the specific objectives of the collection, note its central concepts and themes, and, in the end, speculate on the future use of computers in family therapy. But first it might be important to briefly discuss the rationale for this collection: to face the skeptics right away.

Why should we be interested in computers in general and in psychotherapy practice with families in particular? As the hypothetical staff members assert above, computers are impersonal, time-consuming to learn, and have questionable relevance to human services which require sensitivity to feelings. This collection is based on the assumption that computers are, indeed, an important and useful tool for the clinician. Just as television revolutionized education and video recordings revolutionized clinical training, the microcomputer has the potential for revolutionizing clinical practice, especially family therapy. Most certainly, however, computer technology has already dramatically improved research, assessment, and diagnosis (Apter & Westby, 1973; Slavin, 1982; Schwartz, 1984).

OBJECTIVES

As noted earlier, the purpose of this work is to provide a comprehensive overview of the interface among psychotherapy, computers, and the family. Accordingly, four over-arching objectives which are linked to the organization of this collection are to: (1) discuss and illustrate the current and future impact of computers on family life in general and families seeking psychotherapy in particular; (2) highlight the utility of computers to family clinicians in terms of office and clinical case management; (3) describe and demonstrate computer-assisted assessment and diagnosis; and (4) review the current and future potential for computer-assisted family therapy and family therapists training.

ORGANIZATION AND CONTENT

This collection includes 11 papers written by scholars from a variety of disciplines. Most are practicing psychotherapists who utilize computers in their work on a daily basis. The papers are arranged in this collection, to a large extent, according to the objectives noted above.

The first paper, by Roland Wakefield, "Computers, Family Empowerment and Psychotherapy: Conceptual Overview and Outlook," as noted earlier, suggests that families with computers have increased and will continue to increase significantly in the future. As a result clinicians who work with families or with individuals about family matters must become more acquainted with computer technology not only to improve their own practice, but to understand more fully the lives of their clients. Wakefield notes, for example, that computers lead to empowerment for families, since it enables them to be in touch with and more fully manipulate their world from their own home. He cites government estimates that by 1990 home computers will be nearly universal. And as early as 1987 home computer educational materials will account for 70% of the billion dollar computerized educational materials which will be used largely in the home. The "downside" of this computer revolution in the home, however, is the emotional friction among family members as a result of its empowerment. As a result psychotherapists can play a key role in helping the family adjust to this technological revolution, while, at the same time, taking advantage of it as a clinical resource.

The next paper, by Karen Levitan and Elizabeth Willis, "Barriers to Practitioners' Use of Information Technology Utilization: A Discussion and Results of a Study," acknowledges the great potential of computers for psychotherapy and reports on a recent survey of current utilization of computers by psychotherapists. Their survey is the first of its kind. Given the growing power and influence of computer and information technologies, they assessed not only utilization, but also the perceived barriers to utilization. Their findings were both encouraging and discouraging. Irrespective of the potential benefits, their survey revealed that relatively few clinicians are currently using computers. Yet, the apparent barriers to utilization appear to be temporary, since most of the reasons given for not buying and using computers are cost (57.8%) and size of practice

(54.7%). It appears that it is only a matter of time until both the price and applicability reaches a satisfactory level for most clinicians to seriously consider using a computer in their work. Indeed, this notion of clinician applicability is especially important in their summary of the individual interviews they conducted with a portion of the survey sample. Perhaps most telling is their observation that most of those they interviewed were not very concerned about "how to keep structured records and data in a form that could be used for more effective diagnosis, planning, evaluation, norm development and research" (p. 13). With greater emphasis today on outcome research and accountability—especially from clients' employers and health insurers, the need for such structure will certainly increase. Thus, the utility and utilization of computers will increase.

The next paper illustrates such utilization. Philip H. Friedman's essay on "The Use of Computers in Marital and Family Therapy" discusses one psychotherapist's experiences in incorporating this new technology in clinical practice with families. His initial interest in computers was primarily assessment: to administer various psychometric tests to his clients using the computer and to provide them with a printout of the results quickly. Moreover, he was interested in the inter-relationships among the various instruments he was using and the change in scores throughout the treatment program. Simple enough. His essay, however, notes his progress in gradually learning and applying state-of-the-art computer technology in his private practice, in addition to assessment: client information and education, clinical case notes, financial record-keeping and billing, games, communication, statistics, and marketing/media relations. His précis of the adoption of computer technology into clinical practice is simply an inventory of pleasures. He notes the challenges and limitations of this new technology—indeed the extraordinary frustrations, especially as a neophyte. It is an interesting profile of one clinician in private practice who has discovered that this new computer technology is cost-effective and enhances the quality of his clinical services.

The fourth paper also discusses the introduction and utilization of computer technology in clinical practice, but at a clinic level in the process of clinical training. "A Computer Data-Based Management System for a Family Therapy Clinic," by D. Eugene Mead, and associates presents one clinic's experience of computerizing clinical assessment, practice, and training. Mead describes Brigham Young University's Marriage and Family Therapy Clinic and its need for a computer system which is both flexible and complex. Similar to Friedman's system, ideal for individual therapists in private practice, BYU's system enables clinicians to utilize the computer to perform many clinical functions. In addition, however, the BYU system enables numerous clinicians to enter various kinds of clinical notes in English prose (versus "computereze") organized around a Client Data Base and Treatment Plan. The program then, together with various assessment data, provides various clinical decision options for the clinician. These data are not only useful to the individual clinician, but also to clinical supervisors as they monitor student clinician and case progress. Also described is the system's utility as a clinical research tool.

The next group of papers, 5-8, focus on computer-assisted assessment whereby clients interact directly with the computer. Larry Constantine, in "Computer-Aided Assessment: Design Considerations," first discusses the challenges of assessment in psychotherapy, especially when focusing on interpersonal relationships and systems. Next he discusses an approach to selecting an assessment system that is right for the clinician by first choosing the problem, then selecting the applications, such as intake data collection, tests and measures, games and tasks. He then discusses basic designed considerations for putting together clinical needs with technological capabilities. Here he discusses and illustrates the meaning of computer systems being "user-friendly" and goes on to discuss more technical matters relevant to family assessment, such as modularity, hierarchy, generality, and programming style. The latter part of the paper presents two diverse illustrations of systems of computer-aided assessment: the PARA (Paradigm and Regime Assessment) and the Micro-Kvebaek. He shows quite elegantly that computer-aided assessment can go well beyond current measurement techniques. Indeed, such systems have the potential for changing the nature and effectiveness of psychotherapy in general and family work in particular.

The next paper, by David H. Olson, begins where Constantine's paper ends, presenting a method of assessing relationships in families. "Microcomputers for Couple and Family Assessment: ENRICH and Other Inventories," begins by promoting the numerous advantages of computers for both the clinician and clients. After reviewing computer hardware options necessary for computer-assisted assessment, Olson briefly notes both the basic functions of computers in clinical practice and the range of computer-assisted inventories available. The latter section of the paper is an extensive overview of the 125-item ENRICH program of marital relationship assessment. The description includes the measure's history, method of development, estimates of reliability and validity, and the types and meaning of scores generated from the instrument.

Similarly, Marlene W. Lehtinen and Gerald W. Smith present anther computer-assisted marital assessment program in their paper, "MATESIM: Computer-Assisted Marriage Analysis for Family Therapists." They begin with a brief case study of Mike and Mary who seek marital therapy and then note the importance of precise and accurate information about the marital system for developing an effective therapy program. After noting the basic rationale, assumptions, and theoretical basis for the MATESIM program, Lehtinen and Smith note the process of developing the program and its current, two-version structure. MATESIM

I, they explain, is similar to Olson's PREPARE, in that they both allow individuals to make more informed mate selection decisions. MATESIM II, in contrast, is used by therapists to obtain and analyze information about the marital relationship. One unique feature is the "therapist reference" which allows the therapist to compare his or her priority weightings of various marital characteristics with other marital therapists.

The final paper in this group focusing on assessment is "The Multiple Vantage Profile: A Computerized Assessment of Social Organizations in Family Therapy," by Brent J. Atkinson, Paul N. McKenzie, and Bradford P. Keeney, presents another type of computer-assisted family assessment. In contrast to Olson's assessment, this assessment program is exclusively for the family in treatment. After discussing the importance of assessing the "full complexity of social organization of systems in treatment" they note their rationale for developing a computer-assisted assessment system for marital and family therapy. Their Multiple Vantage Profile (MVP) was designed to measure the social organization of families in treatment by assessing member perception of emotional closeness in family dyadic relationships, including relationships between the family therapist and each family member. Following discussion of data collection methods, the authors discuss methods of data organization and utilization in the course of clinical intervention, including changes in perception. The final section of the paper discusses the role of the therapist as part of the system in treatment, a role which has been widely recognized as important, but rarely analyzed.

In the ninth paper in this collection, "Knowledge Utilization and Decision Support Systems in Family Therapy," Gerald J. Bostwick, Jr. presents another way computers can be useful to clinicians. Recognizing the quickly expanding knowledge scholarly and clinical literature in psychotherapy of family treatment, Bostwick provides a brief overview of a framework for identifying, synthesizing, and applying this knowledge to clinical practice. This framework is based on earlier knowledge utilization approaches and includes a series of steps which culminate in the development of information immediately useful to the practitioner. The process includes five major steps, beginning with identification and recording of substantive findings and ending with deducing practice guidelines (i.e., prescriptive statements which guide intervention). The latter section of the paper demonstrates the utility of computers in facilitating the process of knowledge utilization, especially in family therapy, using a decision support system (DSS). Bostwick illustrates such a program, described as the Family Therapy Information Consultant (FTIC), as a fictitious therapist utilizes the system to assist her in the initial stages of treating a family.

Nicholas S. Aradi, in his paper "The Application of Computer Technology to Behavioral Marital Therapy," discusses the beneficial use of the computer in the three major facets of behavioral marital therapy (BMT): the intake interview, assessment, and treatment. Similar to Lehtinen and Smith, Aradi argues that a behavioral therapy is ideal for computerization since both require specificity and assume a cognitive, algorithmic process of human behavior. Similar to previous chapters in this collection (e.g., Olson, Constantine, and Friedman), Aradi notes the general advantages and disadvantages of computerizing clinical practice. In the latter section of his paper, he discusses the ethics of computerization of psychotherapy. He notes, for example, that clients should be given the option of using or not using computer-assisted therapy and not assume that everyone would perceive its use as de-humanizing or anxiety producing. He rejects the concern about confidentiality in computer use, since it is a problem which is both manageable and not limited to computers.

The paper, "Teaching Systems Psychotherapy with Micro-computers: A Creative Approach," by Randy Gerson, extends computer technology to psychotherapy training. After a brief discussion of the general limitations and advantages of "dumb computers," Gerson notes that "systems psychotherapists" should be especially impressed with computers, since they are "concerned with the interactional and non-linear flow of information that occurs within family systems." One relevant application he describes is THE FAMILY RECORDER, a computer program which generates genograms. Especially relevant to teaching about and illustrating family structure and transgenerational patterns in families, a genogram is a multi-generational diagram of family relations. Next, Gerson describes a computer program for training in family therapy by simulating family interaction. The interactional program allows the trainee to manage a simulated family and learn about the possible likely reactions a family may have to his or her different therapeutic interventions. The final section discusses the future of computer technology—especially software—which will be available to families in the near future. Such technology will enable families to become much more autonomous; be able to educate, analyze, and maintain important records for themselves. Here we come full circle and return to the notion of family empowerment promoted by Wakefield in the first paper of this collection.

The Epilogue, written by John Constantine, discusses the promise of computer technology for family treatment in the future. He suggests, for example, that programs similar to those used with video-arcade type games would be useful in family research and assessment and psychotherapy training. He speculates on the potential for developing "expert systems" for improving computer-assisted psychotherapy and the utility for treating sexual dysfunction, and the potential for working with children.

At the end of this collection we have included a 93-term glossary to assist the reader with the new, and often baffling, terminology of computers. We hope that the Glossary and this introduction is useful to you in reading this collection and managing the challenges of the information age.

REFERENCES

Apter, M. J., & Westby, G. (Eds.). (1972). *The Computer in Psychology.* New York: John Wiley & Sons.

Pinkerton, G. L., & Raffoul, P. R. (1984). Professional colleagues: Confronting the attitudes of professionals toward microcomputers. In M. D. Schwartz (Ed.), *Using computers in clinical practice: Psychotherapy and mental health applications* pp. 61-66. N.Y.: Haworth.

Schwartz, M. D. (Ed.). (1984). *Using computers in clinical practice: Psychotherapy and mental health applications.* N.Y.: Haworth.

Slavin, S. (Ed.). (1982). *Applying computers in social service and mental health agencies: A guide to selecting equipment, procedures, and strategies.* N.Y.: Haworth.

Computers, Family Empowerment, and the Psychotherapist: Conceptual Overview and Outlook

Rowan A. Wakefield

ABSTRACT. Driven by rapid technological advances and a dynamic marketplace, widespread use of microcomputers by families and psychotherapists is inevitable by the end of the decade. Availability of self-help programs based on artificial intelligence expert systems for most family needs normally provided by professionals, and the use of home computers as a new communications medium will give families broad new powers in the emerging information society and change significantly their relationship to services providers, including psychotherapists. The nature of this new relationship is examined, including problems caused by computer use, as well as opportunities created by computers for both families and psychotherapists.

The *Journal of Psychotherapy & the Family* meets an urgent need which is well documented by Levitan and Willis (pp. 21), and which we have frequently discussed in the *American Family*—namely, the need to fill the knowledge gap between the great potential of the microcomputer on the one hand, and what is known and even less used of that potential, on the other, especially by families and psychotherapists. I also see a real value in the emphasis of this first issue on clinical applications, rather than on office management applications.

As editor of *American Family,* my primary concern over the past several years has been the impact of increasing home computer use on families, on the professions who serve them, and on technology and society at large. There is little cohesive research to date on any of these subjects because the home computer revolution is so new, and it is dif-

Rowan A. Wakefield has an AB degree from Williams College. He is president of American Family, Inc., an affiliate of the Youth Policy Institute at the National Center for Family Studies at The Catholic University of America. He is a director of the World Future Society, Bethesda, Maryland; a member of the advisory board of the Family Therapy Practice Center, Washington, D.C., and the family affiliate of the national computer network of the Equal Relationship Institute, Los Angeles, California. As senior editor of *American Family,* the national newsletter on family policy and programs which he founded in 1977, he writes a monthly column on Families and Telematics. His mailing address is Youth Policy Institute, Cardinal Station, Washington, D.C. 20064.

ficult to track recent and current research, since it is scattered across so many academic disciplines. *American Family* (1984a) has, therefore, been functioning as an informal information clearinghouse on such research in progress, some of which I draw on for this chapter.

There are dozens, if not hundreds, of introductory books on computers for home and business use, and an even greater number of computer-related magazines and newsletters. Two books that I have recommended to my readers are *The Personal Computer Book,* by Peter McWilliams (1982), and *The Complete Handbook of Personal Communications: Everything You Need to Know to Go Online With the World,* by Alfred Glossbrenner (1983).

In this introductory chapter I will present a conceptual overview and a forecast of how the computer will inevitably become a "member" of the family. We suggest here that computers are empowering families in a variety of ways, and changing the relationship of the family and the psychotherapist.[1]

THE COMPUTER FAMILY MEMBER:
AN EMPOWERER OF FAMILIES

The home computer will rapidly become a member of the family for many reasons. First and foremost, the computer and the family have the potential for an ideal marriage. Indeed the family may be the only institution in society with the ability to take advantage of virtually all of the computer's potentials: as a fast calculator, an information organizer par excellence; with a word processor, as a typewriter with a powerful and versatile memory; as an entertainer, guardian of the home, and baby sitter; and as an aid in household management and finances.

Moreover, using increasingly sophisticated expert systems programs, it can function in the role of tutor and teacher, doctor, lawyer, therapist and counselor, accountant, travel agent, and stockbroker, as well as in a variety of other professional roles.

In the fields of music and the arts, it can stimulate creativity in promising new areas for all family members by enabling them to develop musical scores and draw pictures. When linked to the world's telecommunication systems, the home computer opens up a whole new domain of communications: within the extended family, with the community, with the whole world. Linked to encyclopedic information sources and rapidly increasing data bases, having access to complex but affordable simulation programs, and in direct contact with elected representatives and government officials, the home computer can greatly increase the family's participation and importance in the political process. Finally, many of the wide array of business programs which are available, and which are constantly being refined, are ideal for use in work done at home and in home business, a part of the economy projected to burgeon in the next decade.

In the second place, an aggressive marketplace and technological advances are creating home computer buying nearly irresistible, with appeals to parents to help their children prepare for college and a career. There is an inevitability about the computer's influence on the family and the psychotherapy. The Census Bureau, for example, projects 96.8 million American households by 1990, with as many as half earning more than $20,000 annually. This strong, magnetic marketplace can make home computers almost universal by 1990, especially as they become even more powerful, more versatile, smaller, and easier with which to communicate. This will happen as the Japanese, in particular, penetrate the low-cost end of the market, and as more utilitarian programs become available for virtually every type of family activity.

Thus, it is expected that the home computer will change from a novelty or luxury to a necessity. We are already seeing the emergence of both of these trends, with the number of computers in homes increasing from almost zero at the decade's beginning to about 14 million this year. The home and personal computer software market is more than doubling in size each year.

EDUCATION/HOMEWORK

How will computers be used in the home? Last year families bought about $300 million worth of home education computer programs. Schools bought barely one tenth of this amount. Even though the quality of many home computer education programs is poor, it appears that the situation is steadily improving as competition increases and home and school users become more sophisticated. Indeed, Futures Computing[2] the Richardson, Texas market research firm, projects a billion-dollar educational software market by 1987, with home computer use accounting for 70 percent of it. *American Family* (1984b) projects an even larger home education computer market.

The home computer phenomenon is so new that there is no definitive research yet on its impact on families. Several preliminary studies using small, relatively nonrepresentative samples do indicate increased time spent on school homework in families with computers compared to children without them. This trend shows up in studies by Giacuinta, Ely and Smith-Burke (1984) of the New York University School of Education, Health and Nursing, and Arts Professions, and by Vitalari and Venkatesh (1984) at the Graduate School of Management at the University of California at Irvine. In this study, for example, 24 percent of the families spent increased time on homework. Perhaps more important,

67.4 percent of the families showed a decrease in time spent watching television, the biggest single change in time use among all the families studied by the Irvine researchers.

FRICTION

Introduction of the computer into the family environment may cause friction for a variety of reasons. In the first place, its use requires time in amounts frequently underestimated. That time must come from other family activities, time together with other family members, as more time is spent alone with the computer. All of these changes can cause friction as they alter family life-styles. As Vitalari and Venkatesh (1984) show, some of these changes in time use are quite marked (see Table 1).

Another possible cause of friction is competition for access to the computer, again a result of time limitations. Preliminary studies, such as research done at the University of Houston by David Gottlieb and Christopher Dede (1984), do not indicate this to be a major source of family problems. Increasingly families will acquire more than one computer and evolve rules for computer use where there is competition. We should be aware that for children, access to computers at school is limited to about a half-hour a week on the national average. This is in stark comparison with home use, especially if the child is persuasive.

Efforts toward identifying ways in which increased home computer use will alter family life-styles and values over time should prove a fruitful

Table 1

Changes in Time Allocation in Families With Home Computers

	Decrease	Same	Increase
Watching television	67.4%	31.4%	2.5%
Hobbies	43.4	48.0	8.6
Sleeping	26.3	73.0	.8
Outdoor recreation	22.1	76.7	1.2
Leisure (time with family)	18.9	76.9	4.3
Reading (not comp.)	17.6	69.8	12.6
Leisure (time with friends)	15.5	73.9	10.6
Time spent alone	11.9	53.5	34.6
Studying homework	6.9	69.0	24.1

activity for researchers. And their results will have important implications for psychotherapists working with families who use computers.

AS BUSINESS ASSISTANT IN WORK AT HOME

Use of the computer for home business—for consulting, operating an independent family or home business, or working at home for an outside employer—is increasing, with most users being women: single parents, displaced homemakers, mothers in dual-earner families, retirees, and others. Self-employment among women, much of it is home based, is increasing rapidly—currently at a rate 6 times the rate for men (Gillis, 1983).

Marion Behr (*American Family,* 1983), vice president of the National Alliance of Home-Based Business Women, estimates that as many as 15 to 20 million women are potential home-based workers. She believes that use of the personal computer has turned home work from an activity viewed as marginal or trivial by economists, to one that increasingly must be viewed as real business. Some experts project that home work may account for 25 percent to 35 percent of all paid work by the year 2000.

Working at home with the computer may cause friction and increasing stress, primarily because of the lack of socialization opportunities—the cabin fever syndrome. This is especially true for women working at home and caring for small children at the same time, an option some women prefer to placing their children in child care facilities, or choose because they have no alternative.

Some professionals and companies have found partial solutions to this problem. AT&T is experimenting with an executive program which involves working part-time at home, while linked to the office by computer, and working part-time in the office. Other dual-career professionals I know can afford to spend more time socializing in the evenings and on weekends as a result of the increased productivity of working at home. They spend no time commuting and less money on luncheons and clothes.

AS SURROGATE PROFESSIONAL

American Family (1984b) estimates that about half of the 1990 $12 billion home computer software market will be used for what is termed ''self-help'' programs in education, health promotion and medicine, therapy and counseling, and legal financial religious, and travel services. Indeed, in virtually every area where professionals have developed computer programs in their fields, most of them never intended their programs for direct consumer use. Many of the assessment tests developed for use by mental health professionals would fall into this category. We touch on the computer as surrogate clinician later in this chapter.

There are already on the market do-it-yourself-at-home legal software programs for preparing simple divorce agreements, living together contracts, powers of attorney, and various business contracts. There are programs that enable you to prepare your income tax returns. In the religious field there are more than 155 companies marketing software. While much of it deals with church administration, there is a growing amount, some of it dependent on the entire Bible stored in an interactive computer program, designed to help meet individual spiritual needs. Of the self-help areas mentioned, some of the greatest growth will occur in the health promotion/medical fields. We estimate this conservatively to be a $1.8 billion market by 1990.

The United States Surgeon General (1979) recently estimated that increasing life expectancy is 70 percent dependent on the information we get and use, 20 percent dependent on genetic factors, and only 10 percent dependent on intervention of the traditional medical system. The rate at which Americans over the past decade have been acquiring and using health promotion and disease prevention information to change their life-styles has confounded the experts, and has seriously thrown off national life expectancy forecasts.

There is already a brisk home computer software market for diet and exercise programs, with more sophisticated health risk appraisal programs and diagnosis and treatment programs entering the market. A recent survey by the American Library Association (Roose, 1984) of use of on-line programs in libraries shows some surprising results. The leading use was by lay people tapping into the National Library of Medicine data base, seeking information they were unable to get from their physicians. As home computer use with modems increases, families can access this information directly from their homes, as well as tapping information from a large variety of other computerized public domain information sources (e.g., local libraries, phone directories, department store catalogs).

THE HOME COMPUTER AS FAMILY COMMUNICATOR

Little is known about the use of home computers for communications purposes, since relatively few home computer users as yet have modems for access to other computers through telephone lines. But the use of the computer as a family member may bring very great benefits within the family and in the family's relations with the world outside. Although the popular stereotype of the computer presents it as fostering isolation, dehumanization, and fragmentation of the family, there is growing evidence, largely anecdotal in the absence of any substantive research as yet, that this is not true. Indeed, just the opposite may be true.

I know several grandparents who share their computers with their grandchildren when they visit, or network with them at other times. ''The family who computes together, stays together,'' they tell me.

The home computer can be and is being used to make and develop personal acquaintances through networking, computer conferencing, use of specialized computer bulletin boards, and various special users' groups offered by the new information utilities such as The Source[3] in McLean, Virginia, and CompuServe[4] in Columbus, Ohio. These activities present new avenues for personal communication and opportunities for enduring relationships at a time when many other forces in our high tech society seem to mitigate against personal communication and relationships.

Though potentially dehumanizing, on-line computer communication is by nature egalitarian. No one knows if you are old or young, black or white, rich or poor, male or female (if you don't give your name), or handicapped. This permits almost pure intellectual communication, an important and often powerful form of human interaction, and one providing a potentially solid foundation for subsequent relationships, including personal meetings.

For many—the homebound, the widow, the elderly, the divorced, and the single person—on-line communication can and does reduce loneliness.

The growing popularity of computer dating services such as Dial-Your-Match Bulletin Board and The Source's Dial-A-Date (Chin, 1984) demonstrates a variety of advantages of the computer as a facilitator of human relationships:

1. Getting to know someone via computer is less risky and intimidating than traditional dating.
2. Strong feelings can develop, demonstrating that this kind of communication is much more powerful than most people realize.
3. Users can develop legitimate emotional ties, often leading, for example to marriage.
4. ''This type of medium enhances your candor of opinion . . . . Because no one sees you, you are freer to express yourself to others,'' writes Elaine Kerr, author with Roxanne Hiltz of *Computer-Mediated Communications Systems* (Chin, 1984, p. 29).

DEFINING NEW SOCIAL STRUCTURES

At universities where universal student ownership of computers has been mandated, some faculty and administrators are noticing apparently significant changes in social structures in the dormitories. There is a tendency to move away from class (freshmen, sophomores, etc.), race, or gender groupings, toward pairs and groups with shared interests revealed by computer uses. This is fostered by cooperation on joint programs accessed through the university's mainframe computer.

USE AS AN OFFICE RESOURCE

There are now computer programs to meet virtually all the office needs of the mental health professional: data base systems in patient care, computerized medical records, laboratory and drug information systems, integrated clinical and administrative systems, and billing and payroll systems. And there is also a growing number of professional associations and publications to help keep the mental health professional current on what's available or being developed. The recently incorporated American Association for Medical Systems and Informatics,[5] periodicals such as *Computers in Psychiatry and Psychology,*[6] *Physician's Computer Monthly,*[7] *Journal of Medical Systems,*[8] and *Journal of Clinical Computing,*[9] and books such as *Applying Computers in Social Service & Mental Health Agencies* (Slavin, 1982), *Using Computers in Clinical Practice* (Schwartz, 1984) are examples. Electronic data bases such as those of GTE Telenet's Medical Information Network[10] and the National Library of Medicine[11] provide on-line access to administrative and clinical literature, drug and disease information, and information on medical procedures.

Of growing importance are those computer systems offering total integration of administrative and clinical functions, such as that developed by Wesleyan Computer Data Processing, Inc. of Corpus Christi, Texas, which specializes in medical office hardware and software. Its totally integrated Medical Officer Management (MOM)[12] offers computer programming in BASIC, medical record keeping, and on-line data base management allowing multiuser, simultaneous access. It provides rapid CRT entry and recall, a fool-proof backup system, extensive documentation of programs to allow the last user to make minor modifications and expansion of all MOM functions. MOM can be used by single or multiple providers, permitting integration with other medical disciplines, such as pharmacy, laboratory services, physical therapy, and nursing. MOM is capable of storing appointments for 99 providers and monitoring their accounts payable and receivable separately or cumulatively.

THE COMPUTER AS A CHANGE AGENT

On the basis of a recent extensive survey, Levitan and Willis (pp. 21) note a significant lack of understanding of computer technology among mental health practitioners, and to the relative scarcity of practitioners who are beginning to use computers extensively for office management and clinical purposes.

In the fall of 1983, *American Family* (1984a) conducted a much smaller, but future-oriented survey of mental health professionals with actual computer experience. We compiled the views of 23 psychiatrists, psychologists, social workers, and other mental health professionals. We were especially interested in the role of psychotherapists who have extensively used self-help computer programs with their clients. Understandably, responses varied widely. All saw the potential for computers changing the routine of therapists and counselors. They noted such activities as intake interviews and histories, assessments, diagnosis, treatment, and patient self-education being especially appropriate for computer assistance. In addition, several saw advantages in family-generated computer programs for teaching and professional training, as indicated in others in this volume.

At one extreme were those who saw increasing family use of mental health self-help programs, with or without professional guidance, as an opportunity to raise the quality of professional services. They expressed the following ideas:

1. As families take over simpler and more routine services (like intake exams), the professional (a) would have more time to keep up with important new developments in the field, for example, in mind and brain research; or (b) could spend more time with clients on more serious problems, or could see more clients.

2. Professionals could produce and market quality computer programs for family use with and without professional guidance, thus helping assure a high level of quality in the mental health software field, and extending greatly the number of families and individuals who could avail themselves of the professionals services.

3. Our one artificial intelligence authority foresaw the computer, using expert systems, taking over 85 percent of the professional's services, leaving only 15 percent—the "real expertise,"—for the human professional. With the advent of the next generation of computers, he foresaw inroads being made on the 15 percent!

The "moderates" in our survey each saw specific instances where family or family members could constructively use self-help programs, usually with professional guidance. In addition to intake exams, these included assessments, histories, and some diagnostic and treatment programs, including a variety in sex therapy, parenting, anxiety and depression treatment, and client education, with the latter used to deal with alcohol and drug abuse, sexual dysfunctions, and some family violence cases. Several saw the computer's value in marriage analysis and marriage preparation, as do the authors of some of the following chapters. There was general agreement on the value of computer programs for family use for health promotion and disease prevention.

In contrast, others were deeply concerned about the computers' "invasion" into the uniquely personal relationship of the therapist and client, and who thus saw increasing family use of self-help programs as (a) a potential danger to families, and (b) a threat to jobs in the profession.

A few of these professionals, incidentally, saw computer networking as a very effective way of keeping abreast of new developments and interacting with peers.

Other issues raised by those surveyed included: (1) the urgent need for an objective evaluation system for the proliferating mental health software on the market; (b) ethical issues arising from the use of the computer; (c) questions of confidentiality; (d) privacy; (e) security; and (f) quality control of software.

FUTURE OUTLOOK

Expanded use of home computers by families can lead to new and exciting forms of family empowerment. This will require taking advantage of the computer's great versatility, of the growing number of practical computer programs for virtually every type of family activity, and of the computer's power as a communications medium. Such expanded use can lead to greater family self-reliance, and to more effective family and individual participation in society's social economic, educational, cultural, and political processes. This trend means bringing back into the family those functions which had gradually been assumed by large public and private institutions and bureaucracies since the beginning of the industrial revolution, functions such as work, education, and health care. What is now important is the fact that these functions can be brought back into the family without necessarily sacrificing job security, literacy or life expectancy. Indeed, many of these functions may be enhanced when carried out within families, aided by the computer.

Thus family empowerment means a change in the relationship of families to professionals. Aided by improving computer technology and more sophisticated programs, families will have more control over their environment and the services they buy. For psychotherapists, this can mean a rising level of professional standards and performance. As empowered families use computers to perform the more routine functions, such as assessment and diagnosis, psychotherapists will have more time to devote to the more difficult and challenging tasks in treatment, which require face-to-face contact.

Moreover, it may also mean spending more time on problems generated by increasing family use of computers. In addition to the stresses caused by the introduction of this new technology into the family, there are problems arising from the shift in authority in families as the young teach their elders about computers. There are problems of computer addiction and networking addiction, problems of a widening gap between the information-rich and the information-poor, and the problems of increased isolation and of fragmentation of the family. On the other side, there is potential for using the home computer to improve family relationships by forcing people to come to grips with time spent together. Computer use may also result in less time spent passively in front of the television, and more time spent thinking, linearly or otherwise, with interactive computer programs.

But it can also mean using computers more extensively in office management and in clinical practice to work more efficiently on these newly generated problems or on more complex older ones.

Expanded family use of home computers can mean greater opportunities for research by the family psychotherapist. Continuing family and societal changes suggest an urgent need for much greater understanding of the impact of home computer use on families, of the changing relationship of professionals to families, and of the emerging new role of empowered families in society.

So far we see very little research into the home computer revolution. What there is focuses mainly on the impact of high technology on families. This is important and needs to be pursued, but we also need research on the changing relationship of the family/clients to the professional, and on the emerging new role of empowered families in society. In this last need, incidentally, the Japanese appear to be interested and are undertaking some studies.

Will empowered families develop a form of superindividualism, especially as they use the great communications potential of the home computer? Or will they use their power for the common good? Playing out the former scenario could lead to a realization of the French historian de Tocqueville's fears that American individualism, growing unchecked, could end in a form of democratic anarchy. What will be the role of the family psychotherapist in this unfolding drama?

NOTES

1. My perspective is that of a journalist and editor of *American Family,* not a scholar.

2. In *Personal Computer Educational Software Market,* March 17, 1983, by Future Computing, Inc., 900 Canyon Creek Center, Richardson, Texas 75080.

3. Source Telecomputing Corporation, 1616 Anderson Road, McLean, Virginia 22102.

4. Compuserve, 5000 Arlington Center Blvd., Columbus, Ohio 43220.

5. AAMSI, Suite 402, 4405 East-West Highway, Bethesda, Maryland 20814.

6. *Computers in Psychiatry/Psychology,* 26 Trumbull Street, New Haven, Connecticut 06511.

7. *Physician Computer Monthly,* American Health Consultants, Inc., 67 Peachtree Park Drive, NE, Atlanta, Georgia 30309.

8. *Journal of Medical Systems,* Plenum Publishing Corporation, 233 Spring Street, New York, New York 10013.

9. *Journal of Clinical Computing,* 166 Morris Avenue, Buffalo, New York 14214.

10. *GTE Telenet Communications Corporation,* 8229 Boone Blvd., Vienna, Virginia 22180.

11. MEDLARS Management, National Library of Medicine, Bethesda, Maryland 20209.

12. Wesleyan Computer Data Processing, Inc., 3138 South Alameda, Corpus Christi, Texas 78404.

REFERENCES

American Family. (1983). VI:2, p. 6.

American Family. (1984a). Impacts of home computer use on professions serving families. Monograph No. 1: Mental Health Professions. Washington, D.C.: Author, January.

American Family. (1984b). 1990 home computer software market forecast No. 2: The $3 billion educational software market. Washington, D.C.: Author, June.

Census Bureau. . . .

Chin, K. (1984). Dial your match: Looking for Mr. Right. *InfoWorld,* July.

Giacuinta, J. B., Ely, M., & Smith-Burke, T. (1984). Educational Microcomputing at home: A comparative analysis of twenty families. A paper presented at the National Institute of Education Conference on "Computers in the Home," Washington, D.C., June 7-8.

Gillis, P. (1983). *Entrepreneurial Mothers,* Noted in USA Today, December 19.

Glossbrenner, A. (1983). *The complete handbook of personal computer communications: Everything you need to go online with the world.* New York: St. Martin's Press.

Gottlieb, D., & Dede, C. (1984). *The social role of the personal computer: Implications for familial mental health.* Policy Discussion Paper Series. Houston: Center for Public Policy Discussion.

McWilliams, P. (1982). *The personal computer book.* Los Angeles: Prelude.

Roose, T. (1984). Who are the consumers? What are the questions? *Library Journal,* February 1, 154-155.

Schwartz, M. D. (1984). *Using computers in clinical practice: Psychotherapy and mental health applications.* New York: Haworth.

Slavin, S. (1982). *Applying computers in social service and mental health agencies: A guide to selecting equipment, procedures and strategies.* New York: Haworth.

United States Surgeon General. (1979). *Healthy people: The Surgeon General's report on health promotion and disease prevention.* Washington, D.C.: DHEW (PHS) Publication No. 79-55071.

Vitalari, N., & Venkatesh, A. (1984). *Computing in the home: Shifts in the time allocation patterns of households.* Irvine: Public Policy Research Organization, University of California, Irvine.

Barriers to Practitioners' Use of Information Technology Utilization: A Discussion and Results of a Study

Karen B. Levitan, PhD
Elizabeth A. Willis

ABSTRACT. This article examine the barriers to therapists' utilization of microcomputer technology by describing the results of a preliminary study. A mail survey to a convenience sample primarily in the Washington, DC, area, plus in-depth interviews, a literature review, a technology assessment and professional networking served as complimentary methods for data collection. The results focus attention on two areas which are generally foreign to the community of therapists: the marketplace and management training. Concluding recommendations outline steps that therapists, educators, and system and software developers might take in reducing the barriers to microcomputer technology utilization.

One of the major themes of this issue is that the practice of family therapy in an information based society requires the therapist to be both knowledgeable about the computer, especially as it impacts families, and also comfortable with the computer, knowing how to handle its constraints and take advantage of its capabilities. This theme has been explored in detail by Wakefield and Messolonghites (1984) and discussed in the popular computer press by Caruso (1984). Among the most prominent reasons cited for incorporating the computer into family therapy include: the increasing use of computers by families for family tasks, addressed in detail by Scharf (1984); the proliferation of self-help software available to families for stress management, alcohol and drug abuse, health promotion (Wakefield and Messolonghites; Caruso); and the capacity of the computer for organizing and managing the information

Karen B. Levitan is founder and President of the KBL Group, Inc., 808 Pershing Dr., Suite 100, Silver Spring, MD 20910, and served as project director of the study reported in this issue. Dr. Levitan holds a PhD in information systems.

Elizabeth Willis is a Senior Associate with the KBL Group, Inc., and served as task leader of the study reported in this issue. She has a BA in sociology-psychology and is combining fifteen years of experience in health and human services with information technology applications.

The authors acknowledge the statistical assistance from Diane Griffin Shook.

This study was supported in part by a grant from the Alcohol, Drug Abuse and Mental Health Administration, National Institute of Mental Health (3R43MH38934-01S1).

storage, retrieval, and manipulation tasks associated with the professional and office practices of family therapists (*American Family* 6(8), Sept. 1983).

The projections are challenging, interesting, and promising. They are projections, however, and must be compared to the realities of the current scene. When we look at the numbers of therapists using computers, we find a relatively small percentage. It is widely acknowledged by mental health practitioners that their field has been slow to use extant information technologies (Greist, 1982; Schwartz, 1978; Taintor, 1982). In searching the literature we found no national survey of computer ownership in the fields of psychology and psychiatry. During the course of the research presented below, we were in contact with a number of newsletters and journals addressing computerization in mental health fields. The subscription rates to each of these publications, while growing, still represent less that 1% of the 100,000 psychologists and psychiatrists who are members of their respective national associations. Such information represents a reasonable indicator of interest and activity level in the use of computers in this field.

Practitioners' work, whether in family therapy or other areas, is so inextricably tied to information processing and so dependent on information resources that use of information (especially microcomputer) technologies can and will have significant impact on their practices. What is keeping the majority of therapy professionals at arms length to the computer? What types of barriers stand in the way of practitioners' effective use of information technologies? How do practitioners perceive such barriers? And what can be done to remove such barriers?

In this article we address these questions by examining the results of one part of a preliminary study conducted by the KBL Group, Inc.,[1] to explore the utilization of microcomputers by private practitioners in psychology and psychiatry. Utilization of the technologies is an interative learning process which requires both systems thinking to design, select and configure the technologies into proper systems, and also management thinking to plan, implement, operate and control the technologies as resources in the office practice. As seen in the title of this article we are concerned not just with microcomputers or software *per se,* but with information systems technologies as applied to the work of therapists. As Boulding (1978) notes, technology is "know how." Microcomputers are tools to enhance users' information work. They operate as systems of equipment and software, which are used effectively only when managed as resources.

These systems often require dozens of person years of effort to design, develop and produce, embodying accumulated "know-how" in systems design and operations. Consequently, computerized information systems require a great deal of user time to learn and understand well enough to be used as extensions of human information processing ability. To utilize information technologies effectively requires the practitioner not only to continuously specify information requirements and evaluate/select/configure systems from extant products and services, but also to apply information management techniques which will convert the system into a professional resource in the practitioner's office. Technology utilization brings together the perspectives of system developers with the perspectives of end-users.

The extent to which this utilization process is understood and implemented by practitioners was the primary focus of a six month study conducted from October 1983 to April 1984. In the course of this study we looked at such barriers as time, cost, dislike of technology, current use of information resources, and status of hardware and software systems technologies relevant to practitioner applications.

APPROACH AND METHODOLOGY

The advantages and disadvantages of the various social science data collection techniques prompted us to use several in order to obtain both breadth and depth of results. Use of mail and literature surveys, interviews, demonstrations, and informal networking allowed cross-checks and validation of different findings.

For the most part, our sampling was constrained by factors of time and budget. A questionnaire survey was designed and pretested, and then mailed to a convenience sample of: 1083 psychiatrists who are listed in the 1982-83 Directory of the Washington Psychiatric Society; 1040 psychologists, of which 655 are licensed clinical psychologists in the Maryland Psychological Association, 297 are licensed clinical psychologists in the Virginia Psychological Association, and 88 are licensed clinical psychologists in Virginia who are not yet members of VPA. In addition, to insure that we receive responses from computer users as well as non-users, questionnaires were sent to 575 individual subscribers to *Computers in Psychiatry/Psychology.*[2] The total mailing was sent to 2,698 practitioners, to complete and return within six weeks.

We received a 19% return rate. We project that the length of the questionnaire, which was four pages, plus the mailing dates and deadline (Christmas holiday season), as well as the impersonal means of contact, were factors that influenced the rate of return. Generalizations from these data, of course, are limited, due to the limitations of the sampling. However, they do provide indicators about the microcomputer utilization process and the types of barriers affecting practitioners use of the technologies.

Of the total respondents (551), 318 (63.1%) were certified under Psychology Doctoral level, 36 (7.14%) under Psychology Masters level, and 150 (29.65%) under Psychiatry. Seventy-four percent (74%) of the total respondents were male, and the largest percent (59.76%) fell in the 30-45 age range (301). General adult was the largest client population of our sample, with 49.08% (239) of total respondents; with 66.66% (96) psychiatrists and 41.69% (143) psychologists practicing in this category. In regards to computer ownership, 38.74% (191) of total respondents owned/leased a computer; 61.25% did not.

In addition, a review of the technology was conducted, based upon the requirements identified in the first sections of the study. Hardware and peripherals which would operate clinical and business applications, as well as appropriate software were reviewed. A catalog of available clinical software was compiled, distribution channels explored, and specific products which served as examples of typical kinds of applications identified to be of interest were seen on-site, and reviewed. These reviews included applications such as business and accounting designed specifically for mental health practitioners, testing, on-line interviews, report writing and biofeedback.

METHODOLOGY AND FINDINGS
FROM QUESTIONNAIRE SURVEY

The mail survey was conducted to define and profile practitioners' information needs and uses, as well as to document the current status of their microcomputer technology use. The questionnaire design for the survey was guided by an initial literature review which identified practice characteristics and areas of information needs and uses.

The questionnaire was pretested; the final draft consisted of four pages of questions covering the following: (1) demographic data, including type of certification, primary and secondary work settings, and specialties; (2) activity and practice characteristics, including clinical assessment procedures; and (3) use and experience with computers. Computer users were asked about specific systems and software in use, and were asked to rate how well their computer systems assisted them in conducting various office management and clinical assessment tasks. Non-computer users were asked to identify factors significant to their not having purchased a computer, to indicate interest in learning more about computers to specify their preference between manual and computer methods for conducting various tasks. Finally, all respondents were asked to indicate the functions for which they currently use the computer and/or for which they project interest in using computer technology in the future.

Reasons for Purchasing a Computer

The responses to a number of the questions begin to provide a profile of the attractions and barriers to computer use. Questionnaire respondents who were computer users were asked about reasons for buying a computer system. The most outstanding reason cited for buying a computer system was "interest in computers" for 74.56% (137) of computer owners. The next most cited reason was "need to improve office management," cited for 44.81% (82) of computer owners. The least often cited reason included "media/advertising" (4.37%), "stimulus from colleagues" (13.11%), and tax benefits (21.86%).

Reasons for Not Purchasing a Computer

Respondents who did not own/lease computer systems were asked about reasons for not purchasing the technology. Three factors were cited most frequently. The first was cost, cited by 57.8% of the total respondents. This was followed by 54.67% of the total indicating that their practice was "too small to justify" a computer. For this factor, however, there was a difference in response between psychiatrists and psychologists. Seventy-three percent of psychiatrists, but only 46.91% of psychologists felt that their practices were too small to justify a computer. The third most dominant factor was "lack of knowledge about computers," reported by 45% of all respondents. Time was also cited as a barrier to computer ownership. Thirty-seven percent of the total respondents felt that the lack of time to research the technology was a barrier to them. Only 16.33% believed that the amount of time it would take to learn a system was a barrier to purchase and use, however.

Only 13.62% (41) of total respondents indicated that "dislike of technology" was a factor in not owning a computer. Additional factors included lack of appropriate software (19.33%), lack of systems dedicated to therapeutic practices (15.95%), and a dislike of technology (16.33%). These last four factors were clearly a minority view.

Respondents perceived cost as the greatest barrier, followed by the belief that their practices are too small to justify computer use. These responses convey the message that computers must be cost effective to be justified, and that they are not cost effective for a small practice.

Lack of Knowledge

Nearly half of the respondents believed that their lack of knowledge about computers was a major barrier. In addition 37% did not feel they had the time to find out more about computers. These factors are intricately connected. The less one knows about computers, the more time it takes to evaluate, select and implement effectively. The less one knows of a computer's capability, the less equipped one is to judge its usefulness as a tool.

An overwhelming number of total respondents (75.25%) were interested in learning more about computers, however, practitioners are aware, then, that they are not as knowledgeable as they need to be to effectively use this technology, but most are open to learning.

Current and Future Priorities

To get at the extent to which psychotherapists appreciate the scope of applications available to assist them in their daily practices, we asked them to indicate practice functions for which they currently use or have future interest in using computer technology. The functions were divided among office management tasks; practice procedures including testing, case histories, and interviews; research/writing; education; and communication. Responses were coded in four categories: (1) neither "Current Use" nor "Future Interest"; (2) "Current Use" only; (3) "Future Interest"; and (4) both "Used Currently" and "Future Interest."

Of the respondents who were computer owners/leasers, 20% (91) of total respondents reported using word processing software, 15.3% of psychiatrists checked billing receipts, 12.7% of psychiatrists checked accounting, and 11% of psychiatrists checked patient registration. For every other function in every category from office and practice management to research, education and communication, both psychologists and psychiatrists reported well under 10% in current use. Few respondents were using the computer for more than one task. It is clear that computer use among practitioners is very limited. While 38.74% of total respondents were computer owners, far fewer had actually begun to use their systems in their practice. Only a handful were using their systems for more than one task or function. With few exceptions, integrated multitask business and clinical systems were simply not in use with the practitioners in this survey.

All respondents, both current computer users and non-users were also asked to indicate their future interest in using the computer for specific tasks. Four office management tasks were the only functions which a majority or even close to a majority of psychiatrists and psychologists indicated a future interest in using computer technology for. The most popular was billing and receipts, which was of interest to 60.1% of respondents; 55.8% indicated an interest in accounting, 52.3% in computerized insurance claims, and 49.8% in word processing. The interest here is not surprising: these are straightforward business functions which would be reasonably easy to adapt to the computer. Three other office functions were of much less interest: payroll, indicated by 29.4% of total respondents; appointments, at 32.9%; and office management reports, which were of somewhat greater interest at 34.4%. These results again are not unexpected, since small practices would not have as great a need to computerize these office functions compared to the previous four.

Fifteen additional tasks were queried, however, again resulting in a minority expressing interest. These are functions which could be described as clinical and professional development in nature. Of greatest interest was online literature searching, of interest to 48.6% of the total. Computerized assistance with DSM-III was of interest to 43%. Computerized testing was rated of less interest also; 40.9% were interested in on-line intelligence tests, 35.5% in achievement tests, 32.9% in aptitude tests, 32.5% in neuropsychological tests, 30.9 in aptitude tests, 26.8% in behavioral assessment, and 23.9% in projective tests.

A number of other clinical functions received a small, but consistent response. On-line case histories were of interest to 36.4% of the total, patient education to 35.4%, use of games and graphics in therapy to 30.5%, and use of on-line interviews for 24.8%. For all of these we again see a small but consistent interest in exploring the potential of the computer in clinical work.

The last category of questions dealt with professional development tasks. On-line continuing education was of interest to 32.9%, staff training to 22.1%, and the use of computers for statistical analysis to 54.2%.

What we can conclude from these responses is not necessarily a resistance to technology, but rather a lack of appreciation of what and how the technology can expand the practitioners' capabilities in many aspect of practice. This list can also be read as an indicator of where the professional community stands in its perceptions about information technologies as tools to aid the psychotherapist. For all that we may hear about the computer revolution, actual usage is miniscule. Interest is much higher. Many therapists may not yet have enough background to be able to define their needs in terms of microcomputer technologies, but the curiosity is present.

METHODOLOGY AND FINDINGS
FROM IN-DEPTH INTERVIEWS

The sample of ten interviews was intended to be used as case studies, providing depth to the data obtained from the questionnaire. Information from a sample of this size and from a community whose work is so individualized is most useful in determining overall issues and needs that transcend specific technology applications.

Interview Objectives and Protocols

Interview protocols were developed for both computer users and nonusers. The interviews were semi-structured, permitting flexibility in the amount of discussion devoted to each practice function, depending upon its importance to the practice and relevance to this study. In some practices, for instance, client records were virtually non-existent; recordkeeping was inconsistent with the therapeutic style of the clinician. In other practices, client records were highly structured, detailed and central to the therapeutic work. A great deal more time would be spent on describing record keeping practices then in this latter case.

The user interviews were conducted with the following objectives:

— To determine current computer use the practice, defining applications and user-satisfaction.
— To define system specifications, and the motivation for purchasing that specific system.
— To define future needs, as perceived by the clinician.
— To discuss specific strategies the clinician sees as being effective in overcoming continuing barriers.

The non-user interview objectives were:

— To determine the practitioner's attitudes towards microcomputers.
— To explore the practitioner's operating procedures and the information requirements of those practice functions.
— To define current barriers to computer use, and the most effective personal strategies for overcoming those barriers.

All interviews covered at a minimum the following subject areas: background, computer orientation, systems specifications (where applicable), current manual practice functions, current computerized practice functions (as appropriate), applications of future interest, and attitudinal factors such as barriers, motivation, feedback from colleagues, impact of technology on the practice and on the profession.

Clinician Priorities

Clinicians varied widely in their concerns, the applications of interest, their therapeutic and managerial style and needs. Some were primarily interested in business applications, to the exclusion of the clinical; others focused on the reverse; still others had interests which spanned many areas. All of the practitioners, user and non-user, were seeking small, integrated, multi-function systems. None had yet found systems, (i.e., hardware, software and interfaces), that adequately met the diversity of their information needs.

The Barriers to Computer Use

Time and Money. Virtually every interviewee cited time and money as the greatest barriers to developing and using information system technologies. Good application ideas were seen as costly to develop, purchase, or install, and took a great deal of time to master. If a manual system was working well, most were inclined to leave well enough alone. Users found that even after investing considerable time into choosing systems they believed were appropriate to their practice, they often still had to change "how they did things" far more than they wanted to in order to use the software.

Finding the Right Software. The frustration and cost of purchasing software which might then prove to be inadequate was seen as a significant barrier. While business software was perceived as being available, clinical software was difficult to find and evaluate. Much of it was of suspect quality. Moreover, these products are often not available locally for hands on testing.

Finding Help. Attempts at self education had met with varied success. Those with successful systems had reported devoting large amounts of time over the course of several years to its development and refinement. They felt, however, that it had been worth it, both because of the benefits they had reaped, and because working with computers was fun. They all expressed the desire to have access to a resource to learn how to develop their systems, but wanted that resource to be able to address their specific professional needs. They felt that computer stores, classes and user groups were too general in nature to be highly useful.

Ethical Concerns as a Barrier. Numerous issues and ethical concerns were raised throughout this study. Concerns about confidentiality, the patient-therapist relationship, computerized testing, for example, were repeatedly voiced. It is significant that interviewees discussed these issues as concerns to be addressed and overcome rather than as barriers to effective information technology utilization.

The Impact of Attitudes and Style

The process of defining requirements in an organized and comprehensive manner occurred rarely, even though this is the critical first step in systems design. The clinicians we spoke to were, for the most part, very receptive to this process and reported their growing awareness of the need to either begin or to further describe at least some of their functions in terms of information use, information resources and management needs.

Those users and non-users who currently utilized structured information in their clinical practice eagerly sought out a variety of clinical applications, viewing each as an additional tool to their practice. They had already begun to view information as a resource. Other clinicians, who described their treatment style as "intuitive," believed that the computer would be detrimental to their relationship with their clients.

Highly structured client records, and a desire to find a way to put them on-line were reported by two users and two non-users. One user expressed a need to develop more consistent manual record keeping formats, with hopes of later putting them on-line. The remaining five kept few or unstructured notes, and did not consider records appropriate for computerization. All ten interviewees currently handled most of their clinical functions manually, however, having not yet found a practical alternative on the computer. Four of the five users utilized word processing software extensively, in an ever increasing number of ways ranging from letters to reports to self-generated forms, educational material, research and writing.

One interviewee continued to keep business functions manually, despite using a computer extensively for testing. The five non-users managed their business in-house via office staff, or in one case, alone. Four of the non-users were satisfied with their manual systems; the clinician who personally handled these functions planned to computerize them soon. The four remaining users either had all or many of their business functions on-line. While some were less than pleased with the software available, they found any computerized system superior to the alternative.

DISCUSSION

It is not possible to point to one factor as the major barrier to practitioners' utilization of information technologies. This is so because the technologies are used as systems and resources in a professional practice and involve both the users and the producers of information technology products. We must look not simply at the attitudes and perceptions of practitioners, nor only at costs, capabilities and performance of the technology. To break down barriers and increase effective utilization of the technology will require understanding from *both* users and producers of what is technologically possible and also what are users' information needs, desires and constraints.

It is interesting that questionnaire respondents did not give much weight to the status of software and systems dedicated to their practice needs as reasons for not purchasing a microcomputer system whereas interviewees discussed their frustrations of searching for and even using systems that were not targeted specifically for their practice needs. From an outside perspective, it is clear that both the accessibility and capabilities of software and system products are significant factors in either facilitating or obstructing practitioners' utilization of the technologies.

As the interviewees indicated, channels of distribution and access to specialized software applications and systems are severely limited. Such limitations increase frustration and time to research systems before purchase, as well as to get help while learning them. These products are not available in commercial outlets for software and systems. Trade shows and conferences offer marketing possibilities, but are costly for vendors, especially those who are sole practitioners themselves. In fact, the applications software products come from a wide range of sources, including both sophisticated, well-developed companies and individual professionals resolving highly specialized practice applications. While some software developers indicated future integration of software packages, no current system reviewed for this study took full advantage of the programming and interface capabilities available on the current 16-bit microcomputer equipment and operating systems. More effective use of current technology in "psych" products and more efficient modes of access and distribution would certainly ease technology utilization for the community of practitioners.

Another major barrier to effective computer use can be described in terms of practitioners' understanding of and attitude towards information processing and information resources. We did not find a resistance to the technology. We found lack of experience with the technology. And more significantly, we found a lack of appreciation of the intellectual and practical contributions that well organized information resources make to their work, their businesses and their professional lives. Before successfully implementing a microcomputer system, a practitioner must be able to specify what information is to be entered, how it must be organized and described, and for whom and for what it will be used; i.e. they must have some sense of appreciation for information management.

The clinicians we surveyed and interviewed ran the spectrum of those who were highly structured in their clinical methods, and their use of records, data, and other information to the analytically oriented, who for the most part did not consider structured information relevant to their therapeutic work. The former group naturally used information in ways that are easily converted to the computer. The latter, by orientation and training, were not likely to find clinical computer applications appropriate.

The middle ground of therapists, however, were likely to use a variety of clinical methods, and at least some of the time do use data from tests, interviews, and other sources in deciding on and conducting treatment. From their responses, however, it did not appear that they think in terms of how to keep structured records and data in a form that could be used for more effective diagnosis, planning, evaluation, norm development and research. Some we spoke to were discovering limitations and problems that eventually arose from the lack of easily accessed and organized patient information, and were beginning to view their information needs with a new eye. This is an important first step.

The same problem existed, to a lesser extent, with business, research and professional development applications. Casual attitudes towards managing business affairs were common. Those who successfully converted their business activities to a computer expressed surprise and delight over the ease and insights gained in managing their practice. Their fundamental decision, however, was not to purchase a computer, but rather to use information as a resource in their work. The computer became their ally and facilitator.

Time and cost were also discussed as significant barriers to computer use. Therapists who have defined even one simple function they want to computerize face the constraint of the time required to learn what may be a formidable body of information before that system or application is working for them. The findings from this study repeatedly point to the need for a more efficient, effective way to go through the entire process. The lack of time and money did not stop those with inherent interest from buying a system. It did inhibit their full use of it, however. From our sample of questionnaire and interview respondents, we conclude that concerns about time and money are more likely to prevent or delay the purchase of a system among those who know less about computers and the use of organized information.

Those who were most pleased with their computers approached both time and money with a realistic eye. They implemented their system by developing one application at a time, building upon their own experiences and knowledge. This measured planning effectively diffused problems of cost and increased their likelihood of success with additional applications.

Many interviewees expressed frustration over the gap between the systems they envisioned and the available products. We believe that this gap makes time and cost more significant barriers now than they will be in the future.

We also found that what is perceived to be a barrier varies somewhat with the kind of application. Business applications, including word processing were of greatest interest, and the reported barriers were primarily time, money and finding appropriate systems. Clinical applications such as on-line testing, on-line patient interviews, patient education, games, etc., elicited a much stronger negative response. There was a clear division between those who felt no conflict with having clients use a computer for some "psych" services, and those who did. In the latter group, such conflict was a clear barrier to effective use of the technology.

The barriers to the use of the computer for professional development and research also included factors beyond time and money. There was often little familiarity with what is available or possible. In the case of research, there was a desire to share data among practitioners in ways that while technically possible, have not yet been developed.

It is significant to note that most of the non-users in this study cite the desire to save time and money as the primary motivation in purchasing a system. However, most user respondents indicated they had not saved time or money in any immediate sense. In spite of this, they were still pleased with the changes and improvements computer technologies brought to their work. We conclude that the more experience and exposure to information and computer technologies, the lower, at least, some of the barriers become.

CONCLUSION

What can be done to break down practitioners' barriers to information technology utilization? Considering the results of this study, a more active, constructive use of computer/information technologies by family therapists and other practitioners must involve more active and direct communication between the user community and the producer community, as well as strong leadership from the professional and educational sectors.

We found a naive perspective on the part of therapists regarding what it takes to produce a micro/information system which is useful to psychotherapists. The process involves not merely developing bug-free software, but taking that software to market—i.e., making it accessible for demonstration and testing; updating and upgrading it so that it will continuously be able to run on a wide variety of hardware systems using advanced microprocessing technologies. For example, producing and marketing a computer game for arcade use should involve very different techniques than producing and marketing a computer game for use in a family therapist's office. The same can be said for a wide spectrum of business and clinical applications programs. The user community must begin to use the technologies so they can feed back to the producer community what is effective and what is not. The producer community must be structured so that user feedback plays a major role in product development. In short, a more sophisticated appreciation for a service-oriented marketplace—from both users and producers of the technologies—would go a long way in initiating constructive utilization.

With respect to therapists' education and training, we found two distinct, but interdependent areas needing attention from professional and educational leaders: management as applied to the entire practice of psychotherapy (business, clinical, and professional practices); and management as applied to the information resources which support activities in each of these practice areas. Psychologists and psychiatrists lack training in management and do not see themselves as managers of even their own practices. They must be educated to understand this so they can effectively manage the microcomputer as a professional resource. They need to become more aware of the activities, relationships, tasks and business systems and resources that are integral to their work life so they will appreciate how a computer can help them manage them more easily. With the exception of Richard Kilburg's essay on "The Psychologist as Manager" (1984), we found no writer or organization, no user or vendor, dealing with the significance of management to the therapist and the important relationship between effective management and effective use of the microcomputer as a resource. These are voids to be filled by creative professional and educational leadership.

Attention to the marketplace and attention to management require new skills from family therapists and other practitioners. How will these skills be developed? A long-term commitment is required to initiate several long-term, learning processes:

1. Software producers need to be on top of the system technologies for entering, processing, storing, and reporting information and incorporate such technologies into their products for practitioners.
2. Software producers need to design systems not from a computer operating point of view, but from the *information* user point of view. Their emphasis must be on the system as a professional resource.
3. Practitioner users need to be educated to appreciate the management and information processing and information resource aspects of their professional lives. Courses in graduate and undergraduate and continuing education programs should recognize and include information management, science and technology as part of the curriculum.
4. Practitioner users need hands on training with microcomputer information systems and applications specific to their clinical and office functions.
5. New, professional channels of distribution need to be developed to provide practitioners with access to psych software and system products and services.

NOTES

1. The KBL Group, Inc. is a private research and consulting firm offering services for 'Knowledge Based Living.' For more information contact them at: 808 Pershing Drive, Suite 100, Silver Spring, MD 20910.

2. *Computers in Psychiatry/Psychology* is a journal edited and published by Dr. Marc Schwartz, 26 Trumbull Street, New Haven, CT 06511.

REFERENCES

Boulding, K. (1978). *Econodynamics.* Beverly Hills, CA: Sage Publications.
Caruso, D. (1984). Room for one more? Families adjust to the inevitability of home computers. *Infoworld,* September 3, 1984, *6*(36), 24-27.
Greist, J. H. (1982). Conservative Radicalism: An approach to computers in mental health. *Computers in Psychiatry/Psychology, 4*(3), 1-3.

Kilburg, R. (1983). The psychologist as a manager. In B. D. Salels (Ed.), *The Professional psychologist's handbook* (pp. 495-537). NY: Plenum Press.

Scharf, P. (1984). *Computer-age parenting.* NY: McGraw Hill.

Schwartz, N. (1978). Why do psychiatrists avoid using the CRT? *Computers in Psychiatry/Psychology, 1*(4), 10.

Taintor, Z. (1982). Information systems are too important to be left to non-clinicians. *Computers in Psychiatry/Psychology, 4*(1), 1-3.

Wakefield, R. & Messologhites, L. (Eds.) (1984). *The home computer, families, and the mental health professions.* Bethesda, MD: American Family, Inc.

The Use of Computers in Marital and Family Therapy

Philip H. Friedman, PhD

ABSTRACT. This paper summarizes the author's experience using a computer in marital and family therapy in six major areas: (1) client intake and records, (2) assessment/evaluation/tracking client changes, (3) client feedback, (4) client information and instruction, (5) financial records, and billing (6) other uses including games, communication, statistics and marketing/media. Also discussed is the author's initial purpose for buying a computer, the joys and frustrations of using a computer, and the client, therapist and computer interaction. Finally, the paper summarizes future trends and emphasizes that "high tech" and "high touch" can go hand in hand to contribute to excellent clinical service in a reciprocal, beneficial and synergistic way.

My initial purpose for buying a computer in the Fall of 1982 was to see if I could administer psychological assessment questionnaires to clients (individuals, couples and families) on a computer, to graph the results and give feedback to clients, both at the initial session and subsequent sessions. At that time I had developed an *Integrative Psychotherapy* approach to conducting treatment (Friedman, 1980a, 1980b, 1981, 1982a) and a comprehensive assessment system for tracking changes in client progress over time (Friedman, 1982b, 1982c). I was also interested in the intercorrelations between the different measures I was using (stress, well-being, self-esteem, marital satisfaction, family cohesion, etc.).

Since I was somewhat concerned about how much time and money would be involved and how much expertise I would need, I initially bought an inexpensive Texas Instruments 99/4A computer, selling for about $225 at that time. Since this was my first experience with a com-

Philip H. Friedman is an assistant clinical professor at Hahnemann University and Director of the Center for Integrative Psychotherapy and Training (CIPT). He is an Approved Supervisor for the AAMFT, co-chairperson of the AFTA (American Family Therapy Association) task force on Integrative Marital and Family Therapy and a member of the AFTA task force on computers in marital and family therapy. Dr. Friedman maintains a private practice in Philadelphia and Plymouth Meeting, PA. He can be contacted c/o CIPT, P.O. Box 627, Plymouth Meeting, PA 19462.

Most of this work could never have been accomplished without the tremendous assistance, devotion and skill of my wife, Teresa, who did much of the word-processing and filing for me and whose support has been invaluable in the development of this entire project. And Thomas Grady of Computer Professionals in Norristown, PA, has been of incalculable help to me.

puter, I was delighted with the cartridges you could buy and easily plug into the computer. I soon purchased a statistics package for $45 (Texas Instruments, 1980) and was thrilled to see the Texas Instruments (TI) computer crunch out dozens of correlations within one-tenth to one-hundredth the time I could have done it by hand or pocket calculator. As a clinician, supervisor and trainer of marital and family therapists who had done relatively little "hard" research in recent years, the convenience and speed of the statistics program was an eye-opener and quickly sold me on the value of a computer for use in my office or home.

Although I used the TI computer for some filing and storage over the next 8 months, in addition to statistics, I soon discovered that I would need a more powerful computer to do the kinds of things I really wanted to be able to do; for example, extensive filing, wordprocessing, graphing and assessment. By that time, however, my enthusiasm and confidence in the use of computers had grown considerably despite the expected frustrations and anxieties that my new professional tool generated. Moreover, I really valued the new skill I was learning and like a new skier, tennis player or dancer, each higher level of skill I achieved markedly enhanced my sense of competence and pleasure.

In June of 1983 I bought an Apple IIe computer with two disk drives, an Okidata printer and six major pieces of software (computer programs on disk). These computer programs on disk permitted me to do many of the things I had originally hoped to do on the computer. In the last 10 months I have used my Apple computer in six major areas in my private practice with clients in general and with couples and families in particular. Some of these areas are further discussed in the excellent book, *Using Computers in Clinical Practice* (Schwartz, 1984).

The six major areas in which I have used my computer are: client intake and record keeping; assessment, evaluation and tracking client changes; client feedback; client information and education; financial records and billing; plus a variety of other uses which include using games with children, communicating with referral sources and clients, producing workshops and training, statistics and developing marketing/media materials. In the remainder of this article, I will first discuss the general sequence of events between my client(s), myself and the computer and then my use of the computer in each of these areas (some more extensively than others). Finally, I will share my personal experience with using the computer in my clinical practice and the future directions I expect to see the field take.

CLIENT, COMPUTER AND THERAPIST INTERACTION

In order to give an overall sense of the use of the computer in my full time private practice, I will briefly describe the sequence of events that involve my client(s), myself and my computer. My client(s) are previously told over the phone that they will have some questionnaires to fill out when they come to the first session. Consequently, when they arrive I greet them and ask them to fill out some questionnaires and forms. One person is seated at the computer in the waiting room and is given brief instructions on how to use it. Since most of the programs are self-explanatory, this only takes one minute or less. The client is then asked to complete one or more questionnaires on the computer. If there is more than one client, I will either ask the other one(s) to fill out paper and pencil questionnaires or I will talk with the other client(s) in my office. After 20-45 minutes I will usually alternate and ask the other client(s) to fill out the computer questionnaire(s). During the first hour, I also have the client(s) fill out an intake form asking for basic information about their personal, marital and family background. This information is later transferred to a computer filing system. The computer questionnaire can usually be scored immediately and the results discussed in the first interview session. Occasionally, the results will be scored and interpreted by the computer after the session is over and the results discussed in the second session if it appears appropriate to do so.

At the end of the first and subsequent sessions, I record the appropriate billing information on a sheet of paper. The billing information can also be transferred to a computer form, daily, weekly or monthly and calculations obtained for monthly billing. Since I require clients to pay at the end of each session, the billing information is mainly for insurance company purposes or as receipts for client(s) who request them. Clients are readministered questionnaires (sometimes shortened versions) at various intervals. The questionnaires are scored and the data stored session by session or every few sessions. After a certain number of sessions, the data which has been transferred to a specialized computer file is graphed by the computer. The graph is shown to clients and the changes that have occurred are discussed with them. This is usually done approximately every 6-10 sessions. Occasionally clients, especially young children or teenagers, will be given computer games to play while I talk to their parents. At other times, educational or instructional information on marriage or family life will be printed out on the computer from the material stored on disk and given to clients. Incidentally, my initial session is a consultation session and frequently takes one and one-half to two hours, including filling out forms and questionnaires. Subsequent sessions last 50 minutes.

CLIENT INTAKE AND RECORDS

Very gradually, over the last ten months, I have developed an intake form that provides me with some basic information about my couples and families. The form is printed out by the computer (at less than 2 cents per copy) and can be filled in by the client in pen or pencil and then transferred to the computer on a software program called PFS-File (Software Publishing Corp., 1983a) or it can be filled out by the client directly on the computer using the keyboard and screen. All client information and forms can be stored on a disk.

The advantage of keeping client records on the computer disks is that it saves space, is very orderly, can be easily modified and updated, can be printed out whenever you want to, and permits filing the data in numerous ways. For example, I can rapidly instruct the computer to sort my client records by age, sex, marital status, name, number of children, income of client or total income, insurance company, referral sources, etc. I can then print out a copy of the data in less than one minute. This can frequently be useful in clarifying and organizing information about my client population. In addition, I keep one copy of each print-out in the client's file and one copy in a general file of all clients.

I have also utilized a Psychological/Social History Report (Rainwater and Coe, 1982a) software program as part of my intake procedure with couples. It takes about 40 minutes for clients to answer the 91 questions posed in multiple-choice format on the computer. The questions cover a variety of areas of the client's past life, such as relationship with parents, school records, education, family income, relations with peers, problems as a child, military history, and parents' marital status plus recent life history information on marital status, income, children and current problems. The attractive aspect of the Psycho-Social Report is that clients like filling it out on the computer and they become more introspective about their lives. Within minutes after it is finished, the computer organizes all the information and prints out a two page professional looking report.

The disadvantage is that filling out the report takes too long (about 40 minutes). Also, it cannot be used with less than 91 items and two or more members of a couple or family cannot fill it out at once, unless you can afford more computers. Though not ideal, having the other partner fill out assessment questionnaires or talking individually to each person while their partner fills out the Psycho-Social Report on the computer avoids this problem. The other limitation is that the Report is not designed explicitly for couples and families. It omits some important questions I would like to see included; for example, questions on marital and family history such as dates of key deaths, births, illnesses, celebrations and emotional events surrounding them.

ASSESSMENT/EVALUATION/TRACKING CHANGES

As previously mentioned, I routinely give a battery of questionnaires to my clients. These include a stress symptom questionnaire, the SCL-90 (Derogatis, Lipman, and Covi, 1973) a well-being questionnaire (modified from Bradburn, 1969) and a self-esteem questionnaire (Hudson, 1982) or (Rosenberg, 1965). In addition, couples routinely receive the Locke-Wallace Marital Adjustment questionnaire (Locke and Wallace, 1959), the Spanier Dyadic Adjustment questionnaire (Spanier, 1976; Spanier and Filsinger, 1983) and the PAIR Intimacy Inventory (Schaefer and Olson, 1981). Families receive the Moos Family Environment questionnaire (Moos and Moos, 1981) and/or the FACES II questionnaire (Olson, Portner, and Bell, 1982) or occasionally both.

All of these questionnaires are re-administered at various time intervals (Friedman, 1982b, 1982c) during treatment in order to track changes occurring over time. Generally, the individual measures of stress and well-being are given every session or every other session, while the marital, family and self-esteem measures are given every fourth or eighth session. It was my hope that many of these questionnaires could be administered, scored, stored, graphed and then the graph of changes occurring over time fed back to my clients by the computer. To date, this goal has only been partially achieved. I quickly discovered that only one of the assessment tools I used was available as a computer software package, and that was the SCL-90 (Duthie, 1983). Even so, the SCL-90 program I obtained was only partially satisfactory for my needs.

I started to explore the use of several other psychological assessment software packages, such as the MMPI (Rainwater and Coe, 1982b; Smith, 1983) and the Beck Depression Inventory Report (Harrell, 1982) and to administer these to couples or families over time since these software programs were commercially available (at approximately the 10th session they would be re-administered). I found that the MMPI software program was very comprehensive but generally took too long to administer for routine use over time (50 minutes to one hour 10 minutes) and was more pathology-oriented than I preferred. For my purposes, the interpretations did not sufficiently focus on client strengths.

However, my computer could score as many as 75 scales within 10 minutes and within 15-20 minutes, score all the scales, graph the major scales and print out a complete interpretive report. Moreover, pre-post changes were often dramatic within less than 10 sessions. The Beck Depression inventory (20 items) took very little time to administer but also added very little to the paper and pencil version.[1]

In the absence of programs specifically designed for marital and family therapy, data are stored and sometimes scored from the paper and pencil self-report measures (marital, family, well-being, self-esteem, stress). I do this by transferring the scores from the paper and pencil questionnaires to a carefully designed electronic spreadsheet called Visicalc (Visicorp, 1983). Visicalc lists rows and columns and can do mathematical calculations easily. Not only can subtotal scores be stored, but summary scores can be instantly calculated. The data can be saved on disks. Moreover, graphs can be made by graphing the data on the Visicalc spreadsheet using a graphing program such as PFS Graph (Software Publishing Corp., 1983b). The graph of changes taking place in therapy can then be printed out and given to the client, sent to a referral source or stored in a client's file. Not only is this easy to do but updating the data and graph is relatively easy and not very time-consuming. It is also possible to store smaller amounts of data directly on the graphing program (e.g., PFS Graph) and graph out changes whenever you so desire.

Having graphed client changes by hand in the past, I can say that this method saves enormous time and is much more attractive and effective. It also provides the marital or family therapist with a fairly rapid way to see visually whether his/her treatment works. Traditionally, marital and family therapists and psychotherapists in general have either not had or not utilized a semi-objective way to measure the changes occurring during treatment in their clinical practice. With the use of currently available, easily administered and scored assessment devices and with the aid of a computer, this is now possible. The graphs demonstrate pictorially and dramatically the changes occurring over time for the therapist and client(s).

One other promising computer software program I have recently received is called CASPER or Computer Assessment System for Psychotherapy Research and Evaluation (McCullough and Farrell, 1983). This program permits the clinician to track ongoing changes in a wide variety of client symptoms over the course of therapy and to store the data on disk session by session. A graphing module may be available for this program in the future and would be a great asset. Personally, I have discovered that usually within 13 sessions or less, very substantial changes occur in levels of perceived well-being and self-esteem, marital adjustment and satisfaction, and family cohesion, expressiveness, independence, organization and control. Hopefully, in the near future, many of the good marital and family measures will be available for administering on the computer. Clients generally seem to like filling out questionnaires on the computer more than filling them out by hand.

CLIENT FEEDBACK

As mentioned in the previous section, I regularly share results of the assessment questionnaires with my clients, both in terms of interpretive reports and graphs of changes occurring over time. When the interpretation comes from a computer, most clients seem to be more impressed with the explanation. Generally, clients are more impressed with the magnitude of changes that have taken place in their lives when they see them graphed over time and can then receive a computer print-out of the graph to take home with them. The graphs of changes occurring over time demonstrate the client's perception of shifts in their level of stress, well-being, self-esteem, marital satisfaction, family cohesion and family adaptability. Many clients are very impressed with the visual print-outs (perhaps those clients who process information visually as opposed to auditorily or kinesthetically). Some clients find the visual feedback interesting but are not impacted strongly by it. There are a few clients, however, who don't seem to care one way or the other. Occasionally, a client is irritated by the whole approach. With these clients, it may not be useful to continue with the assessment-computer approach at all. It is always important to be sensitive to the client's needs, expectations and feelings when utilizing any assessment approach with or without the computer.

CLIENT INFORMATION AND INSTRUCTION

Certain types of educational information can be easily typed on the computer with a word processing program such as Apple Writer IIe (Apple Computer, Inc., 1983) or PFS Write (Software Publishing Corp., 1983c) and then multiple copies run off on the printer. Although this can also be done by a typewriter, with the word processor, even a relatively poor typist like me can make additions or deletions to the information and then run off perfect, multiple copies. For example, I often talk to couples or families about the "weed" and "seed" approach to modifying attitudes. The "weeds" or negative attitudes need to be identified and rooted out and the healthy "seeds" or positive attitudes need to be planted and nourished. The "weeds" correspond to the cognitive distortions discussed by the cognitive therapists and the "seeds" correspond to healing attitudes. On several occasions I have modified the list of "seed" attitudes on the word processor, stored them on disk, printed a new set of copies and given them to clients, all within a very short period of time.

Almost any type of educational material can be stored on disk and copies made, when appropriate, to distribute to clients (e.g., material on communication rules and procedures, homework assignments, imagery and relaxation instructions). Of particular value, for example, might be self-help, instructional software programs that couples and families could use to educate themselves on various aspects of communication, self-esteem, intimacy, sexuality, and parent-child relationships. A number of different psychological or educational software developers are currently writing, or are about to release, programs that may be of considerable benefit to couples and families (e.g., Psycomp, 1984). It will, of course, be an empirical question as to whether information provided via a computer and monitor is more useful or beneficial than information provided verbally or in printed form.

FINANCIAL RECORDS AND BILLING

Using the "Visicalc" spreadsheet program, I have been developing a set of financial statements that record my month to month income from various sources, number of patients and supervisory hours, amount billed, amount paid, amount owed, number of sessions, and fee per hour. Because an electronic spreadsheet program such as "Visicalc" can instantly calculate all the figures, store them on disk and print out one or more copies, I have found the computer a more efficient and organized way of keeping my financial records, once I took the time to learn the spreadsheet program.

I have also constructed a form on my PFS File program explicitly for billing. It has my name, address, telephone and state license numbers on it and can easily be filled out with the client's name, address, telephone number, diagnosis, dates of sessions, fee, amount paid and owed. Copies of the bill are easily printed out for insurance companies, for giving to clients and for keeping records of client billing. The computerized bill creates a very professional appearance. In addition, I have recently been using the computer to send monthly billing statements to the health maintenance organization (HMO) that I deal with regularly. My information is sorted on "Visicalc" which permits me to instantly obtain sums of calculations across all clients for the fee, amount paid by the client, amount owed by the client, amount billed to the insurance company, amount paid by the insurance company and so on. The "Visicalc" file also keeps records of diagnoses, referral source and other information. The information is stored on disk and one or more professional-looking copies can easily be printed. The information is then available for monthly financial records on my clients, in an orderly way.

OTHER USES

Recently, I have experimented with the use of standard computer games such as "Zork" or "Dungeon and Wilderness Campaigns," with couples or families. On occasion, I will ask one or more family members to stay in the waiting room while I talk to their spouse, child, parent-child or marital subsystem. Rather than tell the waiting family member(s) to sit quietly or read, I now ask them if they would like to play a game on the computer. So far they have always said, "Yes." Within a minute or two they are playing their first computer game and usually loving it. On one or two occasions I even asked my adult clients to try their hand at "Eliza" (Grumette, 1982), the simulated therapist that asks questions, has the client type in responses, and answers with non-directive probes. Almost anything on the computer seems to intrigue most clients and the games delight the young and old alike. Whether there is any therapeutic benefit to this, besides temporarily relaxing clients and creating some excitement and fun, I have yet to determine. However, it is clear to me that there is substantial potential for creating games that have an explicit educational and quasi-therapeutic function, not only with teenagers but also with adults.

The word processing programs available for the Apple IIe, such as AppleWriter or PFS—Write, are ideally suited for typing letters, reports, articles, ads, and designing pamphlets and brochures. AppleWriter is a somewhat more sophisticated wordprocessing program than PFS-Write. However, I have found PFS-Write much easier to use, less likely to cause complications, and it has the advantage that what you see on the computer monitor is what is printed out by the printer; an important feature not available on AppleWriter. Recently Apple announced the release of AppleWorks (Apple Computer Inc., 1984), a computer program that integrates word-processing, data-base management and an electronic spreadsheet. AppleWorks may well be the program of choice for the Apple computer in the future because of its integrated capacities. In any case, using the word-processor, it is relatively easy to type a letter or report, correct spelling and typing errors, modify what I have written, rearrange sentences, omit or add words and then almost instantly print as many copies as desired. With the flexibility and speed of the word processor, my typist or I can then send letters and reports to clients or to referral sources.

The word-processing programs can be used to flexibly create many documents. Some of these documents can be used to announce new services to referral sources or to advertise workshops to the professional public. Combined with a filing system such as PFS File, it is possible to store addresses and phone numbers in a file, have the computer print out mailing labels from the file and then send out announcements typed on the word-processor and duplicated on the attached printer. For example, I have sent out announcements for my newly formed "Attitudinal Healing Center" (Friedman, 1984). These announcements were created, printed and addressed using my computer. I have also sent articles and ads to the "Philadelphia Inquirer" newspaper and to local radio and television stations.

There are several packages available on the software market that can rapidly calculate various statistical programs, for instance, means, standard deviations, correlation coefficients, analysis of variance and multiple regression coefficients. Using a statistical program, which I bought for $45, my Texas Instrument computer, did marvelous things for me in seconds. I calculated numerous correlation coefficients between different measures of stress, well-being, self-esteem, depression and marital and dyadic adjustment for males and females, all within a fraction of the time

I could have done it by hand or pocket calculator. Moreover, I did it within the confines of my office, usually between client sessions. Even more sophisticated statistical programs are available for the Apple IIe and other computers (for example, Stats Plus, 1983; Belanger, 1983).

CONCLUSION

Throughout this article I have spoken highly of the use and potential use of the computer in marital and family therapy, in psychotherapy in general, and in clinical practice. I have not, however, spoken of the enormous time I have spent playing with, learning about, reading about, experimenting with and being frequently exasperated with the computer. There have been many occasions when I thought I would never look at a computer again or wondered why I had been so foolish to waste my money in the first place, or just wanted to kick the machine. There have been countless occasions of frustration after frustration, learning how to make a program run that was "presumably" so clearly explained in the manual. I have called software companies in Florida and California more than once in order to try to correct a software program that did not seem to work properly. The saving grace in all of this, for me, has been my local Apple dealer. He has provided excellent service, advice and support over these 10 months, both on the telephone and in person. I say this because he has been like a partner to me in this exciting adventure and without his support or someone like him (a computer users' group or a more experienced friend) I could never have accomplished what I have done, let alone maintained some degree of sanity in regard to my computer. I highly recommend that any new user cultivate a close working relationship with a nearby computer support person or system.

Needless to say, I have been excited throughout this whole period of time with the possibilities for the use of the computer in clinical practice and feel that I have just scratched the surface. I believe strongly that one of the megatrends (Naisbitt, 1982) in our society is what has been called "High Tech/High Touch." The human contact with the couples, families and individuals I see represents the "High Touch" side of the coin and I believe the computer represents the "High Tech" side of the coin. They can, I believe, go hand in hand to contribute to excellent clinical service in a reciprocal, beneficial and synergistic way.

The use of the computer in psychotherapy in general and in marital and family therapy in particular is in its infancy. More powerful, lower priced and easier to use computers and computer software will soon be available. Assessment and educational programs specifically tailored for marital and family therapy will be developed and assessment tools that permit several people to use the computer simultaneously will probably emerge. The unique interactive ability of the computer will no doubt be utilized more frequently and integrated with audio-visual devices such as videotape or laser-discs. The teleprocessing ability of the computer that permits it to tap into large data banks of information or special assessment reports via telephone lines will be readily available and possibly less expensive. The ability of the computer to monitor biofeedback, psychofeedback and eventually family feedback devices will, I think, be a great asset. Uses not currently dreamed of will be developed within the next 5-10 years. These "High Tech" advances will occur side by side with advances in releasing human potential, solving relationship problems and in transforming the capacity for human beings to love one another (Jampolsky, 1979; 1983). The advances in "High Tech," as Naisbitt has said in his book, *Megatrends* (Naisbitt, 1982), will be accompanied by equal and complementary advances in "High Touch." Computers are "High Tech." Human relationships and compassion are "High Touch." They can, and most likely will, develop together to benefit our clients in a more efficient, effective and humane way.

NOTES

1. I have discussed with some computer programmers the possibility of writing assessment programs that would be more appropriate to marital and family therapy and would be made commercially available. I already know of at least one professional group that has developed these computerized assessment tools for "in house" use only. Hopefully, some of the assessment developers will computerize their marital and family assessment tools and make them commercially available in the near future.

REFERENCES

Apple Computer, Inc. (1983). *AppleWriter IIe.* Cupertino, CA: Apple Computer.

Apple Computer, Inc. (1984). *AppleWorks.* Cupertino, CA: Apple Computer.

Belanger, R. (1983). *Stat-systems.* P.O. Box 98, Odessa, FL: Psychological Assessment Resources (PAR).

Bradburn, N. (1969). *The structure of psychological well-being.* Chicago: Aldine.

Derogatis, L. R., Lipman, R. S., & Covi, L. (1973). The SCL-90: An outpatient psychiatric rating scale. *Psychopharmacology Bulletin, 9,* 13-28.

Duthie, B. (1983). *SCL-90-R: Computerized scoring and interpretation.* Wakefield, RI: Applied Innovations, Inc.

Friedman, P. (1980a). Integrative psychotherapy. In R. Herink (Ed.), *Psychotherapy handbook* (pp. 308-313). New York: New American Library.

Friedman, P. (1980b). An integrative approach to the creation and alleviation of dis-ease within the family. *Family Therapy, 7,* 179-195.

Friedman, P. (1981). Integrative family therapy. *Family Therapy, 8,* 172-178.

Friedman, P. (1982a). The multiple roles of the integrative marital psychotherapist. *Family Therapy, 9,* 109-118.

Friedman, P. (1982b). Assessment tools and procedures in integrative psychotherapy. In A. Gurman (Ed.), *Questions and answers in the practice of family therapy.* (Vol. II, pp. 46-49). New York: Brunner/Mazel.

Friedman, P. (1982c, March). *An integrative approach to the assessment and outcome of psychotherapy.* Paper presented at the National Mental Health Center's Conference, New York, NY.

Friedman, P. (1984, February). The Attitudinal Healing Center of the Delaware Valley. In S. Verato (Ed.), *New Frontier Magazine.* Philadelphia: New Frontier Education Society.

Grumette, S. (1982). *Eliza.* Los Angeles: Artificial Intelligence Research Group.

Harrell, T. (1982). *Beck depression inventory report.* P.O. Box 98, Odessa, FL: Psychological Assessment Resources (PAR).

Hudson, W. W. (1982). *The clinical measurement package: A field manual.* Homewood, IL: The Dorsey Press.

Jampolsky, G. (1979). *Love is letting go of fear.* New York: Bantam Books.

Jampolsky, G. (1983). *Teach only love.* New York: Bantam Books.

Locke, H. J., & Wallace, K. (1959). Short-term marital adjustment and prediction tests: Their reliability and validity. *Journal of Marriage and Family Living, 21,* 251-255.

McCullough, L., & Farrell, A. (1983). *CASPER: Computerized assessment system for psychotherapy evaluation and research.* Providence, RI: Butler Hospital.

Moos, R., & Moos, B. (1981). *Family environment scale manual.* Palo Alto, CA: Consulting Psychologists Press.

Naisbitt, J. (1982). *Megatrends.* New York: Warner Books.

Olson, D. H., Portner, J., & Bell, R. (1982). *FACES II: Family adaptability and cohesion evaluation scales.* St. Paul, MN: Family Social Sciences, Univ. of Minnesota.

Psycomp. (1984). *Self-help software.* P.O. Box 994, Woodland Hills, CA.

Rainwater, G., & Coe, D. S. (1982a). *Psychological/social history report.* Indiatlantic, FL: Psychologistics, Inc., P.O. Box 3896.

Rainwater, G., & Coe, D. S. (1982b). *MMPI report:* Indiatlantic, FL: Psychologistics, Inc., P.O. Box 3896.

Rosenberg, M. (1965). *Society and adolescent self-image.* Princeton, NJ: Princeton University Press.

Schaefer, E. S., & Olson, D. H. (1981). Assessing intimacy. The PAIR inventory. *Journal of Marital and Family Therapy, 7,* 47-60.

Schwartz, M. (Ed.). (1984). *Using computers in clinical practice.* New York: Haworth Press.

Smith, B. (1983). *MMPI: Computer version.* P.O. Box 98, Odessa, FL: Psychological Assessment Resources (PAR).

Software Publishing Corporation (1983a). *PFS: File.* Mountain View, CA.

Software Publishing Corporation (1983b). *PFS: Graph.* Mountain View, CA.

Software Publishing Corporation (1983c). *PFS: Write.* Mountain View, CA.

Spanier, G. B. (1976). Measuring dyadic-adjustment. New scales for measuring marriage and similar dyads. *Journal of Marriage and the Family, 38,* 15-28.

Spanier, G. B., & Filsinger, E. E. (1983). The Dyadic-Adjustment Scale. In E. E. Filsinger (Ed.), *Marriage and Family Assessment.* Beverly Hills, CA: Sage Publications.

Stats Plus. (1983). *The statistics series.* Northridge, CA: Human Systems Dynamics.

Texas Instruments. (1980). *Statistics.* P.O. Box 2500, Lubbock, TX.

Visicorp. (1983). *Visicalc.* San Jose, CA: Software Arts Products Corp.

A Computer Data Based Management System for a Family Therapy Clinic

D. Eugene Mead, EdD
Michael W. Cain, MS
Karen Steele

ABSTRACT. This study describes a computer-oriented data based management system designed to be used in a large marriage and family therapy training clinic. The problem was to design a system which would be flexible enough to allow therapists to communicate accurately about their cases as they move between faculty supervisors with diverse theoretical backgrounds. The system was designed to be acceptable to therapists and allows them to enter most of their notes in English prose. Coded entries are kept to a minimum. The system is considered a minimal data system with the gathered material limited to information which is useful in making critical clinical decisions. Information is organized around a Client Data Base, a Treatment Plan which consists of a Problems, Goals and Interventions List, and Progress Notes. The system is also useful for administrative reports and clinical research.

INTRODUCTION

As with many large psychotherapy clinics, the Marriage and Family Therapy Clinic at Brigham Young University has a diverse faculty with many different theoretical backgrounds. This diversity is both an advantage and a problem. The advantage is that therapists in training receive education in a variety of theories and techniques. This prepares therapists to be more flexible and creative in meeting the needs of their clients (Strupp, 1981). The disadvantage is that therapy records have tended to

D. Eugene Mead is a former Chairman of the Family Sciences Department at Brigham Young University and now serves as Coordinator of the Marriage and Family Therapy Clinic, Brigham Young University, Provo, UT 84602. He is a Fellow, Clinical Member, and Approved Supervisor in the AAMFT and he is also a member of the American Psychological Association.

Michael W. Cain is a family therapist at the Southwest Counseling Service, Rock Springs, Wyoming. Mr. Cain is an associate member of the American Association for Marriage and Family Therapy.

Karen Steele received her degree from the Tennessee Technical College, Lexington, Tennessee. Ms. Steele is currently employed as a systems analyst.

49

be structured and maintained in a variety of ways. This inconsistency also precluded full use of the records for clinical research.

What was needed here and elsewhere is an open and flexible data based management system for client records. An open system will not be predetermined by a specific theory of therapy which dictates a certain set of terms and measures. Rather the system would allow therapists of various "schools" to overlay their theoretical model on the general data base structure. A flexible system will not constrain therapists unduly in the way they enter case notes. Nor will it constrain them from making changes in treatment plans as new facts are discovered in the course of therapy.

A computer oriented system was selected to facilitate use of the records for research. In selecting a computer oriented system several issues needed to be considered. First, most computer data management systems have failed when the users were not consulted and their work styles not accommodated (Byrnes & Johnson, 1981; Dow & Jakielo, 1981; Johnson, Godin, & Bloomquist, 1981; Kahn, Ramm, & Gianturco, 1981; Mezzich, Dow, & Coffman, 1981; Mezzich, Dow, Rich, Costello, & Himmelhoch, 1981).

The main users of this system are therapists. Thus, it was considered important to build a system which would allow therapists to include all the richness of English prose in their case notes and treatment planning. At the same time it was important to use the computer to compile critical information in a form which can easily be handled for research and administrative reports (Green & Attkisson, 1981). The second issue considered was that the data based systems can become too cumbersome. Therefore, it was decided that the system should be a minimal data system gathering only information deemed essential for making clinical decisions about the case (Hedlund & Wurster, 1982; Magnussen, 1982).

This paper describes an open and flexible computer oriented data based management system for a family therapy training clinic. The system operates in a Digital Equipment Corporation VAX 11780 with a VMS operating system version 3.7. The computer program is written in Datatrieve which is Digital's data base management language. While the system was developed for a specific training clinic the model may prove useful to other similar clinics and to practitioners in private practice. A similar system is being designed to operate in an IBM-PC.

A DATA BASED MANAGEMENT SYSTEM

The data based management system described here consists of three parts: (1) the client data base, (2) the treatment plan, and (3) the progress notes (Meldman, McFarland, & Johnson, 1976; Ryback, 1974; Tomm &

Sanders, 1983; Weed, 1970). Each of these components will be described below.

The Client Data Base

The client data base consists of the information gathered by the therapist to make clinical decisions about diagnoses, problems, goals, treatment plans, continuing treatments, changing treatments, referrals, and terminations. The initial data base serves as a "time one" evaluation against which later evaluations are compared. The data base is developed out of information from a variety of sources such as referral sources, assessment instruments, laboratory tests, interviews, and observations.

The initial data base is organized in two ways. First, it is written in English prose on the Client Data Base form (Appendix A). The Client Data Base form also serves to initialize the computer record for the data based management system. The use of English prose requires no changes in the therapist's note taking and recording style which is a factor in reducing therapist resistance to the system.

Second, the initial data base is organized around the outline suggested by Tomm and Sanders (1983). It is not expected that the therapist gather all these data prior to beginning therapy, or even by the end of therapy. However, as information is gathered it is recommended that it be added under one of the following categories: *A. Family Structure:* (1) Internal Structure, e.g., Genogram, Household Composition; (2) External Structure, e.g., Social Networks, Geographic Context; *B. Family Functioning:* (1) Instrumental Functioning, e.g., Task Allocation, Daily Routines; (2) Expressive Functioning, e.g., Communication Patterns, Affective Involvement; *C. Family Development:* (1) Specific Problem(s) as described by each family member, e.g., Presenting Problem, History of the Present Problem, Physical Health, Current Drug Use, Mental Status Report; (2) Family Life Cycle, e.g., Relationship History, Sexual History.

It is recommended (Tomm & Sanders, 1983) that the client data base information be recorded in language which is descriptive rather than in abstract concepts. For example: "Mr. B. reported that he feels most 'helpless' when his wife is away from home." Note, too, that the source of the information, Mr. B., was identified in the note. The use of descriptive language rather than abstractions and inferences allows the therapist to return to the notes to entertain new hypotheses. In the example above, at least three hypotheses might be tested against additional data: (a) the husband is depressed, (b) the husband is enmeshed with the wife, and (c) the husband lacks household maintenance skills. Observe that the latter hypothesis would be lost if the notes were simply recorded as the inference "Mr. B. appears depressed due to his enmeshment with his wife."

As the therapist develops the client data base she or he also begins to develop some conjectures about the clinical nature of the problem. These conjectures may be organized into: (a) individual diagnosis, for some or all family members; (b) family diagnosis; and (c) specific problems and goals, again for individuals and for the family as a system. As rival hypotheses are eliminated the therapist narrows upon the clinical problem and begins to hypothesize about a specific treatment program. What is developing is a treatment plan.

The Treatment Plan

The formal treatment plan consists of a list of the problems and goals which are appropriate for each family member in treatment. In addition, the treatment plan contains a list of treatments or interventions which are designed to bring about a change in the corresponding problems or goals.

The treatment plan is recorded in the case notes in two ways. First, the treatment plan is entered in English prose on the Treatment Plan Worksheet (Appendix B). Second, the treatment plan is entered on the Problems/Goals and Interventions List form (Appendix C). The English prose version is for the convenience of the therapist and supervisor. The Problems/Goals and Interventions List is for the convenience of the computer. The two forms are necessary because it appears that therapists do not understand numbers and computers do not understand English.

The therapist may draw upon several sources for assistance in entering numbers on the Problems/Goals and Interventions List. There are two primary sources for the list of problems and goals and one primary source for the interventions. The primary sources for problems and goals are the *Diagnostic and Statistical Manual for Mental Disorders* (3rd ed.) (DSM-III) (APA, 1980) and the *Interactional Diagnostic Manual* (Appendix D). An additional source for the problems and goals portion of the list is the Assessment Instruments Index (Appendix E). The primary source for the interventions portion of the Problems/Goals and Interventions List is the Interventions Index (Appendix F). Use of the DSM-III, the Interactional Diagnostic Manual, the Assessment Instruments Index, and the Interventions Index to enter numerical data in the Problems/Goals and Interventions List will be described later.

The Problems/Goals and Interventions List, i.e., the treatment plan, should not be considered complete until the problems have been rated for severity, the goals have been rated for expected outcome, and a goal achievement date has been established. Setting a goal achievement date is important in maintaining treatment efficiency. Therapists and clients are likely to work harder as the achievement date is approached.

Once the treatment plan has been established the therapist is ready to leave the initial assessment phase of therapy and begin the treatment phase. The hypothesis the therapist entertains in treatment is that a given treatment will influence a given problem or help the clients achieve a specific goal. To determine treatment effectiveness it is necessary to maintain a record which will help the therapist evaluate progress.

The Progress Notes

Progress notes are kept to record the progress being made toward reducing or eliminating a problem or achieving a goal. Just as with the treatment plan two records are kept, an English prose version and a computer version. After each client contact, including phone conversations, interviews, observations, reports by others such as referral sources, and so on, the therapist completes a Progress Notes Worksheet (Appendix G) in English prose and a Progress Notes form (Appendix H).

The goal of the progress notes is to assist the therapist in answering several critical clinical questions. After each contact the therapist must consider whether or not the treatment is being delivered. If the treatment is being delivered, then the therapist must determine if the treatment is having a positive effect, a negative effect, or no effect. Based upon this decision the therapist then decides to continue the treatment, apply another treatment, refer the clients, or terminate the case.

In attempting to determine whether the treatment has been delivered, the therapist will need to consider the amount of the treatment which has been delivered and the extent to which treatment has made an impact on the family's natural environment. Most treatments consist of several interventions and the overall amount of the treatment package which has been delivered will impact upon the critical clinical decisions. For example, treatment of marital conflict may require the therapist to intervene in the family's communication patterns, their problem solving methods, their assertiveness with each other, their relationships with extended family members, and so on. It would be a mistake to expect too much change in the system if only the communication patterns had been treated.

It is also important to consider the events which are occurring outside of therapy as well as the events which occur in the consulting room. Effective treatment makes a difference in the family's system in their natural environment, not just in the therapist's office. The treatment cannot be considered as "delivered" if the clients are unable to put what they have learned or experienced in the therapy session into their lives at home.

It should be clear from the discussion above that assessment or evaluation is a continuous process in the clinical method. Therapists are encouraged to administer assessment instruments as needed to determine progress. Good clinical judgement should be used to determine if the additional testing is needed to provide information for decision making. The need for additional information should be weighed in terms of the costs to the clients in time and dollars. Effective therapy is therapy which helps the clients solve their problems and reach their goals in the least amount of time and at a reasonable cost.

The computer Progress Notes form continues the assessment of the information recorded on the computer Problems/Goals and Interventions List. The goal is to track the relationship between the problems and goals and the planned interventions which were entered on the Problems/Goals and Interventions List earlier. To help accomplish this, the severity of the problem is rated each time the problem is focused upon in the Progress Notes. As stated earlier, the hypothesis being tested is that the treatment, which consists of the planned interventions, influences the client's problems and goal achievements (Nelson, 1981). The data on the Progress Notes form should help us answer this critical clinical question.

INDEXING SYSTEMS FOR PROBLEMS, GOALS, AND INTERVENTIONS

There are several advantages to using specific problem, goal, and intervention lists. One obvious advantage is that such lists can provide index numbers for computer recording. Computers can handle numbers easily for manipulation into administrative reports and for analysis in research. Another less obvious advantage of problem and goal lists is that they provide an alternative form of assessment for the field of family therapy (Tomm & Sanders, 1983). One aim of the problems and goals list is to avoid an abstract, inferential single diagnosis of families. The problem approach eliminates the necessity to label families and individuals while allowing therapists to communicate clearly and explicitly about important aspects of the case. In addition, there are advantages to listing specific interventions which constitute the treatment plan and linking them to specific problems or goals. It provides both clarity and allows more precise investigation of the connections among the problems, the goals, and the treatment.

With the above argument still fresh it is also necessary to state that the descriptions of family problems as opposed to problems of individual persons must come from somewhere. To that end one of the authors (MWC) has begun the Interactional Diagnostic Manual (Appendix D). This manual and its use will be described later in this paper.

In family therapy it is necessary to be concerned with changes at two levels, the level of individual family members and the level of the family system. Although the family system may have the more powerful effect, it is still the individual family members who act (Skinner, 1953). In addition, family therapists are often called upon to give diagnostic evaluations of individual family members for administrative purposes such as classification for mental health reporting and fee collection from third parties. Therefore, the Problems/Goals and Interventions List provides for listing of family system problems and goals and also individual member's problems and goals.

Using DSM-III to Index Problems and Goals. To form a problem and goal list for an individual family member the therapist may use the DSM-III. The DSM-III contains diagnostic criteria for each diagnostic category. Categories are broad general classifications such as "Agoraphobia with Panic Attacks." The DSM-III code for this category is 300.21. The diagnostic criteria provided in the DSM-III for a category describes behaviors or behavior patterns which are often associated with the category. For example, the first diagnostic criteria for agoraphobia with panic attacks is: "A. The individual has marked fear of and thus avoids being alone or in public places from which escape might be difficult or help not available in case of sudden incapacitation, e.g., crowds, tunnels, bridges, public transportation" (p. 227). To further specify a client with this pattern the therapist could list the problem code as 300.21A. Thus to form an index number for an individual family member the therapist uses the diagnostic category code as a root and attaches as many letters and numbers from the diagnostic criteria as are appropriate to specify the problem to be treated.

It is appropriate to note here that the therapist must consciously determine what is and what is not a problem. If the therapist does not specify a problem or does not intend to treat the problem then the problem is treated as if it does not exist at this time. This does not mean that the problem cannot be listed later. It is simply a matter of good clinical practice not to list a problem or possible problem until it is a matter for treatment (Fowler & Longabaugh, 1975).

Using the Interactional Diagnostic Manual
to Form a Problem and Goal List

To form a Problems/Goals List for a family system or subsystem the therapist may use the Interactional Diagnostic Manual (IDM) (Appendix D). The IDM classifies family systems and subsystems in a manner similar to the DSM-III. A category is identified and specific diagnostic criteria are listed where available.

To index a family system or subsystem for a problems and goals list the therapist finds the category in the IDM which applies and uses the category code as a root. Then the therapist applies specific diagnostic criteria as appropriate. For example, a couple which is classified as having a "Vital" marriage would be coded 102.F4. If the couple could be described as sharing most activities and they both agree that their relationship is the highest priority in their lives then the couple would be coded as 102.F413 (IDM, pp. 21-22).

Forming Index Codes for Problems and Goals
Not Found in the DSM-III or the IDM

There are three additional ways to index for a problem or goal list. First, the therapist may specify as a goal the administration of an assessment instrument. Second, the therapist may use scores from an assessment instrument as a problem or as a goal. And third, the therapist may establish a new problem or goal by writing it out in English prose. Here "new" means a problem not described in the DSM-III, IDM, or the Assessment Instruments Index (Appendix E).

If the therapist's goal is to administer an assessment instrument the therapist may turn to the Assessment Instruments Index. The therapist finds the assessment instrument that he or she intends to use and enters the index number into the problems/goals portion of the Problems/Goals and Interventions List (Appendix C). Initial severity is entered as zeros (00.00) and the predicted outcome score may be entered as the goal. Entering the expected administration date as the goal achievement date completes the entries for that problem. As an example, if the therapist is seeing a couple for marital problems, the therapist may ask them to take the Locke and Wallace (1959) Marital Adjustment Test (MAT). At this point their initial severity is unknown, so the therapist enters zeros. The therapist predicts that after treatment they will each score near 100, so she/he enters 100 as the expected goal. Finally, the therapist enters the date he/she has scheduled them to take the test as the goal completion date.

In a similar manner, assessment instruments which have been administered may be entered as problems and goals in the Problems/Goals and Interventions List or on the Progress Notes form. The assessment instrument index number is located on the Assessment Instruments Index and entered. As above, the initial severity is the current score and the goal is the expected outcome score. In our example above after the couple has completed the MAT the problem is entered as their current scores. Let us say the husband scored 70 and the wife scored 64. These scores are entered as the current severity and the goal is set at 100 each. A target date for twelve weeks is set and entered as the goal achievement date. After twelve weeks of treatment the MAT is readministered and if the treatment has been successful the MAT score should be at or near 100.

If the therapist is unsuccessful in locating an index number for the client's problem or goal in the DSM-III, the IDM, and the Assessment Instruments Index then the therapist may write out the problem or goal in English prose. The procedures for specifying a new problem or goal which we recommend are as follows. First, the therapist should provide a short title to designate the classification. The computer program limits this title to 100 characters or less. Next, the therapist should provide a brief, but specific and concrete description of the behavior or behavior pattern which characterizes the problem or goal. The clinic which is using the data based management system would need to have a method established for attaching index numbers to each new problem or goal. We recommend establishing a series of index numbers beginning with a standard identifier such as "N" for new. For example, N001 to N999 might be established as the index numbers to be assigned to new problems and goals. A file of new problems with their index numbers would then be established and shared within the organization.

Forming Treatment Plan Intervention Lists

The treatment plan for the computer consists of the problems, goals, and interventions entered on the Problems/Goals and Interventions List (Appendix C). Each problem is followed by a space to enter the appropriate intervention or interventions. In this way each problem and goal is linked with the intervention which is expected to bring about the remission of the problem or the achievement of the goal. Using the Interventions List (Appendix F) the therapist selects the intervention or interventions which will make up the treatment to be administered. These interventions are entered in the Problems/Goals and Interventions List by their index numbers.

Interventions which are not found on the intervention list may be added in a manner similar to adding new problems and goals. The therapist writes the treatment plan out in English prose specifying the interventions to be delivered. The therapist provides a short title. The current program provides space for fifty characters or less for the title of an intervention. The therapist then provides a clear and specific description of each step in the intervention. It is important that the intervention be described in sufficient detail that others may replicate it should it prove effective. If the new intervention is taken from the literature the therapist should be sure to include a complete bibliographic reference. As with the new problems and goals list it will be necessary to establish a set of index numbers for the interventions. Two methods are available. The new intervention may be added to the Interventions Index (Appendix F) by simply extending the current set of numbers. The alternative would be to develop a new list as described above for establishing a new problems and goals list.

CLINICAL DECISION MAKING
WITH A DATA BASED SYSTEM

As stated earlier the data based management system was designed to help therapists make critical clinical decisions about diagnoses, problems, goals, treatment plans, continuing or changing treatments, making referrals, and terminating cases. This is done by comparing the "time one" information in the original data base as reported in the Treatment Plan Worksheet (Appendix B) and the Problems/Goals and Interventions List (Appendix C) with the "time two" data recorded in the Progress Notes Worksheet (Appendix G) and the Progress Notes form (Appendix H).

The most effective evaluation of the treatment effects would be to have valid and reliable continuous measures of the problems and goals (Kazdin, 1981). Treatment would then be considered complete when the clients reached some predetermined level of reduction in the problems and some predetermined level of achievement of the goals. As described earlier where such measures are available the client's scores at time one may be entered in the Problems/Goals and Interventions List as initial severity scores. The goal achievement scores are the anticipated outcome scores for the measures being used. They are the predetermined criteria for successful treatment. When the Progress Notes indicate that the current severity scores are equal to the predetermined criteria scores the therapist should begin to consider termination of the case. Unfortunately, we rarely have valid and reliable continuous measures of client progress in family therapy. Therefore, what is needed is a systematic and consistent method to rate problem severity when valid and reliable measures are unavailable.

Rating Problem Severity and Expected Goal Outcomes

Therapists often subjectively evaluate the initial severity of a client's problem and then, without formally specifying that evaluation, the therapist applies a treatment and continues to make subjective evaluations of the client's progress. When the client appears to have made satisfactory progress the therapist terminates treatment. A variation on this pattern is to administer pre- and post-test instruments prior to and after completion of therapy. However, even with the pre- and post-tests the continuous session-by-session evaluation of client progress is generally made as a subjective judgement by the therapist.

In an effort to make the therapist's subjective evaluation of client progress more consistent and systematic a Subjective Problem Severity Scale was developed. The severity scale was designed to: (1) provide therapists with a means to rate the initial severity of client problems; (2) provide therapists with a system to establish predetermined outcome goals in terms of the initial severity rating; and (3) provide therapists with a consistent and systematic method of evaluating client progress.

A problem is a situation in which the individual or the family members have no behavior which is immediately available to reduce a state of deprivation or provide escape from an aversive stimulus (Skinner, 1953).

It is assumed that problems exist in varying levels of aversiveness or severity. Extremely severe problems are very debilitating and negatively influence most aspects of the person's life. When the individual or members of the family emit behavior which makes the problem "go away" we call the behavior "the solution." Therefore, with some problems the severity may be reduced to "zero." That is, the problem cannot be identified as a problem by either the client or the therapist.

Fowler and Longabaugh (1975) define a problem as:

> A dysfunction affecting the patient, perceived by the clinical staff (and usually the patient or others meaningful to him) as existing or being imminent, in one or more of the following areas: (a) Physiological, including abnormal physical or laboratory findings, as well as specific diseases; (b) Psychological, as manifested by impaired cognition or feeling states, or both, including abnormal test or laboratory findings; (c) Social relationships or social functioning. (p. 832)

Fowler and Longabaugh point out that the responsibility for determining that a problem is clinically relevant lies with the therapist. It is possible, under this definition, for the client and the therapist to disagree about the existence of a problem. With this definition a problem does not exist if the clinician does not recognize it or does not define it as a problem. Nonetheless, to qualify as a problem the situation must affect the client. If the question "Is this a problem for the client?" cannot be answered in the affirmative then the situation does not qualify as a problem.

When a valid and reliable continuous measure is not available it is recommended that the therapist establish a severity rating by rating the problem according to the Subjective Problem Severity Rating Scale (Table 1). For example, a "Conflict Habituated" marriage in which the problem is interfering with the husband's work because it is "constantly on his mind" might be rated on the severity scale as 7.0. This score would be entered as the initial severity on the Problems/Goals and Interventions List (Appendix C). The predicted outcome in terms of severity would be entered as the treatment goal, e.g., 3.0.

The severity score consists of two digits separated by a decimal point. This allows the therapist to subjectively capture small changes in severity. For example, a therapist may feel that a client has changed but not enough to move from one full point to another. The therapist can indicate this change with any number from "1" to "9" to the right of the decimal. In our example above, the couple may have reduced the conflict exchanged to the point where it is reported to be on the husband's mind "somewhat less and therefore it rarely interferes with my work now." The therapist

TABLE 1

The Subjective Problem Severity Rating Scale

0.0 The problem cannot be observed by the client or the therapist.

1.0 The problem can be observed by the therapist, but is not defined as a problem.

2.0 The problem can be observed by the therapist, but is not reported by the client as affecting the client.

3.0 The problem can be observed by the therapist and the client, but the client does not find the situation aversive enough or depriving enough to be motivated to change.

4.0 The problem can be observed by the therapist and the client and the therapist predicts that there is a high probability that it will become dysfunctional in the near future but the client does not find the situation aversive or depriving enough to be motivated to change.

5.0 The problem is aversive enough or depriving enough that the client seeks a solution, but the problem does not limit normal functions.

6.0 The problem limits some functions in one of the following areas: (a) physiological, (b) psychological, (c) social.

7.0 The problem limits some functions in two or more of the following areas: (a) physiological, (b) psychological, (c) social.

8.0 The problem nearly halts normal functioning in one of the following areas: (a) physiological, (b) psychological, (c) social.

9.0 The problem nearly halts normal functioning in two or more of the following areas: (a) physiological, (b) psychological, (c) social.

10.0 The problem halts nearly all normal functioning.

might score this progress as 6.5 and enter this score on the Progress Notes form (Appendix H).

The Subjective Problem Severity Rating Scale assumes that the greater the severity of the problem the greater the client motivation for change. As the severity decreases changes may be smaller because the client's motivation for change is reduced. For this reason the therapist should keep in mind that a severity outcome of "0.0" may not be realistic. As noted above, in some cases when the client finds a behavior which makes the problem go away, the severity will be zero, but this will not occur with all problems. Therefore, when establishing goals and evaluating progress the therapist should consider the effects of client motivation on potential outcome and termination. It may be assumed that from the point of view of the therapist, many clients terminate therapy prematurely, because they leave when they reach 4.0 or 3.0 on the severity scale. However, in the end the ultimate criterion for successful treatment must rest with the client. Changes in pre- and post-test scores which are of statistical significance are of no significance if the treatment did not make a difference to the client (Barlow, 1981).

CONCLUSIONS

The problem was to develop a data based management system which would be acceptable to therapists, prove useful in helping therapists make critical clinical decisions and would also be capable of providing useful data for administrative reports and research studies. It is believed that the system described in this paper will meet these needs for a large marriage and family therapy clinic with a faculty which represents many theoretical positions. The system appears sufficiently uniform to supply consistent data and to allow therapists-in-training to move from supervisor to supervisor without significant loss in client continuity. At the same time the system enables supervisors to use the data to show the therapists how they can be inductively related to the supervisor's theory of treatment. Moreover it can also show how deductively the theory suggests hypotheses to test in treatment (Burr, Mead, and Rollins, 1973). Considerable research will be needed to determine if any of these assumptions are supported.

REFERENCES

American Psychiatric Association. (1980). *Diagnostic and Statistical Manual of Mental Disorders* (3rd ed.). Washington, D.C.: Author.

Barlow, D. H. (1981). On the relation of clinical research to clinical practice: Current issues, new directions. *Journal of Consulting and Clinical Psychology, 49*, 147-155.

Burr, W. R., Mead, D. E., & Rollins, B. C. (1973). A model for the application of research findings by the educator and counselor: Research to theory to practice. *The Family Coordinator, 22*, 285-290.

Byrnes, E., & Johnson, J. H. (1981). Change technology and the implementation of automation in mental health care settings. *Behavior Research Methods & Instrumentation, 13*. 573-580.

Dow, J., & Jakielo, D. (1981). How to manage the evolution of a computerized information system. *Behavior Research Methods & Instrumentation, 13*, 454-458.

Fowler, D. R., & Longabaugh, R. (1975). The problem-oriented record. *Archives of General Psychiatry, 32*, 831-834.

Green, R. S., & Attkisson, C. C. (1981). A model system for psychotherapy research data management. *Behavior Research Methods & Instrumentation, 13*, 499-510.

Hedlund, J. L., & Wurster, C. R. (1982). *Computer applications in mental health management.* Proceedings—Symposium on Computer Application in Medical Care 6th, 366-370.

Johnson, J. H., Godin, S. W., & Bloomquist, M. L. (1981). Human factors engineering in computerized mental health care delivery. *Behavior Research Methods & Instrumentation, 13*, 425-429.

Kahn, E. M., Ramm, D., & Gianturco, D. T. (1981). TOCRS—The therapy-oriented computer record system. *Behavior Research Methods & Instrumentation, 13*, 479-484.

Kazdin, A. E. (1981). Drawing valid inferences from case studies. *Journal of Consulting and Clinical Psychology, 49*, 183-192.

Locke, H., & Wallace, K. (1959). Short marital adjustment and prediction tests: Their reliability and validity. *Marriage and Family Living, 21*, 251-255.

Magnussen, M. G. (1982). *A computerized clinical data system for child psychiatric facilities*. Proceedings symposium on computer applications in medical care. 6th, 115-119.

Meldman, M., McFarland, G., & Johnson, E. (1976). *The problem-oriented psychiatric index and treatment plans*. St. Louis: C. V. Mosby.

Mezzich, J. E., Dow, J. T., & Coffman, G. A. (1981). Developing an efficient clinical information system for a comprehensive psychiatric institute: I. Principles, design, and organization. *Behavior Research Methods & Instrumentation, 13*, 459-463.

Mezzich, J. E., Dow, J. T., Rich, C. L., Costello, A. J., & Himmelhoch, J. M. (1981). Developing an efficient clinical information system for a comprehensive psychiatric institute: II. Initial evaluation form. *Behavior Research Methods & Instrumentation, 13*, 464-478.

Nelson, R. O. (1981). Realistic dependent measures for clinical use. *Journal of Consulting and Clinical Psychology, 49*, 168-182.

Ryback, R. (1974). *The problem oriented record in psychiatry and mental health care*. New York: Grune & Stratton.

Skinner, B. F. (1953). *Science and human behavior*. New York: The Free Press.

Strupp, H. H. (1981). Clinical research, practice, and the crisis of confidence. *Journal of Consulting and Clinical Psychology, 49*, 216-219.

Tomm, K., & Sanders, G. L. (1983). Family assessment in a problem oriented record. In J. C. Hansen (Ed.), *Diagnosis and assessment in family therapy*. Rockville, Maryland: Aspen Systems.

Weed, L. (1970). *Medical records, medical education and patient care*. Cleveland, Ohio: Case Western Reserve University.

APPENDIX A

Client Data Base

Date (example: 12 Jun 83) _____

Therapist (ex. Cain M) _____ Supervisor (ex. Mead

G) _____

Patient No. (ex. 83-0000-1) ____-_____-_____ Data Gathering Session No. _____

Type of client if determined

(Check one):

____(1) Adolescent Dysfunction ____(2) Child Misbehavior ____(3) Divorce

____(4) Family Conflict ____(5) Individual affect ____(6) Individual Mental

____(7) Marital Conflict ____(8) Premarital ____(9) Reconstituted Family

____(10) Sexual Dysfunction ____(11) Substance abuse

Data Gathering (Tomm & Sanders, 1983). As the information comes in—it need not all be gathered, nor should it be, before one begins—it should be organized into the following areas: (1) Internal family structure, e.g., Genogram, Household Composition; (2) External structure—Social Networks, Geographic Context; (3) Instrumental family functioning—Task Allocation Daily Routines; (4) Expressive functioning—Communication Patterns, Affective Involvement; (5) Description of the presenting problem—History, Physical Health, Mental Status Report; and (6) Family life cycle—Relationship History, Sexual History.

Therapist Notes continued:

Additional Action

Please indicate additional action planned prior to initiating treatment. Check all that apply.

___(1) Additional interviews
___(2) Tests, assessments, checklists
___(3) Observation in the Clinic
___(4) Observation in the Home
___(5) Termination, transfer, refer
___(6) Write up treatment plan
___(7) Other (specify)

Use as many additional blank pages as needed and attach them to this cover sheet.

APPENDIX B

Treatment Plan Worksheet

Date _____

Therapist _____ Supervisor _____

Client Number (ex. 83-0000-1) ____-_____-____

Type of Client (Check one): ___(1) Individual ___(2) Marital ___(3) Family

Problem Type (Check one): ___(1) Adolescent Dysfunction ___(2) Child
    Misbehavior ___(3) Divorce ___(4) Family Conflict ___(5) Individual
    Affect ___(6) Individual Mental ___(7) Marital Conflict
    ___(8) Premarital ___(9) Reconstituted Family ___(10) Sexual
    Dysfunction ___(11) Substance Abuse

Will treatment be in group format? (1) Yes____ (2) No____

Data Base   Hypotheses

                                    1. Etiology   2. Maintenance

Problems/Goals   Treatment

                                    List Interventions

How Will the Treatment   How Connected to
be Evaluated?   Theory?

APPENDIX C

Problems/Goals and Interventions List

Date (example: 12 Jun 83) _____

Therapist (ex. Cain M) _____ Supervisor (ex. Mead G) _____

Client Number (ex. 83-0000-1) _____-_____-_____

Type of Client (Check one): _____(1) Individual _____(2) Marital _____(3) Family
Problem Type (Check one):
    ____(1) Adolescent Dysfunction ____(2) Child Misbehavior ____(3) Divorce
    ____(4) Family Conflict ____(5) Individual Affect ____(6) Individual Mental
    ____(7) Marital Conflict ____(8) Premarital ____(9) Reconstituted Family
    ____(10) Sexual Dysfunction ____(11) Substance Abuse
Will treatment be in group format? (1) Yes_____ (2) No_____

Please use the numbers indicated to designate the subunit to which the problem/goal and
interventions apply. (1) Husband; (2) Wife; (3) Child by birth order e.g., 3.3 is the third
child; (4) Family; (5) Marital Couple; (6) Parent-Child; (7) Siblings; (8) Single Adult.

Prob. No. 1: Subunit No._____ Prob. Code_____ Title_____
Initial Severity_____ Goal_____ Goal Achievement Date_____ No. of Sessions_____
Interventions _____

Prob. No. 2: Subunit No._____ Prob. Code_____ Title_____
Initial Severity_____ Goal_____ Goal Achievement Date_____ No. of Sessions_____
Interventions _____

Prob. No. 3: Subunit No._____ Prob. Code_____ Title_____
Initial Severity_____ Goal_____ Goal Achievement Date_____ No. of Sessions_____
Interventions _____

Prob. No. 4: Subunit No._____ Prob. Code_____ Title_____
Initial Severity_____ Goal_____ Goal Achievement Date_____ No. of Sessions_____
Interventions _____

Prob. No. 5: Subunit No._____ Prob. Code_____ Title_____
Initial Severity_____ Goal_____ Goal Achievement Date_____ No. of Sessions_____
Interventions _____

Prob. No. 6: Subunit No._____ Prob. Code_____ Title_____
Initial Severity_____ Goal_____ Goal Achievement Date_____ No. of Sessions_____
Interventions _____

Prob. No. 7: Subunit No._____ Prob. Code_____ Title_____
Initial Severity_____ Goal_____ Goal Achievement Date_____ No. of Sessions_____
Interventions _____

Prob. No. 8: Subunit No._____ Prob. Code_____ Title_____
Initial Severity_____ Goal_____ Goal Achievement Date_____ No. of Sessions_____
Interventions _____

Prob. No. 9: Subunit No._____ Prob. Code_____ Title_____
Initial Severity_____ Goal_____ Goal Achievement Date_____ No. of Sessions_____
Interventions _____

Prob. No. 10: Subunit No._____ Prob. Code_____ Title_____
Initial Severity_____ Goal_____ Goal Achievement Date_____ No. of Sessions_____
Interventions _____

Prob. No. 11: Subunit No._____ Prob. Code_____ Title_____
Initial Severity_____ Goal_____ Goal Achievement Date_____ No. of Sessions_____
Interventions _____

Prob. No. 12: Subunit No._____ Prob. Code_____ Title_____
Initial Severity_____ Goal_____ Goal Achievement Date_____ No. of Sessions_____
Interventions _____

APPENDIX D

The Interactional Diagnostic Manual

Introduction

Although there is a general agreement among family theorists that families should be viewed as a system there is little other agreement. For example, family therapists cannot agree on the most important variables to study in terms of family behavior. Therefore, each theorist has established an independent set of concepts and nomenclature. The lack of uniformity in the family therapy nomenclature has made classification of family problems difficult.

Purpose

The purpose of this manual is to provide family therapists with a *compilation* of commonly used interactional schemes in a relatively uniform format. The goal is to make it less difficult to make an interactional diagnosis. Two additional benefits are expected from this effort. First, it will begin to provide a common language for family therapists. Second, it will provide for more continuity in research of family therapy. This manual is a beginning effort at compiling family therapy nomenclature. Considerable empirical research will be needed before the widely disparate concepts presented here can be organized into a coherent whole.

Source of Information

There has been no attempt here to create new schemes, paradigms or typologies. Current marriage and family therapy literature has been reviewed and those paradigms which were found to be (1) relatively specific, and (2) could be identified as interactional in nature were included in the present compilation.

Functional vs. Dysfunctional Interaction

One of the strengths of the family therapy field has been the effort to identify both dysfunctional and functional patterns in family systems. Therefore, most of the paradigms included in the Interactional Diagnostic Manual (IDM) make it possible to formulate a description of a healthy or functional family. For this reason, each diagnostic entity will be identified as "functional" or "dysfunctional." This is done in two ways. First, following the title of each diagnostic category will be the term functional or dysfunctional. Second, the code of each diagnostic criterion will include in the fourth digit, a "D" or an "F", indicating dysfunctional and functional, respectively. For example, the "Total Relationship" (Functional) is coded 102.F5, while the "Passive-Congenial Relationship" (Dysfunctional), is coded 102.D3.

Format of Text

Due to the wide acceptance of the DSM-III the IDM was created with a similar format. The information for each diagnostic entity is included under specific headings. Some of the paradigms fit well into this format, while others lacked the information necessary to complete one or more of the descriptions under a specific heading. When this occurred the unused headings were omitted.

The IDM schemes are ordered alphabetically according to author. This differs from the DSM-III where the disorders are organized by diagnostic types. It is hoped that future editions of the IDM can be reorganized on a more logical and useful basis. This will be possible as the field becomes more organized and carefully researched.

These headings and their definitions are given below.

— *Essential Features.* These are the features that the author(s) of each scheme have identified as the most pronounced and/or likely to be seen by the therapist.
— *Associated Features.* These are features that are often present, but not invariably and may be less apparent.
— *Related Schemes or Diagnoses.* Where the diagnosis appears related to another diagnosis in a different scheme, or to the entire scheme itself, the relationship will be identified. This cross-referencing allows the observer to move quickly through the IDM when making diagnoses, as well as the option of making alternate diagnoses.
— *Course.* This will include the long term pattern of events and outcome likely to be associated with the disorder.
— *Impairment.* This suggests what effects the disorder will have on relationships and individuals not identified as a part of the diagnoses.
— *Predisposing Factors.* This is the suggested etiology for each disorder. These should be entertained as hypotheses to be tested. When these predisposing factors are observed in a relationship, the relationship can be considered "at risk." This means that if the current situation were to continue, the relationship would eventually meet the criteria for the diagnosis.
— *Dynamics.* The interpersonal dynamics which were suggested by the authors of each scheme are included. These should be entertained as hypotheses since the definitions depend on the theoretical orientation of the authors.
— *Role Tendency.* If certain essential and associated features tend to occur with persons of a particular role then that tendency will be indicated here.
— *Diagnostic Criteria.* This last heading will always be present since it will provide a list of the features most necessary to make a diagnosis.

Cuber, J. F., & Harroff, P. B. (1965). *The significant Americans.* New York: Appleton-Century.

Five Kinds of Relationships

(John F. Cuber and Peggy B. Harroff, 1965)

102.D1 *Conflict-Habituated Relationship* (DYSFUNCTIONAL)

Essential Features. At first the couple may appear controlled and friendly with one another, but tension and conflict should appear rather quickly and be persistent once revealed.

Associated Features. Children of the couple will likely be aware of the continued conflict, even though the couple may deny it. Issues will seldom if ever be resolved. The content of the arguments will have little effect on the pattern set by the couple. Both spouses will likely express a commitment to the other and a desire to stay in the relationship. Fighting may get quite "colorful," but seldom involves physical abuse.

Related Schemes and Diagnoses. Appears related to Symmetrical relationship (103.D2) and Half-marriage (104.D1).

Course. These relationships often last the life of the couple.

Impairment. Friends and family may avoid association with the couple due to the tendency they have to fight in the presence of others.

Dynamics. The conflict for some of these couples may be the cohesive factor in the relationship and without it the relationship would dissolve. The conflict may also serve as a form of intimacy.

Diagnostic Criteria for the Conflict-Habituated Relationship. 102.D1

A. The couple as a unit will exhibit the following characteristics:
  1. An atmosphere of tension surrounds the couple more often than not.
  2. The couple may first try to conceal their fighting, but when honest with the therapist, they will admit to a high frequency of marital discord.
  3. If the couple has children the children will most likely be aware of their parents continual fighting.

102.D2 *The Devitalized Relationship* (DYSFUNCTIONAL)

Essential Features. There will be a clear distinction between how the couple presently feels about their relationship and how they felt about it in earlier years. Both spouses will suggest that they were deeply in love in the first years of the marriage, but their love has since disappeared. The present relationship will contrast with the earlier years in that there will be little time spent together, most activities will not be shared and sex will be both qualitatively and quantitatively less satisfying.

Genuine interest in children and in the careers of one or both will be retained but this interest will be for different reasons than existed earlier. The intrinsic value of the career(s) will not be shared. Interest will be based most on the career's income value.

To the therapist the relationship will appear dead, lacking any zest or vitality. There will be little tension and little expressed affect. In spite of this the couple will claim there is "something" there.

Associated Features. There appear to be two types of attitudes found in devitalized relationships. One is an accepting, helpless, "that is the way life is" attitude. The other is a resistant, "I don't like it this way" attitude.

Related Schemes and Diagnoses. Appears related to Disengaged System (105.Dx5). The Vital, Devitalized and Total relationships appear to be developmentally related. Most couples probably start out in the Vital mode and then either become Devitalized or move into the Total relationship.

Course. The couples tend to stick together through the rest of their lives.

Predisposing Factors. Some suggest that the devitalized relationship is a developmental stage for marriage which would account for the prevalence of this marital style.

Diagnostic Criteria for the Devitalized Relationship. 102.D2

A. There will be a clear discrepancy between reports of the early years of the marriage and reports of the present relationship.
  1. The earlier marriage will have the following characteristics:
    a. The couple was deeply in love with one another.
    b. They spent a lot of time together.
    c. Each was closely identified with the other.
    d. They enjoyed sex.
  2. Their current relationship will have the following characteristics:
    a. They report no feelings of love.
    b. They spend little time together.
    c. They are each involved in their own separate activities and not identified with each other.
    d. They report little satisfaction in their sexual relationship.
B. To the therapist the relationship will appear "dead."
C. Spouses in the devitalized marriage tend to react to the state of their relationship in one of two ways:
  1. Accepting
  2. Resisting

102.D3 The Passive-Congenial Relationship (DYSFUNCTIONAL)

Essential Features. There is a great deal of similarity between the passive-congenial and the devitalized relationships. The two are differentiated by the fact that the passive-congenial relationship starts out lacking vitality and stays that way. The couple will passively attempt to agree on most things making confict unlikely. Neither spouse will seem jarred or dissatisfied with the relationship and will likely lack any motivation for change.

Associated Features. Both partners will have mostly outside interests as a result of their value in personal freedom and independence. They will often suggest that their relationship is a lower priority item than other interests and therefore it fits in well with their lifestyle.

Related Schemes and Diagnoses. Appears related to Symmetrical Class (103.D2).

Course. Couples may end up in the passive-congenial relationship accidentally or by intention. Either way, since both spouses are usually satisfied with the relationship it does not tend to change to some other type.

Predisposing Factors. Some believe the passive-congenial relationship fits in well with the demands of today's society and is therefore a logical adjustment to such demands.

Diagnostic Criteria for the Passive-Congenial Relationship. 102.D3
A. The couple as a unit will have the following characteristics as a part of their relationship, both past and present:
1. They report a lack of vitality.
2. They have similar interests, but not shared.
3. They are and have been heavily involved in outside interests.
4. They are both basically satisfied with the relationship.

102.F4 The Vital Relationship (FUNCTIONAL)

Essential Features. The partners in this relationship exist for each other. The relationship is the highest priority in their lives. Each will express a lack of enjoyment in activities which the other is not also involved. For this reason all activities that can be are shared. Those activities that are shared are exciting to the couple.

Associated Features. Conflict may occur, but only as a result of a shared priority on which they may differ. These conflicts are settled quickly. This couple may come for therapy for the purpose of eliminating obstacles which keep them from sharing time together.

Related Schemes and Diagnoses. Appears related to Structurally-Connected System (105.F37). The Vital, Devitalized and Total relationships appear to be developmentally related. Most couples start out in the Vital mode and then either become Devitalized or move into the Total Relationship.

Diagnostic Criteria for the Vital Relationship. 102.F4
A. The couple in the Vital relationship will have the following characteristics:
1. Most of their activities are shared.
2. Activities that they do not share, are not enjoyed.
3. They both agree that the relationship is the highest priority in their lives.

102.F5 The Total Relationship (FUNCTIONAL)

Essential Features. The total relationship is, in essence, a matured vital relationship. Conflict will be less in the total relationship since areas of difference have been worked out. The partners will tend to enjoy one another and feel comfortable with each other.

Associated Features. One may often find spouses in the vital marriage involved in each other's careers. One spouse, for example may go with the other on regular business trips even if there is great inconvenience.

Related Schemes and Diagnosis. The Vital, Devitalized and Total relationships appear to be developmentally related. Most couples probably start out in the Vital mode and then either become Devitalized or move into the Total relationship.

Diagnostic Criteria for the Total Relationship. 102.F5
A. The Total relationship will have the following characteristics:
1. They report that most, if not all, important life events are vitally shared.
2. There is practically no pretense between the partners, or between them and the outside world.
3. There are few areas of tension, even though there may have been earlier in the marriage.

Harper, J. M., Scoresby, A. L., & Boyce, W. D. (1977). The logical levels of complementary, symmetrical, and parallel interaction classes in family dyads. *Family Process, 16,* 199-210.

Complementary, Symmetrical and Parallel Interaction Classes

(Harper, James J., Scoresby, A. Lynn, and Boyce, W. Duane, 1977)

103.D1 Complementary Relationship (DYSFUNCTIONAL)

Essential Features. The couple is characterized by an exchange pattern of behaviors that are opposite in nature. For example, if a spouse got depressed following a period of cheerfulness in the other spouse, the interaction would be considered complementary.

Related Schemes and Diagnoses. Appears related to Half Marriage (104.D1), Attaching-Detaching Marriage (104.D2), Sado-Masochistic Marriage (104.D3), and Neurotic Marriage (104.D5).

Diagnostic Criteria for a Complementary Relationship 103.D1
A. Predominant interaction between the partners can be identified as an exchange of opposite behaviors. Examples include: cheerfulness/depression, dominant/submissive, talkative/quiet, and sloppy/neat.

103.D2 Symmetrical Relationship (DYSFUNCTIONAL)

Essential Features. The couple is characterized by an exchange pattern of behaviors that are identical in nature. For example, if spouse A reacted in anger to Spouse B's anger, the interaction would be considered Symmetrical.

Associated Features. Couples identified as habitually symmetrical will likely be very competitive in most areas of their relationship.

Related Schemes and Diagnoses. Appears related to Child Marriage (104.D4), Therapeutic Marriage (104.D6), The Pseudomarriage (104.D7), and possibly the Conflict Habituated Relationship (102.D1).

Diagnostic Criteria for a Symmetrical Couple. 103.D2
A. Predominant interaction between the partners can be identified as an exchange of "identical" behaviors. Examples include: anger/anger, passivity/passivity, withdrawal/withdrawal, sharing/sharing, and touching/touching.

103.F3 Parallel Relationship (FUNCTIONAL)

Essential Features. The couple will exchange behaviors which are different or similar in nature depending on the context of situation in which they occur. The behaviors exchanged should appear appropriate to the situation.

Related Schemes and Diagnoses. Appears related to the Vital (102.F4) and the Total Relationship (102.F5). The parallel interaction class belongs to a higher logical level than complementary and symmetrical because it includes both of those classes in its description.

Diagnostic Criteria for Parallel Relationships. 103.F3

A. Elements of both complementarity and symmetry will be present in somewhat equal proportions.

B. The presence of a complementary exchange or a symmetrical exchange depends on the situation in which the exchange occurs and should appear appropriate to that situation.

Hiebert, W. J., & Stahmann, R. F. (1977). *Klemer's counseling in marital and sexual problems.* Baltimore: Williams & Wilkins.

Commonly Recurring Couple Interaction Patterns

(William J. Hiebert and Robert F. Stahmann, 1977)

104.D1 The Half Marriage (DYSFUNCTIONAL)

Essential Features. There is a difference in the behaviors of each spouse which is easily identifiable. Spouse "A" is retiring, retreating and nonverbal. "A" avoids direct expression of negativity and anger and retires from confrontation in interaction. Spouse "B" is verbal and forward, often confronting and attacking when dealing with disappointments and pain.

Associated Features. Couple experiences frequent ups-and-downs. Sexual relationship will be poor usually resulting in apathy. Spouse "B" tends to be frequently involved in outside activities.

Related Schemes and Diagnoses. Appears related to Complementary Class (103.D1) and Conflict Habituated Relationship (102.D1).

Course. The relationship will likely survive many years but will be highlighted by arguments and separations.

Predisposing Factors. Both spouses have marked dependency needs as a result of poor self-concept and low self-esteem.

Dynamics. Control is a central issue for both since each is trying to get the other to be responsible for their health and happiness.

Diagnostic Criteria for the Half Marriage. 104.D1

A. Spouses appear opposite in behavior with the following characteristics:
   1. Spouse "A" is
      a. passive
      b. retiring
      c. retreating
      d. nonverbal
   2. Spouse "B" is
      a. openly and often expressing anger
      b. attacking
      c. forward
      d. negative
      e. verbal
      f. involved in many outside activities

104.D2 The Attaching-Detaching Marriage (DYSFUNCTIONAL)

Essential Features. Both spouses appear similar in that they are successful in their various roles and quite competent. Spouse "A" will complain that the relationship is not warm enough with too little expression of intimacy. Spouse "B" will complain that spouse "A" tries to get too close. The relationship will have a cyclic pattern with "A" first attempting to get close to "B" and then exploding when this fails. Then after a period of time "A" will try again to get the relationship warmed up.

Associated Features. Spouse "B" may appear rather blah on the surface and will not express what is being felt or thought. Spouse "A" may become hysterical at continued failing attempts at getting the marriage warmed up. Their courtship might be marked with the following characteristics:

1. Spouse "A" was lively, vivacious, fun, strong and independent.
2. Spouse "B" was strong, silent and reliable.
3. Spouse "A" made most of the attempts at cementing the relationship.

Related Schemes and Diagnoses. Appears related to Complementary Class (103.D1).

Course. The pattern set by the courtship described above can continue indefinitely.

Predisposing Factors. Both spouses have dependency needs which are strongly tied to needs for intimacy. Spouse "B" is easily overwhelmed by emotional demands. Neither will have been taught good communication skills.

Dynamics. While both have a need for intimacy each handles it differently. Spouse "A" will continue to pursue "B" in hopes of being rewarded for persistence. Spouse "B" will allow "A" to get close when loneliness is too intense, but then will run in fear of being overwhelmed with intimacy demands from "A."

Role Tendency. Typically Spouse "A" will be the wife and Spouse "B" the husband.

Diagnostic Criteria for the Attaching-Detaching Marriage. 104.D2

A. Each couple will have the following characteristics:
　　1. Spouse "A"
　　　　a. actively pursues communication with "B."
　　　　b. expresses anger at "B" 's unwillingness to communicate.
　　2. Spouse "B"
　　　　a. nonexpressive.
　　　　b. low affect.
　　　　c. complains that other spouse demands too much intimacy.
　　　　d. withdraws from spouse when approached on emotional issues.
B. Relationship has cyclic nature involving:
　　1. "A" tries to get close to "B"
　　2. "B" withdraws
　　3. "A" becomes angry and explodes
　　4. A period of distance between "A" and "B"

104.D3 The Sado-Masochistic Marriage (DYSFUNCTIONAL)

Essential Features. Spouse "A" is very aggressive and abusive to Spouse "B," often expressing anger and hostility towards "B." "A" will belittle and attack "B." "B" appears to accept and even encourages "A" 's attacking. "B" will act as though the attacking they receive is deserved. "A" will often be involved in directing "B" 's affairs due to "B" 's seeming incompetence.

Associated Features. If "B" is the wife, there will be a problem with housework. The home will be extremely disorganized according to "A." The sexual relationship will reflect their interaction style; "A" being rough and abusive and "B" being submissive.

Related Schemes and Diagnoses. Appears related to Complementary Class (103.D1) and Conflict-Habituated Relationship (102.D1).

Course. Sado-masochistic marriages often last a lifetime. There is usually, however, a point at which "B" reaches his/her masochistic limits and explodes and this is the event which will likely bring this couple to therapy.

Impairment. "B" 's ineptness may be carried over into all aspects of "B" 's life, resulting in continual intervention from "A."

Predisposing Factors. Both of these people are dependent on one another but reflect it in different ways. "A" hides it by being in perfect control and running "B" 's life. "B" expresses it through incompetence and reliance on "A." Their dependence is complicated by very low self-esteem and insecurity.

Dynamics. "A" and "B" play on each others low self-esteem. "A" tries to appear to have high self-esteem by being in charge of "B." This fills "A" 's needs. "B" 's self-concept on the other hand is one of helplessness and "A" fills "B" 's needs by taking control. Close evaluation of this couple should reveal that "B" is actually controlling the dynamics.

Role Tendency. The wife in this couple is more likely to take on the characteristics of "B".

Diagnostic Criteria for the Sado-Masochistic Marriage. 104.D3

A. The spouses behaviors will appear interlocked with the following characteristics:
    1. Spouse "A"
        a. is attacking towards "B"
        b. is abusive towards "B"
        c. appears in complete control of self and "B"
    2. Spouse "B"
        a. is submissive
        b. is passive
        c. accepts blame from "A"
        d. appears to be disorganized and inept
B. The couple is likely to argue in front of the therapist, encouraging the therapist to take sides.

104.D4 The Child Marriage (DYSFUNCTIONAL)

Essential Features. Both spouses' behaviors will be very similar to that of children. This will include demands for childish gratifications, temper tantrums, little expression of affection and little time spent together. Each will likely have a group of same sex friends and both will be jealous of the other's friends and their involvement with them. Conflict is usually dealt with through running away to family or friends. When conflict is not dealt with by running they usually fight like kids; throwing things, tearing clothes and yelling.

Associated Features. Each will likely experience life with loneliness. When sick they will be incapacitated and will expect the other to wait on them. They tend to live close to family of origin with high frequencies of intervention from their families.

Related Schemes and Diagnoses. Appears related to Symmetrical Class (103.D2).

Predisposing Factors. Both spouses have dependency needs which they expect to be filled by the other. In essence they are asking the other to finish rearing them.

Diagnostic Criteria for the Child Marriage. 104.D4

A. A strikingly similar pair, with the following characteristics:
    1. frequently fighting.
    2. fighting resembles the fights of children.
    3. expressing little affection
    4. little sharing of friends
    5. both expressing loneliness

104.D5 The Neurotic Marriage (DYSFUNCTIONAL)

Essential Features. The spouses rigidly take on the complementary roles of caretaker and patient. The roles should be very clear but are marked with dissatisfaction. Both will be dissatisfied with the caretakers job and it will show in decreased functioning of the patient. The marriage will appear very lopsided.

Associated Features. Both may appear disappointed and depressed. The caretaker may become angry and both may resent the other.

Related Schemes and Diagnoses. Appears related to Complementary class (103.D1).

Course. The caretaker will be initially successful but eventually will not be able to meet the expectations of caretaking created by the patient and by themselves. In spite of dissatisfaction the roles become so rigid that the prognosis for change is poor.

Diagnostic Criteria for the Neurotic Marriage

A. The spouses will differ markedly from one another, each having the following characteristics:
   1. Spouse ''A'' (the caretaker)
      a. is healthy but tired
      b. feels responsible for the well-being of ''B''
      c. is disappointed in his or her ability to take care of ''B''
   2. Spouse ''B'' (the patient)
      a. is suffering in some way
      b. feels ''A'' is obligated to take care of them
      c. is disappointed in ''A'' 's performance
      d. is depressed
      e. feels helpless
B. These roles will be interlocking and very resistant to change.

104.D6 *The Therapeutic Marriage* (DYSFUNCTIONAL)

Essential Features. The spouses in this marriage are similar in that each is trying to be the doctor of the other. Each will take turns being the patient for the other. A key marker in the relationship is frustration with the other. The frustration usually centers around the other not getting well fast enough, or getting well too fast, or that the other is still trying to doctor them.

Associated Features. The courtship of this couple should standout. They both were likely going through some kind of difficulty when they started dating and they seemed to have rescued each other from the difficulty. At that point each took on the responsibility of taking care of the other for the rest of their lives. The relationship could be characterized as parent/child with very little adult interaction.

Related Schemes and Diagnoses. Appears related to Symmetrical Class (103.D2).

Dynamics. Both have needs to take care of and be taken care of and thus they vacillate back and forth each taking turns being a member of the older generation while the other is a member of the younger generation.

Diagnostic Criteria for the Therapeutic Marriage. 104.D6.

A. This relationship is marked with three characteristics:
   1. Both spouses express a desire to take care of the other, or be taken care of by the other.
   2. The courtship occurred in time of difficulty for both spouses.
   3. Frustration is exhibited by one or both at the job the other is doing as parent or child.

104.D7 *The Pseudomarriage* (DYSFUNCTIONAL)

Essential Features. The couple in this marriage is not bonded. Each spouse will have outside interests which will supersede any interest in the marriage. The key feature will be a lack of intimacy. To outsiders the relationship will seem cool but not hostile.

Associated Features. Many Pseudomarriages are the result of a pregnancy prior to the marriage or some other situation which brought them to marriage before a commitment and a bond was established.

Related Schemes and Diagnoses. Appears related to Symmetrical Class (103.D2) and Passive-Congenial (102.D3).

Course. Unless one of the partners gets lonely or tired of the relationship it could last a lifetime in its pseudo state.

Predisposing Factors. Persons will get involved in this kind of relationship when they have an outside investment which needs the relationship as a payoff.

Dynamics. Since the relationship is not being held together by typical relationship bonds the couple is usually staying together for the convenience of the living arrangement.

Diagnostic Criteria for the Pseudomarriage. 104.D7

A. The key characteristics of this relationship are:
   1. coolness.
   2. lack of intimacy.
   3. priority given to outside interests (e.g., careers).
B. There may be some precipitating event that brought the couple to the altar before a bond could be formed. Premarital pregnancy is a common example.

Olson, D. H., Sprenkle, D. H., & Russell, C. S. (1979). Circumplex model of marital and family systems: I. Cohesion and adaptability dimensions, family types, and clinical applications. *Family Process, 18,* 3-28.

The Circumplex Model of Marital and Family Systems

(Olsen, David H., Sprenkle, Douglas H., and Russell, Candice, 1979)

The Circumplex model developed by Olsen et al. is comprised of two scales; adaptability and cohesion. Four points are identified on each scale. The points on the adaptability scale include: chaotic, flexible, structured, and rigid. The points on the cohesion scale include: disengaged, separated, connected, and enmeshed. A complete diagnosis is made by linking diagnoses from each scale. For example, if a family system is diagnosed as rigid on the adaptability scale and connected on the cohesion scale, the complete diagnosis would be "rigidly connected." The scales described below are unlinked and an "x" indicates where the linking number fits in the code. Complete linked codes are summarized at the end of this section.

Olsen et al. suggest that clinicians keep in mind that the classifications can be applied to entire systems or any subunit of a system.

105.D1x Adaptability: Chaotic System (DYSFUNCTIONAL)

Diagnostic Criteria for Chaotic Systems

A. The system should exhibit at least 5 of the following characteristics:
   1. Assertiveness
      a. passive and aggressive styles of interaction.
   2. Control
      a. limited and/or erratic leadership.
   3. Discipline
      a. laissez-faire attitude
      b. very lenient
      c. inconsistent consequences
      d. erratic enforcement
   4. Negotiation
      a. endless negotiations
      b. poor problem-solving
      c. impulsive solutions

5. Roles
   a. dramatic role shifts
   b. sporadic role reversals
6. Rules
   a. dramatic rule shifts
   b. many implicit rules
   c. few explicit rules
   d. arbitrarily enforced rules
7. System Feedback
   a. primarily positive loops
   b. few negative loops

B. The members of the system will score an average of 199 or greater on the adaptability scale of FACES II.

105. F2x Adaptability: The Flexible System (FUNCTIONAL)

Diagnostic Criteria for Flexible Systems
A. The system should exhibit at least 5 of the following characteristics:
   1. Assertiveness
      a. most members generally assertive
      b. rare aggression
   2. Control
      a. equalitarian
      b. fluid changes
   3. Discipline
      a. democratic
      b. unpredictable consequences
      c. maintained fairly
   4. Negotiation
      a. flexible negotiations
      b. good problem-solving
      c. solutions are agreed upon
   5. Roles
      a. role-making
      b. role sharing
      c. fluid changes of roles
   6. Rules
      a. some rule changes
      b. some explicit rules
      c. few implicit rules
      d. rules often enforced
   7. System Feedback
      a. more positive than negative loops.

B. The members of the unit of analysis will score an average of 183 to 198 on the adaptability scale of FACES II.

105. F3x Adaptability: The Structured System (FUNCTIONAL)

Diagnostic Criteria for Structured Systems
A. The system should exhibit at least 5 of the following characteristics:
   1. Assertiveness
      a. most members are generally assertive
      b. some use of aggression

2. Control
    a. stable leader
    b. leadership is imposed in a kindly manner
3. Discipline
    a. democratic
    b. predictable consequences
    c. imposed firmly and enforced
4. Negotiation
    a. structured negotiations
    b. good problem-solving
    c. reasonable solutions
5. Roles
    a. roles mostly stable
    b. some role sharing
6. Rules
    a. few rule changes
    b. more explicit than implicit rules
    c. rules usually enforced
7. System Feedback
    a. more negative than positive loops
B. The members of the unit of analysis will score an average of 167 to 182 on the adaptability scale of FACES II.

105. D4x Adaptability: The Rigid System (DYSFUNCTIONAL)

Diagnostic Criteria for Rigid Systems
A. The unit of system should exhibit at least 5 of the following characteristics:
    1. Assertiveness
        a. passive-aggressive style of interaction
    2. Control
        a. authoritarian/traditional leadership
    3. Discipline
        a. autocratic
        b. overly strict
        c. rigid consequences
    4. Negotiation
        a. limited negotiations
        b. poor problem-solving
        c. solutions imposed
    5. Roles
        a. role rigidity
        b. stereotyped roles
    6. Rules
        a. rigid rules
        b. many explicit rules
        c. few implicit rules
        d. strictly enforced rules
    7. System Feedback
        a. primarily negative loops
        b. few positive loops
B. The members of the unit of analysis will score an average of 166 or less on the adaptability scale of FACES II.

105.Dx5 *Cohesion: Disengaged System* (DYSFUNCTIONAL)

Related Schemes and Diagnoses. Appears related to Devitalized Relationship (102.D2), Passive-Congenial Marriage (102.D3), and Pseudomarriage (104.D7).

Diagnostic Criteria for Disengaged Systems

A. The system should exhibit at least 6 of the following characteristics:
   1. Emotional Bonding
      a. extreme separateness
      b. lack of closeness or loyalty
   2. Independence
      a. high independence
      b. family members depend on themselves
   3. Family Boundaries
      a. influence and ideas of outsiders unrestricted
      b. closed internal boundaries
      c. rigid generational boundaries
   4. Coalitions
      a. weak marital coalition
      b. poor sibling relationship
      c. blurred generational lines
      d. usually a family scapegoat
   5. Time
      a. time apart from family is maximized (physical or emotional)
      b. rarely spend time together
   6. Space
      a. separate space needed and preferred (physical and emotional)
   7. Friends
      a. mainly individual friends seen alone
      b. few family friends
   8. Decision Making
      a. decisions are primarily individual
      b. no checking with other family members
   9. Interests and Recreation
      a. activities are usually separate
B. The members of the unit of analysis will score an average of 230 or less on the cohesion scale of FACES II.

105.Fx6 *Cohesion: Separated System* (FUNCTIONAL)

Diagnostic Criteria for Separated Systems

A. The system should exhibit at least 6 of the following characteristics:
   1. Emotional Bonding
      a. emotional separateness encouraged and preferred
      b. need for support respected
   2. Independence
      a. independence encouraged and preferred
      b. dependence acceptable at times
      c. many needs met outside of family
   3. Family Boundaries
      a. open to outside people and ideas
      b. clear generational boundaries
   4. Coalitions
      a. stable marital coalitions

    b. stable sibling relationships
    c. fluid generational lines
  5. Time
    a. time alone important
    b. some time spent together
  6. Space
    a. separate space preferred
    b. some sharing of family space
  7. Friends
    a. individual friends shared with family
    b. some family friends
  8. Decision Making
    a. most decisions individually made
    b. are able to make joint decisions on family issues
  9. Interests and Recreation
    a. some spontaneous family activities
    b. individual activities supported
B. The members of the unit of analysis will score an average of 231 to 250 on the cohesion scale of FACES II.

105.Fx7 Cohesion: Connected System (FUNCTIONAL)

Diagnostic Criteria for Connected Systems
A. The system should exhibit at least 6 of the following characteristics:
  1. Emotional Bonding
    a. emotional closeness encouraged and preferred
    b. need for separateness expected
  2. Independence
    a. dependence is encouraged and preferred
    b. independence acceptable at times
    c. many individual needs met within the family
  3. Family Boundaries
    a. some control from outside people and ideas
    b. clear generational boundaries
  4. Coalitions
    a. strong marital coalitions
    b. stable sibling relations
    c. stable generational lines
  5. Time
    a. time together important and scheduled
    b. time alone permitted
  6. Space
    a. sharing family space preferred
    b. private space respected
  7. Friends
    a. some individual friends
    b. some scheduled activities with couple/family friends
  8. Decision Making
    a. most decisions made with family in mind
    b. individual decisions are shared
  9. Interests and Recreation
    a. some scheduled family activities
    b. family involved in individual interests

B. The members of the unit of analysis will score an average of 251 to 270 on the cohesion scale of FACES II.

105.Dx8 Cohesion: Enmeshed System (DYSFUNCTIONAL)

Diagnostic Criteria for Enmeshed Systems
A. The system should exhibit at least 6 of the following characteristics:
1. Emotional bonding
   a. extreme closeness
   b. loyalty demanded
   c. separateness restricted
2. Independence
   a. high dependence of family members on each other
3. Family Boundaries
   a. influence from outside people and ideas restricted
   b. blurred internal boundaries
4. Coalitions
   a. weak marital coalitions
   b. several parent-child coalitions
   c. blurred generational lines
5. Time
   a. time together maximized
   b. time alone strongly limited
6. Space
   a. little or no private space
7. Friends
   a. limited individual friends
   b. couple/family friends strongly encouraged
8. Decision Making
   a. all decisions, both personal and relationship, must be approved
9. Interests and Recreation
   a. most activities and interests must be shared with family
B. The members of the unit of analysis will score an average of 271 or more on the cohesion scale of FACES II.

Linked Codes for Complete Diagnoses with the Circumplex Model

105.D15	Chaotically Disengaged	(DYSFUNCTIONAL)
105.D16	Chaotically Separated	(DYSFUNCTIONAL)
105.D17	Chaotically Connected	(DYSFUNCTIONAL)
105.D18	Chaotically Enmeshed	(DYSFUNCTIONAL)
105.D25	Flexibly Disengaged	(DYSFUNCTIONAL)
105.F26	Flexibly Separated	(FUNCTIONAL)
105.F27	Flexibly Connected	(FUNCTIONAL)
105.D28	Flexibly Enmeshed	(DYSFUNCTIONAL)
105.D35	Structurally Disengaged	(DYSFUNCTIONAL)
105.F36	Structurally Separated	(FUNCTIONAL)
105.F37	Structurally Connected	(FUNCTIONAL)
105.D38	Structurally Enmeshed	(DYSFUNCTIONAL)
105.D45	Rigidly Disengaged	(DYSFUNCTIONAL)
105.D46	Rigidly Separated	(DYSFUNCTIONAL)
105.D47	Rigidly Connected	(DYSFUNCTIONAL)
105.D48	Rigidly Enmeshed	(DYSFUNCTIONAL)

APPENDIX E
Assessment Instruments Index

Code	Assessment Instrument Title
001	Adjective Checklist (ACL)
002	Adlerian Priorities Scale
003	Adolescent-Family Inventory of Life Events and Changes (A-FILE)
004	Allred Interaction Analysis (AIA)
005	Allred Interaction Analysis-Therapists (AIAT)
006	An Adlerian Life Style Questionnaire
007	Analysis of Relationships
008	Areas of Change Questionnaire
009	Assertive Behavior Schedule
010	Beck Depression Inventory (BDI)
011	Becker Adjective Checklist (Patterson Version)
012	Bipolar Psychological Inventory (BIPOLAR)
013	Behavioral Type-A Scale
014	Buss-Durkee Anger Inventory (BUSS)
015	California Occupational Preference Survey
016	California Psychological Inventory (CPI)
017	Caring Relationship Inventory (CRI)
018	Checklist C (Taplin Version)
019	Children's Problem Behaviors Checklist
020	Classroom Environment Scale (CES)
021	Concept Mastery Test
022	Cornell Index
023	Couple Interaction Scoring System (CISS)
024	Couple's Pre-counseling Inventory
025	Depression Adjective Checklists (DACL)
026	Dyadic Interaction Scoring Code (DISC)
027	Edwards Personal Preference Survey (EPPS)
028	Enriching and Nurturing Relationships Issues, Communication and Happiness (ENRICH)
029	Experimental World Inventory
030	Eysenck Personality Inventory
031	Eysenck Personality Questionnaire
032	Family Adaptability and Cohesion Evaluation Scale (FACES)
033	Family Adaptability and Cohesion Evaluation Scale (FACES-II)
034	Family Coping Strategies (F-COPES)
035	Family Environment Scale (FES)
036	Family Happiness Scales
037	Family Inventory of Life Events and Changes (FILE)
038	Family Satisfaction
039	Family Strengths
040	Fear Inventory
041	Fear Survey Schedule
042	Fundamental Interpersonal Relations Orientation—Behavior (FIRO-B)
043	Fundamental Interpersonal Relations Orientation—Feelings (FIRO-F)
044	Group Environment Scale
045	Guilford-Zimmerman Temperament Survey (GUILFORD-ZIMMERMAN)

046	Hill Interaction Matrix (HIM) (HILL)
047	Hill Interaction Matrix-Behavior (HIMB)
048	Hopelessness Scale
049	Interpersonal Conflict Scale
050	Inventory of Marital Conflict (MC)
051	Inventory of Pre-marital Conflict (IPMC)
052	Irrational Behavior Test
053	Jenkins Activity Survey
054	Kuder Vocational Preference Inventory (KUDER)
055	Kvebaek Family Sculpture Technique (KVEBAEK)
056	Leary Interpersonal Checklist (ICL)
057	Lowman's Measures of Family Emotion
058	Marital Activities Inventory
059	Marital Activities Inventory Coding System (MICS)
060	Marital Adjustment Test (MAT) (LOCKE-WALLACE)
061	Marital Attitudes Evaluation (MATE)
062	Marital Communications Inventory (MCI)
063	Marital Expectation Inventory
064	Marital Happiness Scales (MHS)
065	Marital Inventories (MI)
066	Marital Inventories for Latter-Day Saint Couples (MIL)
067	Marital Pre-counseling Inventory
068	Marital/Sexual Happiness Scales
069	Marital Status Inventory (MSI)
070	Marriage Adjustment Inventory
071	Menstrual Attitude Scale
072	Menstrual Distress Questionnaire
073	Milwaukee Academic Interest Inventory
074	Minnesota Multiphasic Personality Inventory (MMPI)
075	Minnesota Vocational Interest Inventory
076	Mooney Problem Check List (MOONEY)
077	Moos Family Environment Scale (MOOS)
078	Multidimensional Assessment and Planning Form (MAP)
079	Multimodal Life History Questionnaire
080	Myers-Briggs Type Indicator (Myers-Briggs)
081	Omnibus Personality Inventory (OMNIBUS)
082	Parent-Adolescent Communication
083	Parent-Adolescent Communication Inventory (P-ACI)
084	Personal Assessment of Intimacy in Relationships (PAIE)
085	Personality Research Form
086	Pleasant Events Schedule
087	Profile of Mood States
088	Psychological Screening Inventory (PSI)
089	Quality of Life
090	Rathus Assertiveness Schedule
091	Reinforcement Survey Schedule
092	Relational Coding Scheme (RCS)
093	Relationship Intimacy Barometer (RIB)
094	Relationship Styles Inventory (RSI)
095	Sex Knowledge Inventory
096	Sexual Activities Inventory
097	Sexual Interaction Inventory
098	Spouse Observation Checklist

099	Status of Women Scale
100	State-Trait Anxiety Scale
101	Strong-Campbell Interest Inventory (STRONG-CAMPBELL)
102	Symptom Checklist 90 Revised (SCL-90)
103	Work Values Inventory
104	Taylor-Johnson Temperament Analysis (TJTA) (TAYLOR-JOHNSON)
105	Tennessee Self-Concept Scale (TENNESSEE)
106	Vanderveen's Family Unit Test (FUT)
107	Vocational Preference Inventory
108	Walker Behavior Checklist (WALKER)
109	Ward Atmosphere Scale
110	Work Environment Scale
111	Zung Depression Scale (ZUNG)

APPENDIX F

Intervention Index

Code	Intervention
001	Abstinence from sexual intercourse, prescribing.
002	Accommodating.
	Actions client has taken. *See* Homework.
	Active listening. *See* Reflecting.
	Affect releasing and controlling. *See* Structuring.
003	Agenda setting. *See also* Goal setting.
004	Allegory, using, in session.
005	Anchoring.
	Antecedents, determining, in session. *See* Discriminative stimuli.
006	Assertiveness training. *See also* Systematic desensitization.
	Assessing. *See* Assessment Instruments Index List (Appendix E).
	See also History taking, Observing.
	Assessment taking,
007	continuous. *See also* Observing.
008	frequency counts. *See also* Observing.
009	permanent record. *See also* Observing.
	pre-posttreatment. *See* Assessing
010	Aversive stimuli. *See also* Punishment.
011	determining.
012	removing.
013	prescribing. *See also* Paradoxical injunction.
	Behavior. *See also* Chaining, Reinforcing, Shaping, Punishing.
014	determining target, in session. *See also* History taking, Goal setting, Observing.
015	Behavioral rehearsal, using, in session.
	Benching. *See* Time out.
	Benevolent sabotage. *See* Crisis induction.
016	Bibliotherapy, using.
017	Body language, explaining or interpreting, in session.
	Ceremony,
018	using, in session.
019	interpreting.

020	Chaining, backwards. *See also* Shaping.
	Chemotherapy. *See* Referring.
021	Clarifying. *See also* Communication.
022	Coaching.
023	Coital positions, prescribing recommended.
	Communication. *See also* Confronting, Listening, Reflection.
024	avoiding punishment in,
025	training "I" messages.
026	training.
	Conditioning. *See* Reinforcement.
	Conflict
	induction. *See* Crisis induction.
	resolution. *See also* Problem solving.
027	Confronting. *See also* Communication.
	Contracting
028	good faith.
029	*Quid pro quo*.
030	training.
031	with clients about therapy.
	Creating alternatives. *See* Problem solving.
032	Crisis induction. *See also* Paradoxical injunction.
	Data collecting. *See* Assessment, History taking.
	Desensitization. *See* Systematic desensitization.
033	Devils advocate, playing, in session.
034	Diagraming. *See also* Education.
035	Direct stimulation of the penis, prescribing.
036	Directives, using, in session.
	Disclosing. *See* Self-disclosure.
037	Discriminative stimuli, determining in session. *See also* History taking.
038	Distraction techniques, prescribing.
039	Dream, analyzing.
040	Educating. *See also* Rationales.
041	Empathizing.
042	Encouraging.
	Evaluating. *See also* Assessment, Data collection, History taking.
043	client reactions to therapy.
044	treatment administration.
045	treatment expectations by clients.
046	Extinguishing behavior.
	Explaining. *See* Educating, Rationales.
	Exploring. *See* History taking.
047	Family of origin, using, in session.
048	Family voyages, using, in session.
049	Fantasy, prescribing.
	Frequency recording. *See* Assessment
	Games
	Confronting. *See* Confronting.
050	interpreting, in session.
051	using, in session.
	Genogram. *See* History taking.
052	Goal setting. *See also* Agenda setting.
053	Go-between process, using the, in session.

Guided imagery, using, in session. *See* Systematic desensitization. *See also* Family voyages.

History taking. *See also* Assessment, Data collection.

    Family structure,

054	genogram.
055	household composition.
056	social network.
057	geographic context.

    Family functioning,
      instrumental functioning,

058	task allocation.
059	daily routines.

      expressive functioning,

060	communication patterns.
061	affective involvement.

    Family development,
      specific problem,

062	presenting problem.
063	history of presenting problem.
064	physical health.
065	current drug use.
066	mental status report.

      family life cycle,

067	individual developmental history.
068	relationship history.
069	sexual history.

Homework,

070	assigning
071	reviewing.
072	Humor, using, in session.
073	Hypnosis, using, in session.

Hypothesis,

074	testing, training clients in use of. *See also* Problem solving.
	testing, in session. *See* Evaluating, Observing.
075	Interpreting.
076	Interrupting.
	Joining, *See* Empathizing.
077	Kegel's exercises, prescribing.
078	Leading.
079	Listening. *See also* Communicating, Empathizing, Reflecting.
	paraphrasing. *See* Reflecting.
080	training.
081	Masturbation, prescribing.
082	Mediating.
	Medical examination. *See* Referring.
083	Metaphor, using, in session.
084	Metacommunicating.
	Mimesis. *See* Empathizing.
085	Modeling. *See also* Educating.
086	Mourning.
087	Multiple impact, using, in session.
	Negative thinking,
088	confronting.

APPENDIX G

Progress Notes Worksheet

Date_____

Therapist_____ Supervisor_____

Client No._____-_____-_____ Session No._____ Session Length (in minutes)__

Type of Client (Check one): _____(1) Individual _____(2) Marital _____(3) Family

Problem Type (Check one):

_____(1) Adolescent Dysfunction _____(2) Child Misbehavior _____(3) Divorce

_____(4) Family Conflict _____(5) Individual Affect _____(6) Individual Mental

_____(7) Marital Conflict _____(8) Premarital _____(9) Reconstituted Family

_____(10) Sexual Dysfunction _____(11) Substance Abuse

Problem/Goal   Current D.B.
                                1. In Session   2. Outside of session
                                                          (Homework etc.)

Treatment (List specific interventions this session)
1. Delivered? How Evaluated?   2. Effects? How Evaluated?

Clinical Decisions
1. Continue Treatment?
2. Change Treatment?
3. Refer?
4. Terminate?

APPENDIX H

Progress Notes

Date (ex. 12 Jun 83)_____

Therapist (ex. Cain M)_____ Supervisor (ex. Mead G)_____

Client No._____-_____-_____ Session No._____ Session Length (in minutes)__

Type of Client (Check one): _____(1) Individual _____(2) Marital _____(3) Family

Problem Type (Check one):

_____(1) Adolescent Dysfunction _____(2) Child Misbehavior _____(3) Divorce

_____(4) Family Conflict _____(5) Individual Affect _____(6) Individual Mental

_____(7) Marital Conflict _____(8) Premarital _____ (9) Reconstituted Family

_____(10) Sexual Dysfunction _____(11) Substance Abuse

Will treatment be in group format? (1) Yes_____ (2) No_____

Treatment Phase: Data Gathering_____Treatment_____Education_____

Enrichment_____Termination_____Follow up_____

Clients present: Husband_____Wife_____Children_____

Information below gained from: Interview_____Phone call_____Other (specify)_____

Problems/Goals and Interventions List Progress

Please use the numbers indicated to designate the subunit to which the problem/goal and interventions apply. (1) Husband; (2) Wife; (3) Child by birth order, e.g., 3.3 is the third child; (4) Family; (5) Marital Couple; (6) Parent-Child; (7) Siblings; (8) Single Adult.

Problems Continued from the P/G and I List

Prob. No._____Subunit No._____Prob. Code_____Title_____
Severity this Session_____Interventions this Session_____

Prob. No._____Subunit No._____Prob. Code_____Title_____
Severity this Session_____Interventions this Session_____

Prob. No._____Subunit No._____Prob. Code_____Title_____
Severity this Session_____Interventions this Session_____

Prob. No._____Subunit No._____Prob. Code_____Title_____
Severity this Session_____Interventions this Session_____

Prob. No._____Subunit No._____Prob. Code_____Title_____
Severity this Session_____Interventions this Session_____

New Problems to Be Added

Prob. No._____Subunit No._____Prob. Code_____Title_____
Initial Severity_____Goal_____Goal Achievement Date_____No. of Sessions_____
Interventions _____
Prob. No._____Subunit No._____Prob. Code_____Title_____
Initial Severity_____Goal_____Goal Achievement Date_____No. of Sessions_____
Interventions _____

Computer-Aided Assessment: Design Considerations

Larry L. Constantine

ABSTRACT. Computer-aided assessment (CAA) is the use of computers to assist or simplify measurement and evaluation in research and clinical practice. In the family field, potential applications range from simple computer simulations of standard paper-and-pencil measures to sophisticated new assessment techniques using computer graphics or interactive dialogue. The development of effective new CAA tools is facilitated by consideration of interrelationships between technical design issues and questions of family measurement and theory. General guidelines for design of CAA systems are discussed and specific examples of working CAA programs are presented.

The application of microcomputers within family studies and family psychotherapy is a developing area with enormous potential. One of the most interesting applications to emerge is that of computer-aided assessment (CAA). First introduced in psychology and psychiatric practice (Cole, Johnson & Williams, 1976; Johnson & Williams, 1978), CAA is the use of computers to assist in the psychotherapeutic assessment or evaluation of individuals, couples, families, and other groups. CAA can simplify ordinary assessment procedures, but it can also make possible exotic new techniques. These methods hold the promise of substantially extending the range of measurement techniques available for family research and clinical practice.

The development of effective new CAA systems for families requires expertise that spans computer program design, family theory, and the practice of therapy. In this chapter, the interaction between "narrow technical issues" on the computer side and "professional, conceptual issues" on the family side will be explored through a discussion of general principles and illustrated through specific applications in the area of computer-aided assessment of families. The emphasis is on applications for so-called microcomputers or personal computers, as these are the systems most likely to be accessible to clinicians.

Larry L. Constantine, LCSW, Assistant Professor of Human Development and Family Relations, University of Connecticut, Storrs, is a Family Therapist in practice in Acton, Massachusetts. A former computer consultant for more than ten years, he was a principal developer of program design theory and techniques now in wide use.

89

In developing computer programs, the complex interactions between application and implementation are often ignored or vastly over-simplified. The resulting computer systems not only offer less for what they cost to build but may even be solutions to the wrong problems. If systems development is primarily approached as a computer programming problem, then the needs of either the psychotherapist or client may become secondary to the particular programming language being used. The opposite approach—specifying in detail the assessment problem to be solved without consideration of the technical programming issues involved in implementing the system—has an equal number of pitfalls. Often an expensive or complicated program is constructed when, by stating the problem only slightly differently, a much simpler system would have been possible. Or a program is developed which solves a problem today but cannot be adapted to the needs which surface tomorrow as research evolves or therapy experience accumulates.

It is not practicable to turn every family researcher or clinician with an interest in CAA into a competent programmer and systems designer, any more than we would expect a programmer to become a trained family therapist before helping on a CAA project. The problems of assessment are those of the family professionals, however, and the initiative to "go the extra distance" must come from their side. Those responsible for developing new applications in the family field must sustain a dual focus on application and implementation and be able to deal deftly and continuously with the complex interactions implied by this double expertise.

Computer programming itself is not inordinately hard to learn. Almost everyone who uses microcomputers sooner or later writes some small programs in a version of BASIC or a similar programming language. This does not, of course, make the writer into a programmer, any more than being able to hammer in a nail makes one a carpenter. A skilled programmer is the master of diverse arcana. The basic principles of sound program design, however, are neither obscure nor excessively difficult to understand.

As in all areas of computer application, the development of computer programs for computer-aided assessment presents a *systemic* problem requiring consideration of a whole and the interaction among its constituent parts, a viewpoint which should be comfortable for most contemporary family therapists and theorists. Just as the multigenerational history of families is reflected in current family process, so the organization of the processes of problem definition and solution development are interrelated and become permanently imbedded in the computer programs we construct. Just as members of families are interrelated by their continued participation in collective activity, so the parts of a computerized system interact to form a whole that could be the solution to a genuine problem or simply the migraine which irritates the entire therapy enterprise.

COMPUTER-AIDED ASSESSMENT:
ANALYSIS OF APPLICATIONS

Choosing the Problem

The first question which should be asked before considering any computer application is: "Why?" In the process, one should consider whether the use of computers can be avoided altogether. If this question is approached with an open mind, many pointless and worthless systems may never have to be programmed.

The list of things computers can do is long; the list of what they cannot do is even more extensive. But the most interesting list is of those things computers could be made to do but might as well be left alone. It is this list that best illumines the appropriate, the effective use of computers. Many hundreds of simple BASIC programs have been written to balance checkbooks, but in truth, in almost every case it is easier to balance a checkbook with a pencil and a pocket calculator than with a computer and a two-bit program. And for the creative cook wanting to keep track of favorite recipes, a simple card-file is almost invariably superior and always cheaper than a data base management system operating on a microcomputer.

The trick is to choose a problem of just the right "size," one which can be expressed straightforwardly but for which the computer offers some special advantage or leverage over a manual procedure. There are few rules of thumb for making this choice, but the range of applications of computers to family assessment illustrates the problem. Using an expensive computer to "act like" an inexpensive paper-and-pencil test is not the most efficient or effective use of a complex machine, although the economics change as computers become cheaper and cheaper. On the other hand, there are sophisticated problems in "artificial intelligence" which are more appropriate as state-of-the-art problems in computer science than as tasks for CAA. An example is expecting the computer to understand and interpret ordinary conversational statements typed by subjects. Trying to get a computer to perform, however clumsily, what is handily done by an ordinary human being, may be legitimate for research at the leading edge of computer science but is likely to be a general waste of programming talent trying to develop working family CAA applications.

Range of Applications

The potential applications of CAA range from the nearly trivial to the unobtainable. At one end of the spectrum, a word processing program can be used as a form of "electric paper" to record anything that a clinician might consider relevant to assess a particular family. Simple though this is, it can be considered to be a form of computer-aided assessment. At the other extreme would be a conversational system which, using ordinary English, "talks" with family members via a video display terminal and keyboard, building a dynamically evolving clinical model of that family. Such a system does not exist at this writing and is considerably beyond current capabilities in both the family field and computer technology.

Intake procedures. Intake procedures are probably the simplest and most basic of potential CAA applications, yet even here the computer can be a valuable partner to the clinician. In the simplest form, a computer-based word processing system could be used by the clinician to record intake notes or clinical evaluations. The word processor, by facilitating easy entry and correction, makes this task less tedious for the therapist than handwritten or typed preparation would be. Furthermore, word processing files become available for easy updating and expansion and for instantaneous incorporation into referral reports or written evaluations which might later be required. Although there are disadvantages and limitations to the simple use of word processors for this purpose (security is a problem, for example), some new capabilities are opened which would not be possible with conventional paper-and-pencil notes. For example, some commercially available file management programs for microcomputers can search ordinary text on computer files for instances of specific words or phrases. Thus the clinician could find out all those client families for which the evaluation notes include the phrase "rigidly enmeshed."

A slightly more complicated application is computerizing the process of client history taking. Filling out long paper-and-pencil forms can be boring to clients; if conducted by the therapist, history taking can be tedious for both. In a computerized version, clients sit before a microcomputer or computer terminal. The CAA program presents a video display showing a series of questions or a visual "form" to fill out. Clients respond by typing their answers directly on a computer keyboard. If the system is designed well, and the client is not intimidated by the computer, the clinician will not have to supervise the process, thus saving professional time. The program can even be made to react conditionally to clients' responses, skipping over certain questions or adding others. For example, questions about children can be omitted for a childless couple and questions about the adoption process can be added if a family has adopted children.

Tests and measures. Computers may be used either for direct assessment of families or to implement computerized versions of therapist or observer ratings. In other words, CAA systems may obtain their responses from either clients or clinicians. In the simplest schemes, CAA replaces or supplements ordinary paper-and-pencil instruments. CAA can consist of nothing more than the computer presenting the subject with each question of a conventional instrument or inventory, then waiting for and recording the response. Even this straightforward use of the computer as "electric paper" can have some advantages over paper-and-pencil administration. Scoring can be essentially instantaneous, and results can be reported to the clinician or added to a research data base almost immediately. No separate keying or entry operation is required to put test responses into "machinable" form. On-line test administration has been shown to be faster than paper-and-pencil approaches and results in fewer errors. Initially, at least, clients report more positive reactions than to equivalent paper-and-pencil tests (Johnson et al., 1978).

Although offering some distinct advantages, the "electric paper" approach does not begin to make use of the real capabilities of the computer. The computer may have easy access to information usually unavailable in conventional paper-and-pencil administration. For example, a CAA system can keep track of the time spent on each item and the number of times subjects changed their minds and corrected their responses. (Any user-oriented system should have provision for the subject to go back and change responses. To be a strict analog to an existing paper-and-pencil instrument, a CAA system *must* have this capacity.)

The best applications are those that take advantage of special capabilities of a microcomputer-based implementation and which smoothly meld the best of what is known of what human subjects can and will do and what the computer can be made to do. For example, a computer can change its display in reaction to different responses from the subject; a piece of paper will always have the same information printed on it no matter where the subject places an "X." Using a computer makes possible tests with branching logic. For example, if a clinician responds to a rating system in a way that would characterize a family as being a closed-type system, the next item might concern enmeshment, while a response indicative of a random-type family might be followed with an item concerning disengagement. The branching logic approach has been used effectively in computer-aided history taking (Psych Systems, 1982), but has seen little application in general instruments especially developed for computer administration.

Games and tasks. Even the simplest microcomputer is capable of much more complex tasks than simply presenting questions and recording responses. The graphics display capabilities of modern microcomputers offer many other possibilities. For example, the well-known RIG/T "train game" (Ravich, 1969) required a cumbersome model train layout in its original form. The strategic patterns of couples were recorded as they operated two toy trains, sending them along a path that included one common section of track. A barrier prevented the couple from seeing each others' moves. It is not difficult to program this game using computer graphics on a video screen to represent the trains moving along their tracks. Various computer implementations are possible: an early version was built around expensive special equipment, but a system has now been written using two less expensive Radio Shack computers. It would even be possible to program this for only one computer by displaying the complete track layout on two interconnected TV screens but covering up half the display on each.

Another example of a computer "game" for family assessment is the computerized version of the Kvebaek Family Sculpture Technique (Cromwell, Fournier and Kvebaek, 1980) described in some detail below. In this system, the computer serves as a medium for family members to play a kind of "board game" developed specifically for family assessment.

BASIC DESIGN CONSIDERATIONS

Designing the Interface

The user interface is where the computer program and the user—whether family member, research scientist, or therapist—interact. What the program looks like to the user and how it behaves are determined by the interface.

Designing a program interface for users who are expected to be members of ordinary families and who may range in age from 4 to 80 requires careful attention to details and a thorough understanding of how people actually respond to various kinds of computer interactions. The basic design principle here should sound familiar to family professions; the object is to maintain clear, concise, consistent communication between computer and user.

Many computer programs or software packages today are claimed to be "user-friendly," an overworked catch phrase in the computer world. In practice, "user-friendliness"often means cutesy messages from the computer and an endless series of displayed "menus" from which the user must make selections to tell the computer what to do next. Users themselves are less impressed by the loquacity than are the programming and sales staffs of the software and equipment vendors. In families, the most verbose member is often the one least attended to, and in using a computer system one soon tires of a program which never shuts up. A typical "user-friendly" system might start every session with:

I AM THE CONTROL SYSTEM FOR THE FUZZIWIG FAMILY
TESTING PACKAGE.

BEFORE I CAN PROCEED I NEED TO KNOW WHO YOU ARE.
PLEASE TYPE YOUR FIRST NAME AND THEN PRESS
"RETURN":

Carol

HELLO, CAROL, I HOPE YOU ARE FINE TODAY. WELCOME TO
THE WORLD OF FUZZIWIG COMPUTER TESTING!
CAROL, I HOPE YOU DON'T MIND WAITING WHILE I SET UP
MY DISK FILES.
THERE, I'M READY! HERE IS A LIST OF THINGS I CAN DO FOR
YOU, CAROL:

MAIN MENU

CHOOSE ANY SELECTION BY TYPING THE NUMBER WHICH
APPEARS NEXT TO THE SELECTION AND THEN PRESSING
"RETURN."
1 — FIND OUT MORE ABOUT THE FUZZIWIG FAMILY
TESTING PACKAGE
2 — START TAKING ONE OF THE FUZZIWIG FAMILY TESTS
3 — COMPLETE A FAMILY HISTORY FOR THE FUZZIWIG
SYSTEM
4 — GET HELP ON ANY ASPECT OF THE FUZZIWIG SYSTEM
WHAT WOULD YOU LIKE TO DO, CAROL?

The dialogue is apt to continue *ad nauseam.*

The format in which information is presented on a video display and
the texts of particular messages are not always carefully planned, as these
are often considered by programmers to be relatively unimportant details.
But, designing a good user interface may not be as simple as it seems. For
example, consider a simple "forced-choice" question format in which
two responses are displayed and the subject is told:

CHOOSE ANSWER 1 OR 2.

Programmers do not always take into account the fact that people are
less well-behaved than computers. What happens if the family member
hits the letter "A" instead of a number? In some programming languages
(most versions of BASIC, for example), it is more difficult to protect the
program from "improper" or unexpected input. The user interface is not
very sound for a family assessment environment if hitting a wrong key on
the computer keyboard can cause the program to lose portions of the
client record files. It may not be any better if hitting the wrong key produces a message on the computer display such as the obfuscatory one an
average programmer might create:

```
 * * *  ERROR 19 - CONTROL CHARACTER, MASKED TO
UPPER CASE  * * *
```

What does this mean to Mrs. Brown or to her 8-year-old son? It is somewhat better to see:

```
I'M SORRY, YOU MADE A BAD SELECTION. PLEASE CHOOSE
ONLY 1 OR 2
```

In a way, however, this still "punishes" the user with the clumsy fingers. Another approach, one programmers seldom seem to think of, is for the program to accept anything, simply ignoring any input until one of the "right" keys is pressed. There is no one "best" interface of this kind, but such details profoundly shape the user interface and are worthy of careful consideration.

For another example, consider a self-administered test requiring the subject to make judgements and to rank order several times. It is well known that such ranking tasks are quite difficult for most subjects to do reliably, especially when more than a few items are to be ranked using pencil and paper. Physically sorting items on cards helps the subject somewhat, but introduces mechanical problems for the administrator and adds extra steps for scoring, steps in which errors are easily made.

In a straightforward "programmer's" implementation of the ranking procedure on a computer, the items might be numbered and displayed in order. The subject is directed to type in a list of the item numbers in rank order, e.g., 5,1,2,4,3. This requires the hapless subject to do precisely the sort of numeric mental juggling that computers are good at but most of us are not. This scheme takes no advantage of any special capabilities in which the computer might excel over the person.

A better interface might display the items unnumbered (to avoid confusion with the numbers of assigned ranks). The subject is directed to enter a rank next to each item. This really offers no advantages over the common paper-and-pencil scheme, which it closely resembles.

Contrast the above with the following scheme to take advantage of the dynamic characteristics of a computer display

The items are displayed unnumbered in the bottom half of the display. The subject is directed to position a cursor (pointer) next to the item which is most like his family and to press the "ENTER" key. The selected item immediately appears at the top of the display and is erased from the bottom half. Next, the subject is directed to position the cursor at the item along the remaining ones which is most like his family. After all items are exhausted, the subject is given the opportunity to rearrange items in the ranked list in a similar manner.

In such a scheme, the user is presented with a dynamically updated *picture* of the items as ranked. The user does not have to figure out which number to press, but only has to move a cursor up or down and press a key to enter the next item in order. (Of course, provision for later rearrangement of ranked items must also be made.)

Designing the Structure

Structure and structural issues regarding the family system have long been of major interest in family studies and family therapy, but not until the late 1960s and early 1970s did the programming field discover the importance of structure. (See, for example, Barnett and Constantine, 1968; Parnas, 1972; Stevens, Meyers, and Constantine, 1974).[1]

The internal structure of a computer program, although normally not "visible" to the user of a system, is important. The structure, among other things, affects how reliable or "well behaved" the program may be, and it shapes and limits what can be accomplished in the future through modifications or "enhancements" to the program. While the subject of program design in its entirety is complex and highly technical, some basic principles can be outlined.[2]

Modularity. Computer programs which are carefully laid out and built from modules—small, independent pieces or sections—take less time to write, are easier to get to run correctly, and are simpler to change later. Nonetheless, many programmers, especially those whose primary experience has been on microcomputers, simply start writing a program at one end and "go with the flow" until they reach the other end. This is analogous to writing a journal article without either an outline or notes on organization and with no divisions into sections or topics.

In computer programming there are technical rules and procedures for deciding what pieces are needed, what goes in what section, and how the sections are to be interconnected into a working whole. Interestingly, one of the major considerations is the "coupling" between modules (Yourdon and Constantine, 1978). Intermodular coupling is analogous to the enmeshment-disengagement dimension in families. Enmeshed programs are every bit as problematic as enmeshed families and just as hard to change! Good design practice produces program "pieces" which work together cooperatively but are interconnected in very limited and constrained ways so that each can be looked at as a more-or-less independent entity.

Hierarchy. The question of "Who's on top?" or "Who's in charge?"

is as central in program design as it is in families, with many of the same issues and similar consequences arising in both areas. It is easiest for most people, for instance, to imagine utopia as a benevolent dictatorship—with themselves in charge. ("Things would run much easier for me in the family if only everybody else would just do things right, the way I want.") It is much the same in computer programming. It is easiest and most straightforward for the so-so programmer to write his solution as a "stand-alone" program, in charge of everything with no need to cooperate or work things out with any other programs. But such "autocratic" programs, though a little easier to write in the first place, are harder to live with. It may be very difficult to get a stand-alone program for the Fuzziwig Parenting Style Inventory to record its scores in ways compatible with the program you use to manage case records; extensive reprogramming may be needed. And when the closely related Fuzziwig Couple Style Inventory is to be computerized, yet another "autocratic" program will probably have to be created.

Generality. Just as the flexibility of a large behavioral repertoire is considered an asset for a family, so is generality often a desirable property for programs. It takes a certain amount of work to write a program to administer and score an inventory like Olson's FACES II; it would take about the same amount to create a program just to handle the similar test called FAMSCAN (Clarke, 1984; Leonard, 1981). But, with careful design and only about 10% more work than to program either one separately, a good programmer could create one system to do both. In fact, an ideal design would create a general-purpose system which would administer and score *any* instrument with simple Likert-type items.

Programming Style

Style is an essential element of written communication. Just as there is an approach to style in writing which leads to clear, simple, direct communication (e.g., Strunk and White, 1972), there are guidelines for programming which favor compact, straightforward, intuitively obvious programs which are easily understood and modified (e.g., Kernighan and Plauger, 1974).

The most important and universal guide to programming style involves a creative "reframing" of the computer programming process. Amateurs and beginning programmers think of a program as a set of instructions written to a computer; experienced programmers and real professionals think of a program as a message written to another person. The addressee is that unknown other programmer who has to figure out what went wrong, or how to change the report format, or how to get the program to print out on a different printer. If the programmer continues to keep this point of view in mind while developing the program (always thinking in terms of writing a message to another programmer), the end product will be substantially more effective and modifiable.

CASES: TWO SYSTEMS
FOR COMPUTER-AIDED ASSESSMENT

The range of possibilities for CAA systems based on sound systems design and development will be shown using two demonstration programs. These systems are to be considered illustrative rather than paradigmatic.

PARA: Paradigm and Regime Assessment

The PARA system is a microcomputer program for use by clinicians to assist in identifying and clarifying features of a family's basic organization. It is implemented as a subsystem to a comprehensive assessment and records management package which can operate with a variety of CAA and file management programs. PARA is written in a high-level programming language (CB-80) for use on any of a large family of microcomputers (those running under a particular widely used operating system called CP/M). No special hardware or machine features are used beyond those present in any computer having a standard video display terminal with a keyboard.

Using the PARA system, the therapist's clinical judgement is invoked to identify a family's basic image of itself as a family—its paradigm—and its methods of organizing its ongoing process—its regime. The underlying theory of family paradigms argues that actual family images and organizations are variants on four basic interrelated themes (Constantine, 1983; 1984; in press). These basic competing themes are defined in terms of certain fundamental dualities of family living, e.g., dependence-independence or stability-change. In the paradigmatic framework, actual families establish joint family images and collective styles of interaction by the way in which they order these issues in importance. Thus a family's paradigmatic preferences are represented by a series of rank orderings of competing priorities. The intrinsic structure of the basic paradigms and their corresponding regimes is most simply represented as a two-by-two matrix, more completely and elegantly as a circumplex or circular fan of variables having two principle components (Wiggins, 1980). For closest consistency with theory, locating a family in this "state-space" requires, in effect, a series of four-fold rankings.

The PARA program presents the clinician with a series of "frames" on the video display, each frame consisting of an incomplete statement about the family and four brief phrases which might complete the statement. These frames were constructed from certain key "clinical indicators" developed by family therapists working within the paradigmatic framework.

In the PARA system, the four alternative descriptive phrases are displayed at the corners of a square region within which a cursor, or position marker, is displayed. The clinician positions the cursor anywhere within the square at a point which best represents his/her clinical judgement about the family in relation to the four descriptors displayed at the corners of the square. The display is, thus, arranged to reflect the underlying logical structure of the paradigmatic model, but the clinician need not even be aware of these theoretical assumptions to make use of the system and to understand its reported results. Each time the clinician positions the cursor and signals the computer to record the position (by pressing an "ENTER" key), scores in two dimensions are recorded.

The system can report to the clinical user in several ways. A visual display can superimpose all the clinician's responses on a single chart (a "scatter plot" showing the dispersion of the clinician's ratings) or can display a single point representing the center of mass (average) of responses, i.e., an overall score of the family's style. These scores are also available as means and standard deviations for the two principal components (ordinate and abscissa) and the four diagonal vectors representing the four basic paradigms. A verbal "profile" report can be displayed on the terminal screen or typed on a printer. This report is constructed from individual phrases. For example:

This family strongly relies on rules and authority but to a lesser extent expects family members to know implicitly just what to do. Its organization and operation seem to be highly compatible with its values, which are moderately consistent across family members.

The PARA system is not a very complex application of microcomputer technology to CAA, but it illustrates careful consideration of a number of design issues. For example, in designing the interface, the structure of the presentation to the user (clinician) was made to correspond strictly to the theory on which it is based, thus making the presentation as intuitive as possible. The system also makes efficient use of communication from the user, deriving a ranking of four items from a single response (position of the cursor). PARA uses the "special abilities" of a computer equipped with a video display, namely positioning of a cursor and graphic display of plotted results. It also takes advantage of human "special abilities," namely the ability to visualize and represent complex judgements by spatial metaphor.

The MicroKvebaek

The Kvebaek Family Sculpture Technique (Cromwell et al., 1980) is a family assessment technique widely used in research and clinical practice. In original form, it is a "board sculpture" (Constantine, 1978) in which family members use small figurines to sculpt their family relationships by positioning them on a mèter-square board marked in a 10-by-10 grid. A problem in the use of the Kvebaek FST is in recording the numerical positions of the pieces after each sculpture, an operation which is both time-consuming and error-prone. Various indices of interpersonal distance must then be computed manually, a tedious task. In fact, for manual scoring of the Kvebaek FST, the conventional formula for distance between two points in a plane is simplified to a sum-of-squares so that no square root need be extracted.

The MicroKvebaek is a demonstration program created by the author to implement a version of the Kvebaek FST as a "video game" on the video display of a microcomputer. It is another subsystem for use with the larger assessment and records management package referred to above. In this version, family members choose "playing pieces" or graphic tokens which represent them on the screen. Family members use "arrow keys" on the computer keyboard or "joysticks" to move pieces around on a displayed 10-by-10 grid. Provision is made for any one member to position all tokens (an "individual sculpture") or for each member to position his/her own token (a "conjoint sculpture"). When all tokens are positioned, the computer records the sculpture. Immediate scores are available computing indices of family, pair, and triad enmeshment-disengagement, as well as indices of individual isolation. Results from the sculpture can be displayed on the video screen or printed out in either a tabular form or as a narrative report. Provision is made for comparison to norms when these become available.

The CAA version of the Kvebaek FST also offers entirely new opportunities for the economical study of family interaction, in this instance the interactive process of conjoint family sculptures. MicroKvebaek actually keeps a complete record of every move made for any token as well as the time when the move was made. Thus, as an automatic side-effect of running the MicroKvebaek, a complete transcript is recorded of the exact sequence in which all moves were made. This transcript functions like a computerized "video tape" which may be "played back" on the computer display at any speed. Viewing a sequence in slow motion can help clarify the precise sequence of events in the sculpture; accelerated playback facilitates visual recognition and study of repetitive patterns in family interaction. A transcript is also a data matrix which can be further processed or manipulated. It can be saved as a file to be analyzed by other programs, such as a statistical package. The transcript is detailed "process data" showing just who moved after whom, what repeated sequences were evident, and how the sculpture evolved over time. Of course, such data could be obtained by video recording of a conventional manual Kvebaek sculpture, but quantifying the raw data from a video tape and converting it to machinable form can be very difficult and expensive. The CAA version of the Kvebaek bypasses these costly and time-consuming transcription problems.

CONCLUSIONS

Developing better tools for the computer-aided assessment of families requires attention not only to matters of family theory and practice but also to questions of programming theory and practice. With careful consideration of the choice of problem, the design of a simple interface, and the use of sound structural principles of program development, better computer-based systems for family work are possible. As the PARA and MicroKvebaek systems illustrate, the special capabilities of microcomputers can be exploited to develop entirely new approaches to family assessment which go beyond present-day measurement techniques.

NOTES

1. The "discovery" that such things mattered in programming constituted a veritable "structural revolution" which swept the programming world. Theories of program complexity and program structure were developed and translated into systematic procedures for designing "good" systems. This meant programs which were easy to build, use, maintain, and modify. For the first time the computer field seriously considered how computer programs were constructed, how the pieces were put together into useable wholes. Although the techniques and approaches are now well established in computer science and advanced computer applications development (Yourdon and Constantine, 1978; Page-Jones, 1980; Stevens, 1981), programming for small computers (microcomputers and "personal computers") has lagged far behind.

2. The reader desiring to pursue the subject in depth and detail is referred to Kernighan and Plauger, 1974; Page-Jones, 1980; Stevens, 1981; and Yourdon and Constantine, 1978.

3. Consider the following passage:

Integral to the comprehensive systemic assessment of the cohesion dimension of family process, the family therapist, counselor, social worker, or other family service professional evaluates the non-linear summation of the permutative relationships among family members taken as dyadic entities, evaluating interpersonal distance by quantitative analog, but also incorporating qualitative factors representing hedonic and anhedonic emotional components not to the exclusion of analytical considerations of rate and nature of meaningful informational exchange.

Any similarity of the above to actual material appearing in contemporary professional journals is purely coincidental. The same basic ideas might be stated:

To gauge the cohesion of a family as a whole, it is necessary to take into account relationships between all pairs. The clinician must consider not just the matter of closeness and distance, but the quality of each relationship: whether it is affectionate or hostile, communicative or closed off.

REFERENCES

Clarke, J. P. (1984). *The family types of schizophrenics, neurotics, and "normals."* Doctoral Dissertation, University of Minnesota.

Cole, E. B., Johnson, J. H. & Williams, T. A. (1976). When psychiatric patients interact with computer terminals: Problems and solutions. *Behavior Research Methods and Instrumentation, 8,* 92-94.

Constantine, L. L. (1978). Family sculpture and relationship mapping techniques. *Journal of Marriage & Family Counseling, 4,* 13-23.

Constantine, L. L. (1983). Dysfunction and failure in open family systems: I. Application of a unified theory. *Journal of Marriage and the Family, 45,* 725-738.

Constantine, L. L. (1984). Dysfunction and failure in open family systems: II. Clinical Issues. *Journal of Marital and Family Therapy, 10,* 1-17.

Constantine, L. L. (in press). *Family paradigms: The practice of theory in family therapy.* New York: Guilford Press.

Cromwell, R., Fournier, D., & Kvebaek, D. (1980). *The Kvebaek family sculpture technique.* Jonesboro, TN: Pilgrimage.

Johnson, J. H., Giannetti, R. A., & Williams, T. A. (1976). A self-contained microcomputer system for psychological testing. *Behavior Research Methods and Instrumentation, 10,* 579-581.

Johnson, J. H., & Williams, T. A. (1976). Using a microcomputer for on-line psychiatric assessment. *Behavior Research Methods and Instrumentation, 10,* 576-578.

Kernighan, B. W., & Plauger, P. J. (1974). *The elements of programming style.* New York: McGraw-Hill.

Leonard, A. S. (1981). *Kantor and Lehr's family type theory: Towards a diagnostic instrument for family therapy.* Master's thesis, The Hebrew University of Jerusalem, Department of Psychology.

Page-Jones, M. (1980). *The practical guide to structured systems design.* New York: Yourdon Press.

Parnas, D. L. (1972). On the criteria to be used in decomposing systems into modules. *Communications of the ACM, 15*(12), 1053-1058.

Psych Systems, Inc. (1982). *Fasttest.* Baltimore: Psych Systems.

Ravich, R. A. (1969). The use of an interpersonal game-test in conjoint marital psychotherapy. *American Journal of Psychotherapy, 23*(2): 217-229.

Stevens, W. P. (1981). *Using structured design.* New York: Wiley.

Stevens, W. P., Myers, G. J., & Constantine, L. L. (1974). Structured design. *IBM Systems Journal, 13*(2), 115-139.

Strunk, W., & White, E. B. (1972). *The elements of style,* 2nd Ed. New York: Macmillan.

Yourdon, E., & Constantine, L. L. (1978). *Structured design: Fundamentals of a discipline of program and system design.* Englewood Cliffs, NJ: Prentice-Hall.

Microcomputers for Couple
and Family Assessment:
ENRICH and Other Inventories

David H. Olson

ABSTRACT. Considerable advances have been made in the development
of valid, reliable, and clinically relevant inventories for marital and family
therapy (Olson, Russell, & Sprenkle, 1980). However, few of these tools
have been systematically integrated into clinical practice. Some of the major obstacles that have limited the clinical use of these inventories are the
difficulty in administering, scoring, printing, and storing these data. Microcomputers can, however, help overcome some of these problems. With
the increasing availability of microcomputers, these inventories can now
be more readily introduced into clinical practice.

This paper will describe some of the advantages of using microcomputers for couple and family assessment. A variety of self-report inventories
that are currently available on microcomputers will be briefly reviewed. A
comprehensive marital assessment tool called ENRICH will be described
to illustrate the type of information that a computer summary can produce
for therapists.

ADVANTAGES OF A MICROCOMPUTER FOR THERAPIST

1. The use of a microcomputer will enable marital and family therapists to conduct a comprehensive clinical assessment in an efficient,
   effective, and systematic manner.
2. The microcomputer system can make readily available a comprehensive range of relevant inventories for assessing premarital,
   marital, and family dynamics.
3. If appropriate diagnostic instruments are selected, this diagnostic
   assessment can provide a wealth of clinically useful information that
   might not emerge for two to three clinical sessions. While these data
   would not replace the clinical assessment by the therapist, a common battery might help focus and direct the therapeutic intervention.
4. In addition to decreasing the amount of time for diagnostic assess-

David H. Olson, PhD, Professor, Family Social Science, University of Minnesota, St. Paul, MN
55113.

ment and increasing the amount of information, assessment on the microcomputer might also serve as a primer for therapeutic change in the clients.

5. The microcomputer can increase the speed of administering, scoring, and storing the data. It would free the professional staff from these responsibilities since it could be handled by clerical personnel with a minimal amount of training.

6. The microcomputer could decrease the cost of administering and scoring these inventories. The initial cost would include a microcomputer, which could also be used for word processing and accounting, and the purchase of the software programs. A variety of purchase options usually are available for software programs. Some software packages are sold at a fixed price and the program can be used repeatedly at no cost. A second option which is more often used with diagnostic tools is that a price is set for a certain number of administrations of each inventory. If used repeatedly, the purchase of the computer and software programs will pay for themselves over a year or two.

7. The microcomputer can also be an efficient way to store the diagnostic findings and can serve as a data base for future analysis. For example, if the inventories were also administered at the end of treatment and at a follow-up period, these repeated evaluations could be used to assess change. It would also be possible to determine the relative effectiveness of the different treatment approaches with different types of presenting problems and relationship dynamics.

8. Annual summaries could readily be prepared which would describe the types of clients, presenting problems, length of treatment, treatment effectiveness, and other relevant clinical information. These data would enable an agency to better evaluate their therapeutic impact and improve their case management.

ADVANTAGES FOR COUPLES AND FAMILIES

1. Because taking the inventories on a computer is more novel and interesting, individuals get more involved in answering the questions.

2. Taking an inventory on a microcomputer also increases the speed of administration and decreases the boredom often involved with most tests.

3. Couples and families enjoy taking the inventories on a computer and are very interested in learning about their results.

4. Clients appreciate the scientific and objective approach used with the computer and greatly appreciate receiving concrete feedback on

their responses. It is particularly helpful in motivating males who are often more reluctant to become involved in therapy.

5. Computer scoring provides them with more immediate feedback.
6. The immediate feedback makes individuals feel like the therapeutic process has begun and motivates them to become more involved in that process.

SELECTION OF MICROCOMPUTER COMPONENTS

Couple and Family Inventories Available on Microcomputer

A variety of couple and family self-report inventories have been developed over the last few years by Olson and colleagues, and most of these are described in the volume entitled *Family Inventories* (Olson, Mc-Cubbin, Barnes, Larsen, Muxen, & Wilson, 1982b). All of these inventories have been scientifically developed over the past five years to maximize their reliability, validity, and clinical utility. National norms based on a sample of 1,000 "normal" families across the life cycle are available for each of these scales. The results from the national survey are published in a book entitled *Families: What Makes Them Work* (Olson et al., 1983a).

Table 1 provides a summary of the couple and family scales developed by Olson and colleagues that are currently available on microcomputer. These scales are designed to assess premarital couples, married couples, families, and also provide a global life assessment. Table 1 indicates the specific scales, content areas, and reliability of these scales. Both the internal consistency (alpha) reliability and test-retest reliability are indicated in Table 1. Content and construct validity is available (Olson, Fournier, & Druckman, 1982) as well as predictive validity (Olson et al., 1983a).

These inventories can be used as a *core battery* and administered to *all* individuals at intake. This diagnostic assessment can, thereby, be integrated directly into clinical practice. The same core battery can be administered at post-test and follow-up to assess change on these various dimensions.

The specific core battery would depend on the status of the relationship. A premarital couple would either take PREPARE or PREPARE-MC (Marriage with Children). A married couple would probably take ENRICH and the Marital Stress Scale. For a family, the couple would do the marriage assessment and also complete the family assessment which would include FACES II, Family Satisfaction Scale, and the Family Stress Scale. If adolescents were involved, they could also take FACES II, Family Satisfaction and Family Stress Scales (Olson & Portner, 1983).

TABLE 1: COUPLE AND FAMILY ASSESSMENT TOOLS

Premarital Assessment	Content Areas	Reliability Alpha	Test-Retest
PREPARE (125 items)	12 Content Areas:		
PREPARE-MC	Idealism	.88	.79
(Marriage with Children)	Communication	.70	.69
(125 items)	Conflict Resolution	.72	.76
	Role Relationship	.77	.83
	Realistic Expectations	.75	.82
	Religious Orientation	.82	.93
Couple Assessment			
ENRICH	14 Content Areas		
(125 items)	Similar to PREPARE:		
	Marital Satisfaction	.82	.86
	Communication	.68	.90
	Conflict Resolution	.75	.90
	Personality Issues	.73	.81
	Role Relationship	.71	.90
Marital Stress	Change and Stressors	.87	.80
(15 items)	in Several Areas		
Family Assessment			
FACES II	Dimensions in Circumplex		
(30 items)	Model		
	Family Cohesion (Togetherness)	.87	.83
	Family Adaptability (Change)	.78	.80
Family Satisfaction	Satisfaction on Circumplex		
(14 items)	Dimension		
	Cohesion and Adaptability	.92	.75
Family Stress	Changes and Stressors in	.90	.80
(20 items)	Several Areas		
Parent-Adolescent	Openness in Communication	.87	.78
Communication	Problems in Communication	.78	.77
(20 items)			
Family Strengths	Family Pride	.88	.73
(12 items)	Family Accord	.72	.79
Global Life Assessment			
Life Satisfaction	11 Content Areas such as:	.92	.65
(40 items)	Family, Friends, Home, Health		
	Education, Leisure, and Finances		

Parents and adolescents could *both* complete the Parent Adolescent Communication Scale and Family Strength Scale.

In summary, the choice of the core diagnostic assessment battery would be dependent on the clinical situation and the type of clientele. It is, however, important to select a core assessment package that is administered at intake for diagnostic purposes and at termination in order to assess change. After the initial assessment, a therapist might choose to have a couple or family complete some additional scales. These supplemental scales would provide additional input into the therapeutic process and could also be repeated at termination. While it might not be possible to compare all couples and families across the supplemental scales, the core battery would provide these essential data.

Although it would be ideal if computer software was written to be compatible with all types of microcomputers, the current practice is that most of the software programs are written for the most popular types of computers. This means that the IBM-PC computer and others that are IBM compatible have a big share of the market, followed by the Apple computers. The programs described in this paper were developed for use on the IBM-PC with 128K memory and two dual density disk drives.

In addition to choosing the microcomputer, the choice of a monitor and printer is also quite important. For most clinical and business applications, a color monitor is not needed, but some programs have color visuals that are rather attractive and interesting. There are basically two types of printers—a dot matrix printer and a letter quality printer. Dot matrix printers are generally less expensive and faster but print is not as clearly defined as with a letter quality printer.

In making choices on the type of microcomputer, monitor, and printer, it is critical to consider the various uses for this equipment. In most office situations, it would be ideal to use this equipment for word processing and accounting. There are a wealth of word processing and spreadsheet programs available for most microcomputers.

If you are planning to use the microcomputer for assessment procedures, you will need to consider whether to purchase a separate unit for this function or whether the computer would be used for a variety of functions. For a small clinic, one microcomputer might be sufficient, but larger clinics might want to allocate a microcomputer exclusively for assessment procedures.

FIVE FUNCTIONS FOR THE MICROCOMPUTER

There are five functions that the microcomputer performs that are useful in doing couple and family assessment. These five functions enable you to administer, score, and print the inventories. They also enable you to store the couple and family data and also perform descriptive data analysis.

There are basically two ways that the inventories can be administered. One method involves having the microcomputer present the inventory items to the individual who answers the questions directly on the computer using the keyboard. The second method involves having the individuals answer the questions in a booklet, and these data are later entered into the computer by some assistant or clerical personnel. The advantage of the first method is that it is more interesting to individuals and they become more involved in answering the questions. The disadvantage is that it ties up the microcomputer so that it cannot be used for other functions. The advantage of the second method is that more people can take the inventory at the same time and a clerical worker could enter the data very efficiently.

The computer programs will score the data and simultaneously store the raw data and/or scored data for later use. The printing can be done on either a dot matrix or letter quality printer on 8 1/2 or 11-inch paper.

The data are stored using a unique couple or family identification number. The raw data and/or scored data for each individual family member are also stored. It is also easy to record whether the data were collected at intake, at termination, and at follow-up.

There are a variety of ways that these data can be used to make a clinical office more efficient. One procedure might be to do an annual summary of the types of couples and families and their presenting problems and dynamics at intake. Another useful analysis would be to assess *change* that occurs between intake and termination and at later follow-up. It would be possible to compare cases that were most successful (produced the most change) compared to those that were least successful. Also, analysis could be conducted to evaluate the cases that terminated early versus those that continued in therapy. A variety of software programs are available which could help provide comprehensive and useful summaries of this data.

MARITAL ASSESSMENT USING ENRICH: AN ILLUSTRATION

ENRICH is a self-report instrument designed to provide a comprehensive assessment of a couple's relationship. The 125 items are organized into 14 content categories. The assessment identifies the specific relationship strengths and work areas for a couple in these 14 content areas.

ENRICH was developed in 1979 and was used in a national survey of 1,000 "normal" couples across the life cycle. The national norms and descriptive findings based on this study are published in a book entitled *Families: What Makes Them Work* (Olson et al., 1983a). More details on the reliability and validity of ENRICH are published elsewhere (Fournier, Olson, & Druckman, 1983; Olson et al., 1982a).

There are two ways ENRICH can be administered. First, an individual can sit at the computer terminal and answer the 125 item inventory. The second option is to respond to the questions on an answer sheet and then have the data entered onto the microcomputer by a clerical person. The computer program then scores the data and prints a 22-page computer summary for each couple. The couple's raw data are then stored for later use.

The 22-page computer summary provides a very comprehensive and detailed summary of the couple's relationship. Individual and couple scores are provided for each of the 14 content categories. Each category is described as either a relationship strength or a work area for a particular couple. A *relationship strength* indicates that they agree on these issues and do not see them as problematic. Conversely, a *work area* indicates that they disagree and have problems in this content area.

An example of a couple profile summary on ENRICH is indicated in Table 2. The male and female scores for four content areas are described, i.e., marital satisfaction, personality issues, communication, and conflict resolution. The right-hand column indicates the percent of positive couple agreement in each area, which could range from 0 to 100 percent. For this couple, they have "possible relationship strengths" in the areas of marital satisfaction and personality issues but have "possible work areas" in the areas of communication and conflict resolution.

In addition to the summary of the individual and couple scores for each of the 14 content areas, a more detailed item summary is provided for each content area. This detailed summary provides analysis of the ten specific items in that content area. Items are classified as either *disagreement, special focus, indecision,* or *positive couple agreement.* Disagreement items are those in which a couple disagrees by two or more points on the five point response scale. Special focus items are those where both individuals indicate some concern about that issue. Indecision items are those where one or both individuals have not made a clear decision about that issue. Lastly, positive couple agreement items are items in which a couple agrees with each other in a positive way on that issue.

An example of the detailed summary for the conflict resolution is presented in Table 3. As previously illustrated in Table 2, the conflict area was one in which they both had relatively low individual scores and they had a low couple agreement score, indicating that it was a work area for them. The detailed summary indicates that they had four disagreement items, one special focus item, two indecision items, and three positive couple agreement items. Table 3 clearly indicates that this couple has difficulty dealing with conflict in a constructive way, and this item summary provides some detailed information on how they currently handle conflict.

We have found that having couples take ENRICH inventory speeds up the diagnostic process but also facilitates getting the couple more involved in the treatment process. Simply answering the 125 items increases a couple's awareness of specific issues and encourages them to begin discussing some of these issues. We have found that they enjoy feedback on the results and that it speeds the process of both diagnosis and intervention.

One of the assets of ENRICH is that it identifies both the work areas for a couple and also their strengths. Too often couples coming in for marriage counseling have not thought about or been able to identify their

E X P A N D E D   C O U P L E   P R O F I L E

THIS COUPLE PROFILE IS DESIGNED TO HELP YOU COMPLETE YOUR COUNSELORS FEEDBACK FORM.
THIS IS A SUMMARY OF THE COUPLE'S RELATIONSHIP STRENGTHS AND WORK AREAS ON ENRICH.

MALE AND FEMALE REVISED SCORES	PCT. POSITIVE COUPLE AGREEMENT

MARITAL SATISFACTION
MMMMMMMMMMMMMMMMMMMMMMMMMMMMMMMMMM 69
FFFFFFFFFFFFFFFF 33

60

HIGH SCORERS (60 OR MORE) ARE HAPPY ABOUT MOST ASPECTS OF THEIR MARRIAGE.
LOW SCORERS (30 OR LESS) ARE UNHAPPY AND CONCERNED ABOUT SEVERAL ASPECTS OF MARRIAGE.

POSSIBLE RELATIONSHIP STRENGTH

PERSONALITY ISSUES
MMMMMMMMMMMMMMMMMMMMMMMMMMMMMMMMMMMMMMM 77
FFFFFFFFFFFFFFFFFFFFFFF 47

60

HIGH SCORERS (60 OR MORE) LIKE THE PERSONALITY, BEHAVIOR AND HABITS OF THEIR PARTNER.
LOW SCORERS (30 OR LESS) ARE CONCERNED ABOUT SEVERAL PERSONALITY TRAITS OR BEHAVIORS OF THEIR PARTNER.

POSSIBLE RELATIONSHIP STRENGTH

COMMUNICATION
MMMMMMMMMMMMMMMMMMMMMMMMMMMMMMMMMMM 71
FFFFFFFFFFFFFFFFFF 36

30

HIGH SCORERS (60 OR MORE) FEEL THEY ARE UNDERSTOOD BY THEIR PARTNER AND ARE ABLE TO EASILY SHARE THEIR FEELINGS WITH THEIR PARTNER.
LOW SCORERS (30 OR LESS) ARE CONCERNED ABOUT THEIR COMMUNICATION AND FEEL UNABLE TO SHARE THEIR FEELINGS WITH THEIR PARTNER.

POSSIBLE WORK AREA

CONFLICT RESOLUTION
MMMMMMMMMMMMMMMMMMMMMMMMM 49
FFFFFFFFFFFFFFFFF 34

30

HIGH SCORERS (60 OR MORE) FEEL THEY ARE ABLE TO DISCUSS AND EASILY RESOLVE DIFFERENCES WITH THEIR PARTNER.
LOW SCORERS (30 OR LESS) FEEL THAT ARGUMENTS ARE DIFFICULT TO RESOLVE, AVOID DISAGREEMENTS, AND FEEL THEY MUST GIVE IN TO THEIR PARTNER.

POSSIBLE WORK AREA

TABLE 2

CONFLICT RESOLUTION

```
********************************************************************
1              2              3              4              5
STRONGLY    MODERATELY    NEITHER AGREE    MODERATELY    STRONGLY
AGREE         AGREE       NOR DISAGREE     DISAGREE      DISAGREE
********************************************************************
```

*** DISAGREEMENT OR DIFFERENCE ITEMS ***

071. M= 5,   F= 3.
SOMETIMES WE HAVE SERIOUS DISPUTES OVER UNIMPORTANT ISSUES.

074. M= 2,   F= 4.
I WOULD DO ANYTHING TO AVOID CONFLICT WITH MY PARTNER.

079. M= 4,   F= 2.
I SOMETIMES FEEL OUR ARGUMENTS GO ON AND ON AND NEVER SEEM TO GET RESOLVED.

112. M= 4,   F= 2.
WHEN WE ARGUE, I USUALLY END UP FEELING THAT THE PROBLEM WAS ALL MY FAULT.

*** SPECIAL FOCUS ITEMS ***

058. M= 4,   F= 4.
WHEN WE ARE HAVING A PROBLEM, I CAN ALWAYS TELL MY PARTNER WHAT IS
BOTHERING ME.

*** COUPLE INDECISION ITEMS ***

010. M= 4,   F= 3.
MY PARTNER AND I HAVE VERY DIFFERENT IDEAS ABOUT THE BEST WAY TO SOLVE
OUR DISAGREEMENTS.

083. M= 4,   F= 3.
WHEN WE HAVE A DISAGREEMENT, WE OPENLY SHARE OUR FEELINGS AND
DECIDE HOW TO RESOLVE OUR DIFFERENCES.

*** POSITIVE COUPLE AGREEMENT ITEMS ***

004. M= 4,   F= 5.
IN ORDER TO END AN ARGUMENT, I USUALLY GIVE UP TOO QUICKLY.

039. M= 2,   F= 2.
WHEN DISCUSSING PROBLEMS, I USUALLY FEEL THAT MY PARTNER UNDERSTANDS ME.

096. M= 4,   F= 4.
I USUALLY FEEL THAT MY PARTNER DOES NOT TAKE OUR DISAGREEMENTS SERIOUSLY.

TABLE 3

113

strengths because they are so involved in the process of focusing on problems. In addition to the overall summary on the 14 categories, the detailed item summary enables a therapist to focus on specific issues that are either strengths or are problematic for a couple.

ENRICH can be used as a standard intake assessment to speed the diagnostic and intervention process. In addition, ENRICH can be administered toward the end of treatment to assess the therapeutic change. It is often very helpful to review the progress and change with a couple. All of these data are stored on the microcomputer so that later analysis can be done based on individual and couple scores. Annual summaries could also be done for all couples who received therapy during that year. In this way, a clinic could evaluate the types of problems the couples present and the amount of change that occurred in each of these areas over the course of treatment.

SUMMARY

The use of microcomputers for diagnostic assessment of couples and families is just beginning to emerge. While there has been a variety of self-report inventories that are relevant for marriage and family therapists, they often have not been integrated in clinical practice. Microcomputers help to overcome some of the limitations and problems of incorporating these inventories into a clinical setting. As a result, microcomputers offer considerable potential for integrating couple and family assessment into the routine of clinical practice.

There are numerous advantages to both therapists and family members if microcomputers are utilized for marriage and family assessment. For therapists, it makes available a wide variety of clinically useful diagnostic tools. It decreases the amount of time for assessment and provides a wealth of information that can be used in clinical diagnosis, in evaluating treatment, and in revising treatment programs.

Family members find taking the inventories on the computer to be a novel and interesting experience. It increases their awareness of relationship issues, stimulates their discussion of these topics, and accelerates their involvement in the therapeutic process.

The ENRICH marital assessment inventory was used to illustrate how a microcomputer program can be used effectively and efficiently with couples. ENRICH and related self-report inventories can provide a wealth of information that can be useful for diagnosis and for treating relationship problems.

The potential uses of microcomputers for clinical settings are only beginning to be realized. Microcomputers have the potential for greatly increasing the efficiency and effectiveness of therapeutic intervention.

We are only beginning to tap the rich potential that this resource has to offer for improving the quality of therapeutic care for individuals and families.

REFERENCES

Fournier, D. G., Olson, D. H., & Druckman, J. M. (1983). Assessing marital and premarital relationships: The PREPARE-ENRICH inventories (Chapter 12). In E. E. Filsinger (Ed.), *Marriage and family assessment* (pp. 229-250), Beverly Hills, CA: Sage Publishing.

Olson, D. H., Russell, C. S., & Sprenkle, D. H. (1980). Marital and family therapy: A decade review. *Journal of Marriage and Family, 42,* 973-993.

Olson, D. H., Fournier, D. G., & Druckman, J. M. (1982a). *Counselor's manual for PREPARE-ENRICH* (rev. Ed.). Minneapolis, MN: PREPARE-ENRICH, Inc.

Olson, D. H., McCubbin, H. I., Barnes, H., Larsen, A., Muxen, M., & Wilson, M. (1982b). *Family inventories.* Minneapolis, MN: University of Minnesota.

Olson, D. H., & Portner, J. (1983). Family adaptability and cohesion evaluation scales (FACES II) (Chapter 15). In E. E. Filsinger (Ed.), *Marriage and family assessment* (pp. 229-250), Beverly Hills, CA: Sage Publishing.

Olson, D. H., McCubbin, H. I., Barnes, H., Larsen, A., Muxen, M., & Wilson, M. (1983a). *Families: What makes them work?* Beverly Hills: Sage Publications.

Olson, D. H., Russell, C. S., & Sprenkle, D. H. (1983b). Circumplex model of marital and family systems VI: Theoretical update. *Family Process, 22,* 69-83.

MATESIM:
Computer Assisted Marriage Analysis for Family Therapists

Marlene W. Lehtinen
Gerald W. Smith

ABSTRACT. MATESIM is a computer automated simulation designed to help therapists analyze marital relationships in a thorough and efficient manner. The program identifies both problem areas and strengths of a relationship by collecting information on clients, analyzing it, organizing it into a useful format, and making it easily retrievable. Information is gathered from clients in 108 different categories considered relevant to marriage. Specific information is collected about each individual and his/her marital values. In addition, the program collects information from each concerning how the partner is perceived and what type of person would be considered the "ideal" marriage partner. The computer then analyzes the relationship utilizing all of this information, as well as a marital therapist ideal based on values associated with successful marriage. From this analysis the computer predicts problem areas in the marriage, areas in which the marriage is especially satisfying, and identifies areas in which the clients can individually direct self-change to improve the overall quality of the relationship. The computer has built-in change routines to allow therapists (without programming skills or knowledge) to alter the program to suit particular needs.

CASE STUDY

Mike and Mary have been married for six months and are experiencing marital problems. They consult a therapist about their difficulties. The therapist takes Mike and Mary individually to a personal computer in the office and begins the MATESIM marriage simulation program. The computer asks each partner a series of questions about his/her values and expectations concerning marriage; his/her characteristics and those of the

Marlene W. Lehtinen, PhD, is an associate professor in the Department of Sociology, University of Utah, Salt Lake City, Utah 84112. Her research and teaching interests are in the areas of marriage and family.

Gerald W. Smith, PhD, is an associate professor in the Department of Sociology, University of Utah. His research and teaching interests are in the areas of computer applications and software development.

117

partner. The computer then runs a detailed comparative marriage analysis for each partner. The computer then runs a detailed comparative marriage analysis for each partner, noting their respective areas of strength and weakness. The computer also notes areas in which each would need to change in order to improve the quality of the relationship. The analysis then describes their values relating to marriage and notes inconsistencies between their values and between the values marriage counselors believe lead to successful marriages.

The above scenario would require approximately two hours time. The detailed, individualized marriage and value analysis could then be used as the basis for developing a self-help program with the marriage therapist.

One of the more difficult tasks facing therapists who deal with couple relationships is to effectively take into account the significant amount of data that have been gathered or that should be gathered. This problem can properly be referred to as information overload. It can best be understood by considering that the human mind is capable of taking into account a much more limited amount of data than are available. One indicator of this problem and of the seriousness of its existence is the fact that many therapists are not even aware that they are failing to properly take into account valuable data that they have in their possession. When faced with overwhelming amounts of information, they tend to focus on some segments of the facts, but to ignore other segments. This ignoring of perhaps critical information is not done consciously in most cases. The segments of information that are focused upon tend to have some feature that causes attention to be drawn to them, such as having occurred most recently or having significant emotional impact. Because the analytical capacity of the human mind is finite, information that is the focus of attention causes the rest of the information to fade into the background and for all intents and purposes to be ignored.

Another indicator of information overload is the fact that therapists are often unaware that they have failed to acquire information that could be critical in dealing with the issues at hand. In the face of the significant amount of data that could be collected, the therapist concentrates on acquiring those bits of information that appear to be of potential benefit. Simple oversight may, therefore, prevent the exploration of valuable lines of questioning.

LITERATURE REVIEW

In addition to the instruments noted by others in this collection (C. F. Olson, Constantine) two different computer-assisted psychological assessment inventories have been reported which assess the marital relationship.[1] These are *Mate* (1982) and *Marriage Problems* (1982). Also two computer games were identified (*Lovers or Strangers* [1982] and *Sexware* [1984]) that allow individuals to answer a series of questions on an Apple computer with the computer comparing the answers with those of a partner and/or an independent reference. In the Lovers or Strangers game the computer graphs how closely the couples are matched in seven areas and how well each person guessed the other person's response. It then prints out an overall compatibility rating. In *Sexware* the computer scores sexual IQ after a person answers more than 200 multiple-choice questions. Along the same line, Weichselgartner (1981) has developed a 20-item adaptive test for individual psychodiagnosis for a programmable pocket calculator.

An interesting study of computerized counseling in which the computer collects general information from a battery of tests and then makes an assessment and diagnosis (Costello, 1982) most closely approaches our MATESIM program. The computer model in this study, however, is not a general model that can be readily adapted by therapists to include additional information and is not currently available for microcomputers.

MATESIM RATIONAL: THEORY OF DECISION ANALYSIS

The decision to get involved in a close interpersonal relationship has both emotional and rational elements. The emotional aspects are the most critical and pre-condition of any rational analysis which may follow. In no way does MATESIM attempt to deal with those emotional-intuitive drives underlying human relationships. Rather it is concerned with other questions: "What are the strengths and weaknesses of my relationships?" and "What can be done to build a better relationship with my partner?"

MATESIM is a new approach designed to help therapists analyze relationships and provide insight to couples so that they can deal rationally with their problems. The model uses the capabilities of the computer to individualize the process of rational decision making in order that it fit the specific needs of each individual.

MATESIM makes the following assumptions:

1. Various aspects of relationships can be analyzed by means of discrete questions with alternative positions describing typical non-sex-specific modes of human behavior, each of which may be more or less desirable to the user.
2. In any given society, some types of behavior are generally considered more effective than others in producing lasting and effective relationships.

3. The user can prioritize traits and behaviors desired in a partner using a scale of 1 to 5.
4. There are three significant considerations related to rational mate selection: the position that best describes the user, the position that describes his/her ideal partner, and the position that best describes his/her actual partner. The best choice generally occurs when all three are the same. This "theory of similarities" contrasts with the "theory of opposites" which states that opposites produce the best relationships because they complement one another.

Based on this assumption, Figure 1 gives a visual demonstration of how the theory of similarities works in comparison to the theory of opposites.

Conflict arises when there are differences between views. The more differences there are, the greater the potential conflict that may arise. A weak person may be attracted to a strong person because of a need for help; a strong individual to a weak individual because of a need to provide help. This only works, however, so long as each placed a low priority on that which the partner lacks.

The theory of complementary needs argues that what partners lack and what they provide one another holds relationships together. Although this may be true, it can also produce dependencies that may be resented and perceived as entrapment. Ideal relationships build upon strengths rather than weaknesses. Differences that were appealing early in a relationship often become significantly less desirable over time.

It is possible, however, for two people to be similar to one another, match one another's ideal, and still have an unsuccessful relationship. This often occurs when the similarities are in areas that have been found to produce problem marriages. Two alcoholics, for example, rarely have what have been considered successful marriages.

The ideal marriage occurs when all four of the above circles merge into one—the self, the ideal partner, the actual partner, and the society ideal.

FIGURE 1

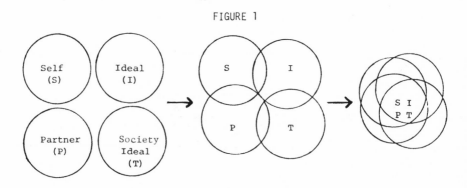

BACKGROUND

Several years ago we developed a general computer model of MATESIM. The model was designed to assist users in making more rational decisions regarding relationships. It did this by first gathering extensive information on a user's characteristics, values, and ideals. This information was then analyzed in the model and compared with similar information obtained from one hundred individuals and from clients submitted by the user. Different types of information were collected from the user depending upon the particular issue the client seeks to resolve. Some users of the model were seeking information regarding dating compatibility, so one version of the program dealt with issues surrounding dating relationships and focused on compatibility of dating partners. Other users were more interested in determining marital compatibility, so a second version of the program was developed dealing with marriage and the factors considered important to marital compatibility. Finally, a small, but significant, set of users desired information on issues having to do with sexual compatibility. This third version of the program, therefore, aided in determining sexual compatibility by comparing sexual preferences and values.

Several significant changes have been made since the original model was developed. The original model was designed as a computer simulation game for us by students in marriage and family classes at the University of Utah (Debenham & Smith, 1979). In the game format, students provided information about themselves and personal friends. This information was collected on standard computer sheets and then optically scanned and processed. The results of the computer simulated marriage were given to the students and formed the basis for discussion of various aspects of marriage. In revising the model we have eliminated the batch processing format needed for completing massive numbers of analyses for a university class in favor of an interactive model in which a user can directly input information into the computer and then run any of a series of different analyses. The program is designed so that a person with clerical skills can input client data or a client can input his/her own information. We have designed the program with a series of menus that allow users to input data and complete an analysis by answering a series of questions in English. Users need have no special knowledge of computers or computer programming to be able to comfortably utilize any aspect of the program.[3]

It has also been important to maintain flexibility in the program. It was determined that in order for a program to be of significant use over time, it must be sufficiently flexible to allow changes in the program. Furthermore, it must be possible for these changes to be made by a user with minimal computer skills. A number of menu driven change routines are included to change the program to suit the current conditions by making simple commands in English.

All variables in the model can be altered with the change routines so that the model can be custom tailored to an individual user's needs. The program parameters can be altered to include any set of scale items a therapist may wish to include. This means that a therapist may elect to use the scale items we have developed (see Figure 2), use additional scale items developed by others, or completely individualize the model with his/her own scales and information. These change routines make the program a potentially powerful tool for use by therapists and researchers.

The earliest version of the model was designed to run on a mainframe computer. It is now available for use on the IBM Personal Computer of compatibles with two disk drives and 512K memory. This makes the program available to persons at home or an independent practice.

To date, we have broken the program into two different programs. Unlike the three versions of the model discussed above that differed only in terms of the specific type of issue being considered, the new programs were developed for a particular audience and, therefore, were designed with specific features and capabilities.

The first version MATESIM I, was designed to allow individuals to make better decisions concerning their choice of marriage partners (Smith & Debenham, 1983; Debenham & Smith, 1979). It allows a user to compare a potential marriage partner with up to one hundred different individuals, taking into account the user's values, ideals, self-description,

FIGURE 2

Sample Item

Age

1. Less than 21
2. 21-30
3. 31-40
4. 41-50
5. Over 50

State your (John Doe) age.
State the age of your *ideal* partner.
State the age of your *actual* partner (Mary Doe).
How important is age to you in a relationship?
(Unimportant) 1 2 3 4 5 (Extremely Important)

Information supplied by the client is either requested in an informational type format or from Likert-type scales. Each person supplies the requested information, from his/her individual perspective, describing him/herself, describing his/her ideal partner, and describing his/her actual partner.

and the expert opinion of a therapist reference. The counselor reference is the collective judgement of a panel of marital therapists. It represents the consensus of the panel regarding the various characteristics and values that contribute to successful relationships and to stressful relationships. The counselor reference can be altered in the change routines, however, to reflect some other significant perspective, such as the values of a particular religion.

The second version of the model MATESIM II, was designed to be used by family therapists as an aid in couple therapy. It is currently being used experimentally by marital therapists in an effort to test its capabilities and its limitations. This version operates by utilizing data on actual couple clients, the bulk of whom are currently married and have sought counseling because of marital problems. Another client segment for whom the program has been utilized is made up of couples who are contemplating marriage.

MATESIM II has been primarily used by therapists to obtain a comprehensive look at particular relationships in an efficient manner. The program functions effectively to identify both problem areas and strengths of a relationship, taking into account the perspectives of both individuals. MATESIM II achieves this by collecting information on clients, appropriately analyzing it, organizing it into a useful format, and making it easily retrievable. As described earlier, one of the serious difficulties faced by family therapists is the problem of being able to keep in mind the wealth of information potentially available on a particular couple in a useful manner.

MATESIM II functions effectively to present the available data in a useful format. It also can be used to suggest avenues for data collection.

MATESIM II

To utilize MATESIM II a therapist requests that both parties of the client couple complete the appropriate MATESIM questionnaire. The current questionnaire utilized for this purpose taps information in 108 areas, shown in Figure 3. These are referred to as categories of analysis and are grouped into nine dimensions of related categories. As noted earlier, by using the change routines, the categories of analysis can include any scale items or information needed by the therapist. The scale items that are currently used have evolved over the past five years from our tests. One of the model's analytical routines runs an analysis of items, indicating items with positive and negative skews as well as inter-rater reliability correlation for each item. The reliability of an item is established by correlating ratings of separate evaluators of the same individual. The program recommends that items failing to receive an inter-rater correla-

FIGURE 3

MATESIM Categories

Dimension I—Physical Characteristics

1. Age
2. Body Build
3. Physical Attractiveness
4. Sexual Attractiveness
5. School Applied Intelligence
6. Life Application of Intelligence
7. Specialized Intelligence
8. Physical Impairments
9. Temporary Illness
10. Mental Illness
11. Chronic Illness
12. Family Line Genetic Deficiencies

Dimension II—Personal Habits

1. Eating Habits
2. Sleeping Habits
3. Television
4. Reading
5. Use of Tobacco and Alcohol
6. Use of Drugs
7. Physical Fitness
8. Language Usage
9. Dress
10. Personal Adornment
11. Manners
12. Cleanliness and Neatness

Dimension III—Work and Economic Orientations

1. Current Education Level
2. Physical Talents
3. Artistic and Musical Talents
4. Consumption Orientations
5. Type of Consumption
6. Focus of Consumption
7. Lifework
8. Job Mobility
9. Locality
10. Economic Stability
11. Investments
12. Personal Financial Organization

Dimension IV—Family

1. Affection
2. Number of Previous Marriages
3. Marriage Motivation
4. Possession-Affirmation
5. Divorce
6. Abortion
7. Number of Living Children
8. Number of Children Desired
9. Motivation for Children
10. Orientation Towards Children
11. Disciplining Children
12. Family Activities

Dimension V—Mental Orientations

1. Goals and Ambitions
2. Need for Self-Improvement
3. Intuition vs. Science
4. Rationality vs. Intuition
5. Romance
6. Feminine vs. Masculine
7. Highs vs. Lows
8. Physical Discipline
9. Behavior Modification
10. Basis of Truth
11. Spiritual Beliefs
12. Good and Evil

Dimension VI—Sexuality

1. Dating Standards
2. Faithfulness After Marriage
3. Communication in Sexual Areas
4. Sexual Interest
5. Sexual Variety
6. Orgasms
7. Sexual Aggression
8. Type of Sexual Experience
9. Extent of Sexual Experience
10. Nudity
11. Physical Privacy
12. Birth Control

FIGURE 3 (continued)

Dimension VII—Personality Characteristics

1. Attitude Towards Life
2. Attitude Towards Others
3. Dependability-Trustworthiness
4. Honesty in Relationships
5. Taking and Giving Criticism
6. Sensitivity to Criticism
7. Problem Solving with Partner
8. Expression of Anger
9. Love
10. Level of Generosity and Caring
11. Self-Sacrifice
12. Level of Independence-Dependence

Dimension VIII—Personal Preferences

1. Religion
2. Political Preference
3. Preference of Social Activities
4. Marriage Preferences
5. Attitude Towards Animals
6. Friendship Choices
7. Class Association
8. Interpersonal Conversation
9. Subject of Conversation
10. Type of Humor
11. Solitude vs. Society
12. Mental Privacy

Dimension IX—Social Characteristics

1. Listening
2. Openness in Relationships
3. Self-Confidence
4. Emotional Responses to Conflict
5. Adaptability
6. Tactfulness
7. Work Roles
8. Decision Control
9. Remembrances
10. Promptness
11. Compassion
12. Forgiveness

tion of .80 be eliminated. The program also recommend elimination of items that fail to discriminate (over 80 percent of the time the item is given the same answer).

As indicated above, MATESIM II is designed to allow flexibility. If the therapist desires to include a particular category or any number of specific categories not covered in the current questionnaire, he/she can easily do this utilizing the change routines built into the program. This allows a therapist to custom tailor the questionnaire to the demands of particular client needs if the questionnaire does not cover a specific area.

A critical feature of the MATESIM program is the utilization of priority weightings. An individual's priority weightings can be likened to their values. Individuals are asked to set a priority weight on how important each of the categories is in comparison to all other categories. This is done utilizing a one to five priority weight scale in which one has the lowest level of importance and give the highest level of importance. The utilization of priority weightings is considered essential to the design of the MATESIM program. As therapists too well know, it is often not the fact of difference between two parties that spells disaster, but the degree of the difference. If, for example, a wife were to describe her ideal partner in the area of physical fitness as being something akin to Superman, but also indicated that on a scale of 1 to 5 this area ranked as a one, a therapist need not be concerned that her husband's level of physical fitness approached that of Caspar Milquetoast. If, on the other hand, she were to have given physical fitness a level 5 priority weighting, the therapist would be more concerned. The program indicates these differences in the analysis.

Each position on the scale for every category may also be given a priority weight on the same system of 1 to 5. It should be noted, however, that this is an optional feature of the MATESIM II program. Although a respondent may indicate how important each of the positions on the scale is to him/her personally, failure to supply this information sends the program into a default mode in which the priority weightings have been preset.

After all of the necessary information has been supplied and entered into the system, the MATESIM II program will analyze the data and provide a printout of the results to the therapist. For the sake of simplicity, let us say the Therapist Jones has requested clients Sally and Robert Long to provide responses to the MATESIM II questionnaire. Assuming that they have gone through this process, the program will carry out the following analyses:

1. A comparison between Sally's self-description and Robert's ideal partner taking into account Robert's priority weightings.
2. A comparison between Robert's self-description and Sally's ideal partner taking into account Sally's priority weightings.
3. A comparison between Sally's self-description and Robert's self-description.
4. A comparison between Sally's description of Robert and Robert's description of Sally.

See Figure 4 for an example of this printout. It should be noted that this is a significantly shortened version of what would be included in this type of analysis.

A complete analysis of a relationship in MATESIM II using all 108 categories utilizes over 30 pages of printout. The sample analysis here takes each dimensional group and indicates the degree to which each partner is similar to the other's ideal and the degree to which they are similar to one another. Similarity is measured by priority weight differences. Large differences between individuals in categories assigned low priorities are considered differently from similar categories assigned a high priority. Since the analysis here is based on priority weightings, a small difference in a high priority area would indicate a significant difference. We are using a scale of 0-25 (a scale of 1-5 with priorities 0-5

FIGURE 4

MATESIM II Analysis
for Sally and Robert Long

Comparison of Sally to Robert's Ideal Partner
(Listed in Order of Robert's Priority Weights)

Dimension I — Physical Characteristics
Sally is 80 percent of Robert's Ideal
Areas in which Sally is significantly different from Robert's Ideal:

1. Age
3. Physical Attractiveness
2. Body Build

Areas in which Sally is similar to Robert's Ideal:

4. Sexual Attractiveness
7. Specialized Intelligence

Dimension II — Personal Habits
Sally is 50 percent of Robert's Ideal
Areas in which Sally is significantly different from Robert's Ideal:

9. Dress
5. Use of Tobacco and Alcohol
1. Eating Habits
11. Manners

Areas in which Sally is similar to Robert's Ideal:

4. Reading
3. Television

(Seven Additional Dimensions Considered)

Comparison of Robert to Sally's Ideal Partner
(Listed in Order of Sally's Priority Weights)

Dimension I — Physical Characteristics
Robert is 90 percent of Sally's Ideal
Areas in which Robert is significantly different from Sally's Ideal:

9. Temporary Illness
4. Sexual Attractiveness

Areas in which Robert is similar to Sally's Ideal:

11. Chronic Illness
1. Age
8. Physical Impairments

(Eight Additional Dimensions Considered)

FIGURE 4 (continued)

Comparison of Sally and Robert Long

Dimension I — Physical Characteristics
    Robert and Sally are 90 percent similar
    Areas in which Robert and Sally are significantly different:

    11. Temporary Illness

    Areas in which Robert and Sally are similar:

    4. Sexual Attractiveness
    7. Specialized Intelligence

Dimension II — Personal Habits
    Robert and Sally are 80 percent similar
    Areas in which Robert and Sally are significantly different:

    7. Physical Fitness
    2. Sleeping Habits

    Areas in which Robert and Sally are similar:

    6. Use of Drugs
    3. Television

(Seven Additional Dimensions Considered)

yielding a priority weighted scale of 0-25). A difference of greater than 5 priority weighted points would indicate a significant difference. Similarity here is considered less than 5 priority weighted points on the scale. The percentage indicating the degree to which each partner is similar to the other's ideal is also based upon priority weights—a score of 100 percent would indicate that in all categories considered, the partner's characteristics were exactly the other's ideal. The therapist can preset the criteria for similarity and difference in the change routines which the priorities are assigned by each individual client.

MARRIAGE THERAPIST REFERENCE

Both MATESIM I and MATESIM II allow for the inclusion of the counselor reference.[2] Marriage therapists, like most individuals, do not generally differentiate between emotional and rational aspects of a relationship. This is often the case because they only see clients at such an advanced stage of emotional involvement that relatively objective, rational analysis is almost impossible. The theories and techniques that have emerged, therefore, are designed to help the troubled, not to facilitate the relatively healthy.

Our approach could be classified as behavioristic. We focus on an interpersonal relationship as a cumulation of specific behaviors that are either rewarding or punitive. The best relationships, we believe, are those that maximize the opportunities for both partners to accumulate rewarding life experiences. Behaviorists suggest that we look at specific behaviors which we have done with the MATESIM questionnaire. This also suggests that some behaviors must be more desirable than others because of their greater tendency to promote rewarding life experiences. We measure this by use of the priority scales for the individual self-analysis and by use of a therapist consensus on generally socially rewarding issues. Finally, behaviorists suggest that optimums are reached when behaviors are modelled or the same.[2]

This allows a therapist the opportunity to hear the opinions of a group of colleagues in order to confirm judgments or to obtain new insights and ideas for intervention. A therapist may also incorporate his/her own professional priority weightings into the model and then routinely utilize this information to help analyze data on the various couples as it is input. Although not shown here, the analysis provides a comparison of the couple's characteristics taking into account both the preset counselor reference and/or the priority weightings of the therapist utilizing the program.

Another section of the analysis compares each individual's personal characteristics with their ideal partner. This analysis can help a therapist identify those areas in which clients are expecting significantly more out of a relationship than they have to offer. This type of information is very useful for pointing out areas in which clients' expectations regarding relationships are not realistic.

The flexibility of MATESIM II allows therapists to utilize the program for research purposes. The program allows the comparison of any number of any number of actual client characteristics and the manipulation of any actual or hypothetical information directly on the personal computer.

LIMITATIONS

Like all simulations that deal with complex human problems, MATESIM has limitations. This does not, however, invalidate its potential usefulness as a means of extending the rational dimension of human life and thereby contributing to a better life for many who take advantage of it. Some of the most obvious limitations of our approach are directly related to the complexity of the subject matter:

1. There are too few questions. Potentially there could have been thousands of question, but limitations of time and cost prevented additional questions from being used.

2. The simulation assumes that the questions given represent the significant issues of concern to most individuals in their relationships. It also assumes that the users can understand the questions and are willing to answer them honestly. In addition, it assumes the individuals have accurate perceptions of themselves and their partners as they answer the questions. Unfortunately, these assumptions may not hold true for all users.
3. The simulation assumes that users have accurate perceptions of their long-term values when they differentiate between issues by means of the priority weight scales. This requires maturity and experience that some users may lack. If such limitations apply, the simulation must be perceived as a teaching tool designed to expand and enhance the thinking process, not as a predictive tool.
4. The simulation assumes that increased knowledge and understanding will lead to behavior change. This assumption is that human willingness and ability to control emotions reflects rational thinking processes. Some people are capable of this, but others may not be. Can better understanding of the problems of a relationship lead to a better relationship? Can such understandings help some individual to terminate a relationship and seek out a better one? For some this will be true, but for others greater knowledge may lead only to hostility and defensiveness when the emotions cannot be controlled and, perhaps, depression and self-devaluation when the user lacks confidence in his/her ability to change.
5. It does not focus on the interaction pattern of the couples.

FUTURE DIRECTIONS

With the revolution in the use of computers that we are currently witnessing, it is anticipated that there will be increased utilization of computer programs in other areas having to do with nonprogrammed decisions. Just as many other areas have benefited from the vast power of modern computer technology, it is anticipated that the future will bring with it increased utilization of computer applications in the field of human relations.

AUTHORS' NOTE

The program will be available in early 1985 for experimental use by therapists. A license fee of $1,000 will be charged for use of the model in beta test. We are currently negotiating with a publisher for release of a limited version of the model without the change routines for use in marriage and family classes at a cost in the $30-$40 range. To be put on a mailing list for additional information, write: Professor Marlene Lehtinen, Department of Sociology, University of Utah, Salt Lake City, Utah 84112.

NOTES

1. We conducted a computerized search of *Psychological Abstracts, Sociological Abstracts,* and *Social Science Research Abstracts* for the past four years to identify any general purpose computer automated models for use by marriage therapists similar to MATESIM.

2. In establishing our therapist reference, we chose five behaviorists whose focus is on cognitive techniques to modify behavior in ways to make life more rewarding. The counselor reference was established by having this group of five marriage therapists assign a priority weight to each scale item and each variable within each scale. The priority weight was based upon the degree to which the therapist believed that the category and each subposition within each category was associated with successful marital relations. The degree of difference between subpositions within each category was also priority weighted by the therapist. A two-round Delphi method was used to initially set-up the counselor reference differences in priority weights between therapists resolved in a general meeting of the therapists. The counselor reference is used in each analysis of the program to indicate the degree to which the relationship would contribute to a successful marriage. In addition, the counselor reference is used to indicate strengths and weaknesses in the relationship and to target areas for additional growth and development. As such, the counselor reference serves as an independent assessment of the relationship from the perspective of the consensus of the panel of five marriage therapists. The counselor reference can be changed in the change routines of the program to allow individual therapists maximum flexibility in the use of the model. A therapist may be willing to compare his or her priority weighting (on a particular couple) with the collective judgment of the panel of marital therapists.

3. Jerry Debenham and Gerald Smith wrote the computer programs described in this article.

REFERENCES

Costello, B. (1982). The application of computerized psychological and educational assessment in South Australia. *School Psychology International, 3,* 195-202.

Debenham, J., & Smith, G. (1979). MATESIM: Simulating decision making in marriage formation. *Teaching Sociology,* 147-160.

Lovers or Strangers. (1982). Alpine Software: Colorado Springs, Colorado.

Marriage Problems. (1982). Consulting Psychologists Press, Inc.: Palo Alto, California.

Mate. (1982). Consulting Psychologists Press, Inc.: Palo Alto, California.

Morgan, N., & Lehtinen, M. (1981). CAPE: Computer assisted police evaluation. *The Police Chief, XLVIII,* 65-69.

Sexware. (1984). Challenge Software: New York, New York.

Smith, G. W., & Debenham, J. D. (1979). Computer automated marriage analysis. *The American Journal of Family Therapy, 7,* 16-31.

Smith, G. W., & Debenham, J. (1983). Mass producing intelligence for a rational world. *Futures,* 33-46.

Weichselgartner, E. (1981). Adaptive, individualized psychodiagnosis based on a pocket calculator. *Zeitschrift für Experimentelle und Ansewandte Psychologie, 28,* 335-352.

The Multiple Vantage Profile: A Computerized Assessment of Social Organization in Family Therapy

Brent J. Atkinson, MS
Paul N. McKenzie, MS
Bradford P. Keeney, PhD

ABSTRACT. This paper describes the use of a computer program for gathering information regarding social organization in family therapy. The method elicits multiple views of relationship structure and addresses all relationships within a treatment system, including those between therapist and family members. Various ways the computer organizes the assessment data are described and clinical exemplifications demonstrate its usefulness to practicing therapists.

In recent years it has been argued that family therapy clinicians and researchers need to be more responsive to assessing the full complexity of social organization of systems in treatment. Several articles have suggested the importance of assessing multiple levels of social organization, including the behavior of individuals, social relationships indicated by dyadic interaction, and social group structures that organize the relations among dyadic interactions (Keeney, 1983; Keeney & Cromwell, 1979; Cromwell and Peterson, 1981, 1983). Further, Gurman and Kniskern (1978) have stressed the importance of assessing these system levels from multiple perspectives. For example, rather than simply assessing the problem of a particular family member from his or her own perspective, the perspectives of other family members, significant others, the therapist or therapy supervisors can be discerned.

Brent J. Atkinson and Paul N. McKenzie are Co-Directors of the Family Therapy Assessment Project and PhD candidates in Family Therapy, Department of Human Development and Family Studies, Texas Tech University, Lubbock, TX 79409.

Bradford P. Keeney is Director of Family Therapy Research and Associate Professor in the Department of Human Development and Family Studies, Texas Tech University, Lubbock, TX 79409.

The authors wish to gratefully acknowledge Paul and Margaret Pauley for financial support of this project.

A more encompassing level of social organization is included when one adopts an ecosystemic approach to assessment. The ecosystemic view (Keeney, 1979) fully acknowledges the participation of the therapist as an active member of the system being assessed and treated. This view suggests that the individual behavior of the therapist as well as the relationships between the therapist and family members are an appropriate domain for assessment. The majority of instruments assessing social organization currently available do not attend to the therapist's participation in the system being diagnosed.

When complexity is addressed through the assessment of multiple levels of the therapist-family system from multiple perspectives, a set of data is obtained which has until recently been nearly impossible to organize. Recognizing this problem, Gurman and Kniskern (1978) presented a model to help researchers prioritize and limit the targets assessed. We propose that recent advances in computer technology provide new ways of managing data in family assessment. Because of the computer's ability to easily handle large amounts of information, it is no longer necessary to eliminate potentially useful assessment data due to limited time and resources.

The computer's efficiency in handling complex sets of data makes it particularly valuable to clinicians. For the data from an assessment instrument to be optimally beneficial to a therapist, it must be readily available so the therapist can use it to guide his actions in the ongoing course of a session. Using computers in the assessment process enables diagnostic information, including graphical displays, to be available to the therapist seconds after the assessment data have been gathered.

In 1982, a special project was formed at Texas Tech University for the purpose of exploring the use of computers in assessment in marriage and family therapy. While initial efforts focused upon more efficiently assessing marital interaction (Atkinson & McKenzie, in press), more recent efforts have been directed toward computer assessment of the whole therapist-family system in treatment. A specific computer program called the Multiple Vantage Profile (Atkinson & McKenzie, 1983) has been developed which illustrates the use of computers in efficiently organizing complex sets of diagnostic data.

THE MULTIPLE VANTAGE PROFILE

The Multiple Vantage Profile (MVP) is a measure of social organization. Specifically it measures how systems in treatment perceive their relationship structure.[1] The MVP assesses relationship structure across dyadic relationships which may be used for making inferences about the organization of the whole family. In addition, the MVP allows the option of assessing perceptions of how the therapist participates in these relationship structures. A unique aspect of the MVP is the method used to assess each relationship from the multiple vantage points of all other members of the system.

The MVP systematically asks each member of the system to indicate their view of the relationship structure of dyads within the system. For example, in a treatment system which includes a family of four and a therapist (mother, father, son, daughter, and therapist) there are ten possible dyadic combinations:

Mother–Father
Mother–Son
Mother–Daughter
Mother–Therapist

Father–Son
Father–Daughter
Father–Therapist

Son–Daughter
Son–Therapist
Daughter–Therapist

In assessing the perceived structure of these relationships, each member is asked to respond to a series of basic statements regarding each of the above dyadic patterns.

1. How close are person 1 and person 2?
2. How close would person 1 like his/her relationship with person 2 to be?
3. How close would person 2 like his/her relationship with person 1 to be?

The first question is designed to elicit perceptions of the *present* pattern of closeness in a relationship. Questions two and three tap perceptions of the level of *desired* closeness in a relationship.

Depending upon the particular computer format used (formats available are described in the next section), each statement is answered either by using the Likert-type scale shown below:

close				distant
1	2	3	4	5

or by manipulating the distance between two stick figures (representing family members) on a computer screen. In this procedure, subjects adjust the distance between the two figures by manipulating a "joystick" which maneuvers two figures on the screen to indicate their perception of closeness in the relationship. An example is given to the subjects to demonstrate that the space between the figures is to be metaphorical for the general level of closeness in the relationship represented by the figures.

The assessment process is complete when each member of the system has addressed all possible dyadic relationships in the system. This process not only helps the therapist hypothesize the general patterns of relationship structure in terms of perceived distance and closeness, but also indicates differences of perception that various family members have about specific relationships. Palazzoli, Boscolo, Cecchin, and Prata (1978) state that these differences of perception are often valuable sources of information about the family, and have pioneered a clinical interviewing technique, called "triadic questioning" designed to elicit these differences between family members.

Computer Options Available

The MVP utilizes computer technology in both the gathering and the organizing of clinical data. Several different MVP programs have been developed, each utilizing different types of computer hardware and processing formats. Each of these formats has its own advantages and disadvantages. Some are more suitable for research purposes, while others have more clinical utility. One format works especially well with younger children, while others require basic sixth grade reading skills. A few of the formats can be administered with an inexpensive home computer. The following is a brief description of the available MVP formats.

1. *Optic Scanning.* This version of the MVP requires family members to complete a questionnaire using a standard computer answer sheet, using the Likert scale previously described. Individual responses are marked and then "read" by a computer via an optic scanner. This computerized scanning system is similar to the grocery store checkout devices used to read universal product codes. The computer is then instructed to organize the data in a manner predetermined by the therapist (e.g., descriptive statistics, graphs, etc.). The advantage of this format is the speed of processing. Most optic scanners can read thousands of computer forms in seconds. Because of this efficiency, most research on the MVP has utilized the optic-scan method. However, the disadvantage of this system lies in the cost and limited availability of optic scanning to most clinical contexts.

2. *Compu-score.* Because most therapists do not have access to equipment necessary to perform optic scanning, another method was developed which involves "reading" family member's responses.

The compu-score method requires that the therapist type in the responses from each MVP answer sheet onto a home computer. A computer program then organizes the data in the manner the therapist desires. Cost factors of this format are minimized since computers are quite often already being utilized by therapists for business or billing purposes. The disadvantage of this method is the time necessary for a therapist or secretary to type in the family's responses (approximately 5 to 10 minutes for a family of five).

3. *Computer Interactive.* This format of the MVP requires that each family member interact with the computer and uses graphic displays that are often entertaining for the family (and therapist). Each individual responds to the computer's questions by manipulating the distance between figures on a computer screen which represent specific members of the system (this process was described earlier). The computer then "reads" the distances between these figures and organizes the data in whatever manner the therapist decides. The advantage to this format is that family members, especially children, are often fascinated by the game-like quality of the MVP. Since this method does not require manual input of data by either optic scanning or terminal input, it is the most efficient format from the therapist's perspective. The disadvantage of this method lies in the time necessary for each family member to complete the task. Unless the therapist has access to several computers, family members must take turns using the computer.

4. *Computer Interactive: No Graphics.* This format is similar to the previous method except no graphics are used. Instead of manipulating figures on the computer monitor, all MVP questions are printed out on the computer screen along with the Likert-type response choices. Each family member responds to the questions by typing in the appropriate answer.

ORGANIZATION OF DATA AND CLINICAL APPLICATION

We have found that the MVP can be valuable both as an initial assessment given before therapy begins, and as an ongoing measure of change administered at several points in the therapy process. Of course, when the MVP is given as a pre-therapy assessment, the therapist and his relationships with family members cannot be included in the assessment because the therapist and family have not yet encountered each other. However, the therapist can be included in all subsequent administrations of the MVP. Some of the ways in which the MVP can help organize clinical data and contribute to the process of therapy will now be illustrated. Our discussion demonstrates how the MVP was used with a treatment family.

The mother of a family of four (mother, father, son and daughter) initially requested therapy, indicating her worry over the son's frequent temper outbursts which had recently escalated to the point that even father could not stop them. The family came to the first therapy session twenty minutes early and completed the optic scanning format of the MVP. The results which follow were available to the therapist before he saw the family.

One of the ways the MVP organizes clinical data is by graphing the average level of perceived closeness in each dyadic relationship. Figure 1 shows such a graph for this family. Note that each bar indicates the *average* perception of closeness for a specific relationship. It is the mean of the perceptions of every family member regarding that relationship. The therapist must be careful in interpreting the meaning of these averages. The computation of an average score is only one means of managing the complexity of all the family data. The cost of this reductive operation is that it may obscure the specific relationship patterns organizing the whole family. On the other hand, differences across average scores may direct the therapist to examine particular relationship configurations that otherwise might be overlooked.

Figure 1 may be interpreted as indicating that family members perceive the relationship between mother and father to be more distant than either the relationship between mother and son or mother and daughter. In addition, the relationship between mother and son may be hypothesized as particularly close, and the relationship between father and son may be hypothesized as the most distant relationship in the family. To the structurally oriented therapist, this profile might further suggest the possibility of a cross-generational coalition between mother and son against father. This information can be used to calibrate and direct the therapist's questions to gather further information which will support or negate this hypothesis about relationship structure. It is important to recognize that the MVP does not "measure" or "prove" the existence of cross-generational coalitions, but may be used by the therapist to build hypotheses from which to operate. Since this process of building and testing hypotheses about family relationship distance, coalitions and alliances is common to several schools of family therapy (Palazzoli, Boscolo, Cecchin, & Prata, 1980; Haley, 1976; Minuchin, 1974), the MVP may be used with a variety of clinical strategies.

Figure 2 presents another form of an average score from which inferences may be drawn that suggest how close each family member is to the family as a whole. From Figure 2 it can be hypothesized that father is the most distant member from the whole family. His score was computed by averaging the scores of each of the dyadic relationships in which father is a member. Scores for the other family members were computer in a

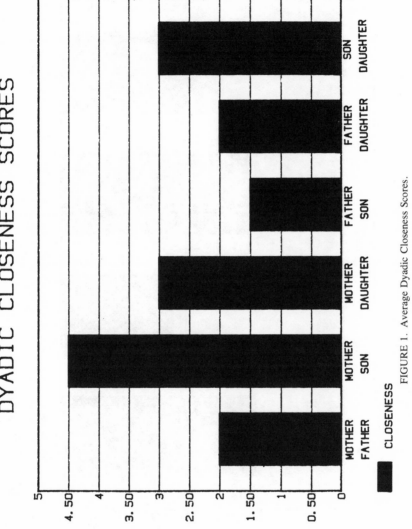

FIGURE 1. Average Dyadic Closeness Scores.

139

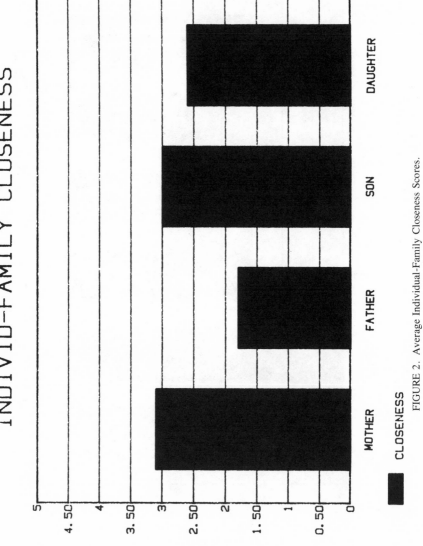

FIGURE 2. Average Individual-Family Closeness Scores.

140

similar fashion. The graph may be seen as supporting the hypothesis that the father is somewhat generally disengaged from the family, and that the mother is more centrally a part of the family.

It is often valuable for the therapist to check whether family members agree or disagree with each other about their perceptions of the various levels of closeness in dyads. Returning to Figure 1, one may hypothesize that the relationship between mother and father was perceived as being quite distant. The present question is, did the family members uniformly see this relationship as distant, or did some see it as being closer than others? The MVP makes this information available by graphing perceptual discrepancy scores. These scores are the mean deviations of family members' perceptions regarding a specific relationship. The perceptual discrepancy scores for the family are illustrated in Figure 3. It can be seen that there is considerable disagreement among family members regarding the level of closeness in the mother-father relationship as compared with the other family relationships. Whenever the therapist locates considerable disagreement among family members, it is useful to go a step further and find out *which* family members are disagreeing. The MVP makes this information available by graphing raw scores.

Figure 4 depicts the raw scores that each family member gave in response to the question, "How close is the relationship between mother and father?" What is immediately obvious is that all family members describe this relationship as very distant except father, who describes it as being very close. Based on this information, a therapist might begin with the simple hypothesis that the father tends to exaggerate or overestimate the closeness of his marital relationship.[2] If so, he may also overestimate (or underestimate) other family relationships.

An immediate way of evaluating the latter hypothesis is to compute the average of the closeness scores that father gives to all the possible relationships in the family. This average score, which represents father's tendency to score relationships in a certain direction (close or distant), can then be compared with the tendencies of other members to score all relationships in a certain direction. These scores are called "individual portrayal scores," because they focus more upon an individual's style of portraying relationships than on the relationships actually being portrayed. Figure 5 illustrates the individual portrayal scores of the family described previously. Here it can be seen that father does tend to, on the average, rate all relationships in the family as being closer than other family members rate them. Not only does he give them higher closeness ratings, but, except for the daughter, he also rates more consistently across relationships than other members, as evidenced by the mean deviations. This graph then gives support to the notion that father may see all family relationships in a different manner than do other family members.

Thus far we have considered various ways of examining how family

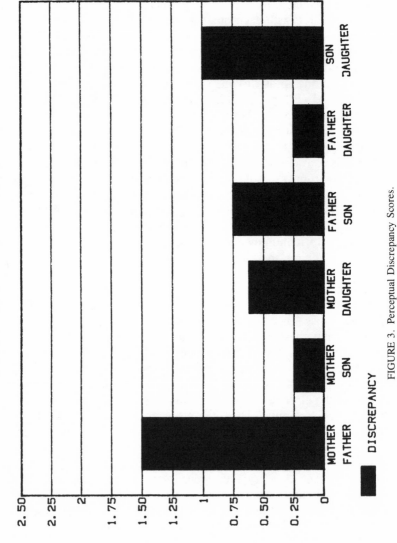

FIGURE 3. Perceptual Discrepancy Scores.

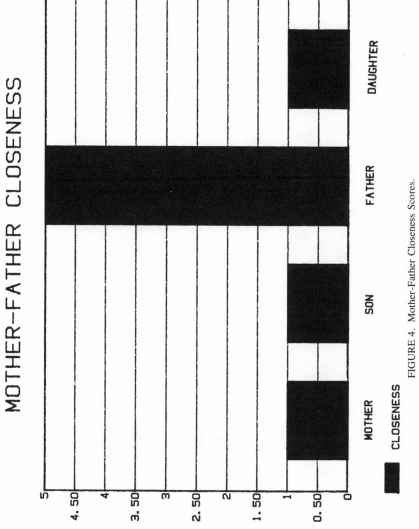

FIGURE 4. Mother-Father Closeness Scores.

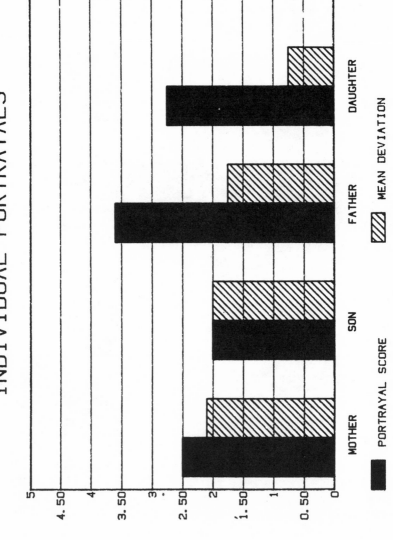

FIGURE 5. Individual Portrayal Scores.

144

members perceive closeness in their family relationships. This information does not indicate how close family members would like their relationships to be. One reason for considering the changes desired by each person is that those who are desiring the most change may be more motivated to change than those who are content with the present level of closeness in their relationship. The MVP makes this information available for each relationship by graphing the discrepancies between how close family members generally perceive the relationship to be, and how close family members generally believe that the members of that relationship would *like* it to be. The "change desired" scores for each dyad are graphed in Figure 6. Notice that there are two scores for each dyad, one for each member of the dyad. For example, looking specifically at the mother-father scores, the first (solid) bar indicates how much change the *mother* would like in the relationship, while the second (striped) bar indicates how much change the *father* would like in the relationship. It can be seen that mother is perceived as desiring a considerable positive change in closeness (more closeness), while father is perceived as desiring a negative change in closeness (less closeness). Looking across the different dyads, it may be hypothesized that father is desiring very little change in any of his relationships.

The change desired scores may be useful to a wide variety of therapeutic orientations. In particular, therapists using the interactional approach (Fisch, Weakland, & Segal, 1982) may be interested in these scores because these therapists often decide to directly work with those members who are most motivated to change.

In addition to gathering information about who wants to change and how much, the therapist may find it useful to have a portrait of the family's view of the changes its members desire. Figure 7 shows this kind of portrait for the family we have been describing. This portrait graphs the present and desired future levels of closeness in a relationship (as perceived by family members) side-by-side for comparison. The solid bars indicate the level of closeness desired by the person whose name is listed *first* in each dyad. The striped bars are the present perceived level of closeness in each dyad, and the open bars indicate the level of closeness desired by the person whose name is listed *second* in each dyad. Portraying the scores this way enables the therapist to see, for example, that if father's goals were reached, on a closeness scale of 1 to 5, his relationship with mother would be at the 1.5 level of closeness. On the other hand, if mother achieved her goal, the relationship would be at the 4.5 level of closeness. The other dyads can be looked at in similar fashion.

With the information gathered about this family through the various MVP graphs, one might hypothesize that the mother is closer to the children than she is to the father, the father is somewhat distant from the

CHANGE DESIRED

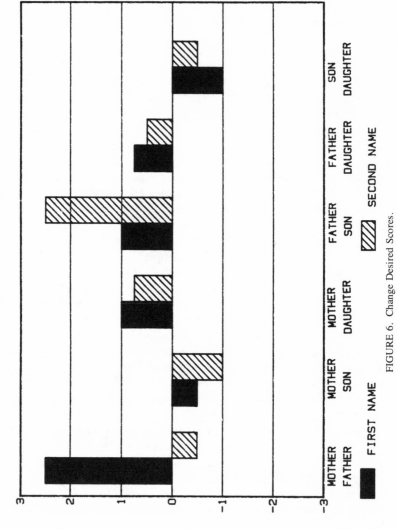

FIGURE 6. Change Desired Scores.

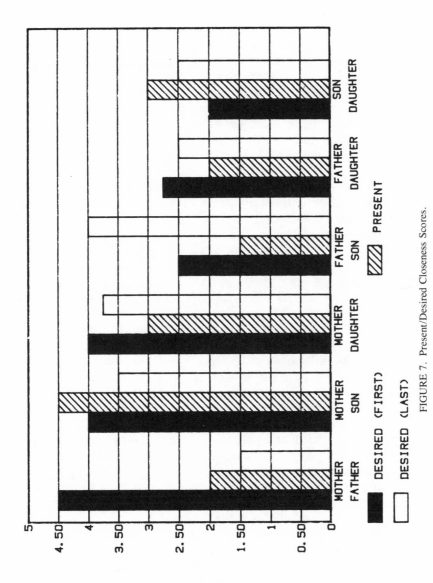

FIGURE 7. Present/Desired Closeness Scores.

147

family in general, the father seems prone to idealize relationships in the family (portraying them as closer than other members think they are), and the mother and children would like more closeness from father, but he has not indicated any intention of getting closer.

With these hypotheses about relationship structures, the therapist is in a position to begin constructing a more general (i.e., systemic) hypothesis about the organizational patterns that stabilize the presenting problem. Based on the information generated by the MVP and the knowledge of the presenting problem, the following therapeutic hypothesis might be constructed. The son's outbursts are part of a repeating organizational pattern where father is engaged to calm the son, subsequently providing mother and son more closeness with father. One consequence of father's move toward the family, however, is that the mother becomes worried by the father's intrusion into her close relationship with the son. She then, in post hoc fashion, criticizes the father's previous handling of the son, resulting in father's distancing from the family again. This hypothesis provides a frame of reference the therapist can use to design a therapeutic intervention.[3]

THE ONGOING MEASUREMENT OF CHANGE

As therapy progresses, the MVP can report changes in any of the types of scores previously described. In the case reported, information was obtained in the first session which led to a hypothesis about the family's relationship structures. The major intervention delivered in the first three sessions consisted of challenging and prescribing the way the family's relationship structures maintained organizational stability (interventions of this sort are described in detail by Keeney & Ross, 1984). In general, the therapist commended the family for coming up with a creative way for father to periodically enter and leave the family. It was then pointed out that the unfortunate cost of this solution was the son's developing antisocial behavior. At the same time, the therapist noted that it was probably best to not interrupt this process until the family was certain they had found an alternative way of preserving their stability.

After three sessions, the family reported that the temper outbursts had stopped. The family again took the MVP, and several changes could be interpreted: Family members rated father's relationships with both children as closer, and father's perceptions of family relationships were more similar to the perceptions of other members, including the view of his relationship with his wife. The family however, still rated the relationship between mother and father as quite distant. Finally, mother's ''change desired score'' regarding her relationship with father had declined drastically.

Since the present degree of closeness did not appear to have changed between mother and father, the therapist was concerned about the sudden drop in the score reflecting mother's desire for closeness with father. This concern, coupled with father's lower marital closeness score, prompted the therapist to explore the marital relationship more directly in the fourth session. He discovered that since father had become more involved with the children, fights had increased between he and his wife. The marital relationship became the focus throughout the rest of therapy.

The MVP was useful in this situation in that it helped alert the therapist to changing patterns in family relationships. More specifically, it underscored problems emerging in the marital relationship as father's relationship with the children changed.

THE THERAPIST AS PART OF THE SYSTEM

The importance of the therapist joining (and separating from) the family system has been addressed in one form or another by most major schools of family therapy. Usually, the degree of joining (and separation) present in a therapist-family system is determined by the therapist or supervisor. One of the contributions of the MVP is that it provides access to knowing how the family may perceive the amount of closeness between themselves and the therapist.

For example, in Figure 8 the perceptions of the therapist about his relationships with family members are listed side-by-side with the average perceptions of the family after three sessions of therapy. The graph indicates that the therapist perceives himself to be more joined with the son than do other family members. The son has always been very polite to the therapist, smiling at him as they interact, even telling the therapist a joke at the beginning of the third session. This information led the therapist to conclude that he was fairly close to the son. However, other family members were present when the son would make fun of the therapist at home, calling him names, and insisting that he was not going to go to the next therapy session. The family's perspective was different from that of the therapist, and the therapist was alerted to this information when he viewed the MVP scores.

In a similar way, the perceptions of the therapist regarding closeness in other family relationships can be compared with the perceptions of family members. This comparison, in addition to noting the different ways in which family members may perceive the therapist's closeness in family relationships, helps remind the therapist of his participation as *part* of the whole therapeutic system. It naturally follows that the therapist may use this class of information to further shape and polish the therapeutic hypothesis that guides his or her understanding and subsequent action.

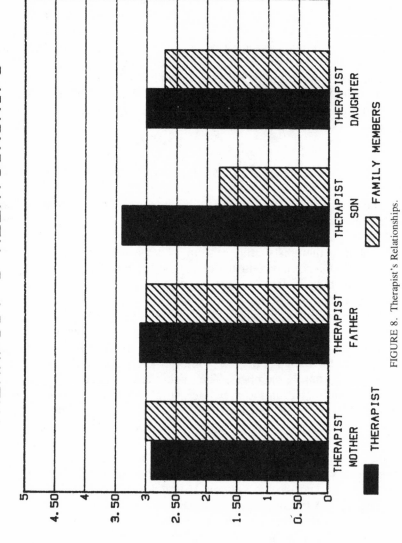

FIGURE 8. Therapist's Relationships.

CONCLUSION

This paper has presented an example of how a computer can be used in the process of assessment in family therapy. The computerized Multiple Vantage Profile generates up to 20 different types of graphic displays for representing assessment data about patterns of family social organization functioning. In addition, multiple perspectives are used in a systematic way to assess relationships within the treatment system. Further, computer processing enables the results from the assessment to be quickly available, thereby contributing to the ongoing organization of therapy.

Before closing it is again necessary to briefly comment on the limitations of using the MVP in family therapy.[4] It is particularly important to remember that the responsibility of interpreting and utilizing the findings of the MVP always falls upon the therapist. The MVP only compares differences of perception across members of a family-therapist system. How these differences contribute to diagnosis and intervention depends on the therapist's own decision-making and epistemology. In conclusion, although computers can never perform therapy, the wider system of therapist-family-computer may become a pattern that helps organize successful therapeutic outcomes.

NOTES

1. Assessment of relationship structure, whether articulated in terms of distance and closeness, emotional bonding, or more generally as family structure, has been a central theme in theories and assessment models of family functioning. It is central to both the Circumplex (Olson, Sprenkle, & Russell, 1979) and the Beavers-Timberlawn (Beavers, 1976) models, as well as the clinical treatment models developed by Minuchin (1974), Haley (1976), the Milan Associates (Palazzoli et al., 1978), Bowen (1978), and Alexander and Parsons (1982).

2. The therapist's hypothesis should never be seen as suggesting any "objective reality" that operates in the family. As Maturana (1978, p. 50) states: "Representation, meaning, and description are notions that apply only and exclusively to the operation of living systems in a consensual domain, and are defined by an observer to refer to second-order consensual behavior. For this reason, these notions have no explanatory value for the characterization of the actual operation of living systems as autopoetic systems, even though they arise through structural coupling. Because a description always implies an interaction by a member of a domain of consensus, the domain of descriptions is necessarily bounded by the ultimate possible interactions of a living system through the properties of its components." In other words, all hypotheses and interpretations of the MVP are strictly in the domain of the observer and can never be held as operative in the observed family system. The usefulness of any therapeutic hypothesis can only be evaluated in terms of its relation to therapeutic interventions and subsequent outcomes.

3. The reader is again reminded that a multitude of hypotheses may fit the description of this particular case.

4. It is beyond the scope of the present paper to discuss the limitations inherent in using measures concerned with dyadic interaction to evaluate more complex relations. Although social scientists have fantasized about the capability of assessing triadic (and presumably quadradic) relations, in the most formal sense, science and logic has not yet constructed anything beyond a dyadic calculus. Warren McCulloch (1965), the father of modern experimental epistemology, often lamented that our understanding of biological processes (including social events) is constrained by our lack of a triadic calculus. Our point is that we are presently limited to formally assessing dyadic relations, although we may make as many inferences as we wish to more complex patterns of relationship.

REFERENCES

Alexander, J., & Parsons, B. V. (1982). *Functional family therapy.* Monterey, CA: Brooks/Cole Publishing Co.

Atkinson, B. J., & McKenzie, P. N. (in press). The personalized Spouse Observation Checklist: A computerized assessment of marital interaction. *Journal of Marital and Family Therapy.*

Atkinson, B. J., & McKenzie, P. N. (1983). *The Multiple Vantage Profile.* Unpublished manuscript, Texas Tech University.

Beavers, W. (1976). A theoretical basis for family evaluation. In J. Lewis, W. Beavers, J. Gossett, & V. Phillips (Eds.), *No single thread: Psychological health in family systems.* NY: Brunner/ Mazel.

Bowen, M. (1978). *Family therapy in clinical practice.* New York: Jason Aronson.

Cromwell, R. E., & Peterson, G. W. (1981). Multisystem-multimethod assessment: A framework. In E. Filsinger & R. Lewis (Eds.), *Assessing marriage.* Beverly Hills, CA: Sage Publications.

Cromwell, R. E., & Peterson, G. W. (1983). Multisystem-multimethod family assessment in clinical contexts. *Family Process, 22,* 147-164.

Fisch, R., Weakland, J. H., & Segal, L. (1982). *The tactics of change.* San Francisco: Jossey-Bass.

Gurman, A. S., & Kniskern, D. P. (1978). Research on marital and family therapy: Progress, perspective, and prospect. In S. L. Garfield & A. E. Bergin (Eds.), *Handbook of psychotherapy and behavior change.* NY: Wiley.

Haley, J. (1976). *Problem-solving therapy.* San Francisco: Jossey Bass.

Keeney, B. P. (1983). Ecological assessment. In B. P. Keeney (Ed.), *Diagnosis and assessment in family therapy.* Rockville, MD: Aspen.

Keeney, B. P. (1979). Ecosystemic epistemology: An alternative paradigm for diagnosis. *Family Process, 18,* 117-129.

Keeney, B. P., & Cromwell, R. (1979). Toward systemic diagnosis. *Family Therapy, 4*(3), 225-236.

Keeney, B. P., & Ross, J. (1984). *Mind in therapy: Constructing systemic therapies.* New York: Basic Books.

Maturana, H. R. (1978). Biology of language: The epistemology of reality. In G. A. Miller & E. Lennenberg (Eds.), *Psychology and the biology of language and thought.* NY: Academic Press.

McCulloch, W. S. (1965). *Embodiments of mind.* Cambridge, MA: M.I.T. Press.

Minuchin, S. (1974). *Families and family therapy.* Cambridge, MA: Harvard University Press.

Olson, D. H., Sprenkle, D. H., & Russell, C. S. (1979). Circumplex model of marital and family systems: I. Cohesion and adaptability dimension, family types, and clinical applications. *Family Process, 18,* 3-29.

Palazzoli, M., Boscolo, L., Cecchin, G., & Prata, G. (1980). Hypothesizing, circularity, and neutrality. *Family Process, 19,* 3-12.

Palazzoli, M., Boscolo, L., Cecchin, G., & Prata, G. (1978). *Paradox and Counterparadox.* NY: Jason Aronson.

Knowledge Utilization
and Decision Support Systems
in Family Therapy

Gerald J. Bostwick, Jr., PhD

ABSTRACT. The knowledge explosion has been a frustrating experience for many family therapists. They have difficulty keeping up with the literature and, oftentimes, determining the relevance of that literature to practice. One approach for dealing with this problem is to teach therapists a systematic process for selecting, reviewing, and translating information into practice guidelines. These guidelines can then be transferred to a computerized decision support system which can be used in a consulting role. As practice guidelines are modified and new ones added, the data base will be able to support more sophisticated types of practice decision-making.

INTRODUCTION

It has become increasingly difficult to stay current in the field of family therapy. Clinicians have responded to the knowledge explosion in a variety of ways. Some have undertaken the monumental task of trying to read everything. Others have turned to specialization, thereby limiting the amount of information they need to process. At the far end of the continuum are those who have stopped keeping up with the literature altogether, relying instead on practice wisdom and feedback from peers. However, none of these strategies for coping with information overload are viable for the accountable professional with a heavy and varied caseload. Specialization may work for the academician, theoretician, or researcher but not for the front line therapists who rarely enjoy the luxury of selecting the types of families they want to work with.

At the same time the author was becoming interested in the problem of information overload in family therapy, he joined a University of Chicago project designed to examine the utilization of knowledge in practice. One aspect of the project addressed the potential use of computers for the identification, synthesization, and application of practice knowledge. This led

Gerald J. Bostwick, Jr. is an associate professor at the School of Social Work, Michigan State University. In addition to his teaching and research responsibilities, Dr. Bostwick also maintains a private family therapy practice. Mailing address: School of Social Work, Michigan State University, East Lansing, MI 48824.

to the exploration of bibliographic services, management information systems, and, more recently, decision support systems.

This paper discusses the development of a systematic knowledge utilization process, the incorporation of computer technology, and the impact that microcomputers have had on our thinking about the potential for using this process in a clinical setting. The concluding section will look at the complementary relationship between the knowledge utilization process and decision support systems. An illustration is provided to demonstrate how such a system can be used to assist family therapists in their work, and the development/implementation of such a system in a family service agency is discussed.

PROCESS OF KNOWLEDGE UTILIZATION

Recognition of the difficulties many practitioners experience in managing the information available to them gave impetus to an examination of knowledge utilization in practice by Edward Mullen, the author, and Nancy Kyte. Our study of the uses of different types of information in practice led to the development of a strategy that systematizes the collection, translation, and application of knowledge (Mullen, 1978; Mullen, Bostwick, & Ryg, 1980).

The process we developed represents a rational and self-conscious use of available knowledge and at the same time reflects the stylistic idiosyncracies of the practitioner. In other words, it brings together the art and science of practice because it considers all types of information, e.g., theoretical, research, and experiential knowledge (Mullen, 1981, 1983). At the heart of this process is the use of knowledge for the identification and development of intervention techniques or practice guidelines.

The knowledge utilization process involves a series of steps which culminate in the development of general and specific knowledge. General knowledge refers to information that can be generalized to (i.e., utilized in) most case situations. An example from the problem-solving paradigm would be the establishment of clear and attainable short-term and long-term goals. Specific knowledge represents an attempt to answer the challenge Kiesler (1971) raised in his questioning of the uniformity assumptions of practice. In short, the belief that clients, therapists, and treatment outcome are homogeneous in characteristics and dimensions is a myth that has permeated most conceptualizations of treatment. Individual differences are not appreciated and this in turn has hindered both the evaluation of practice and the application (i.e., perceived relevance) of research results. In particular, consideration has to be given to specifying which interventions (techniques) and therapists work best with which clients, problems, and situational exigencies.

The knowledge utilization process itself encompasses five major steps:

1. identifying and recording substantive findings
2. recording evidence for the substantive findings
3. forming summary generalizations
4. deducing practice guidelines (i.e., prescriptive statements that guide intervention)
5. developing an evaluation/feedback plan

To explicate this process more meaningfully, the author's personal experiences will be drawn upon to illustrate the use of the theoretical and research literature in the development of practice guidelines designed to reduce the likelihood that a family will drop out of therapy prematurely (Bostwick, 1981).

Step One: Identifying Substantive Findings

The process usually begins with the identification of secondary reviews of the relevant literature. For example, the Gurman and Kniskern (1978) review of family therapy outcome presents cumulative findings and suggests several practice guidelines. However, the author's search of the literature failed to uncover any similarly comprehensive reviews of family therapy dropouts. Therefore, the next step was to examine individual journals and identify primary articles that have discussed or empirically examined the dropout phenomenon. Not unexpectedly, this was an extremely time-consuming endeavor. Although the scope of this particular review was probably more than would be needed to develop practice guidelines, this experience made it quite clear that reliance on primary studies could easily overwhelm the individual clinician trying to survey and use the literature. This factor, additionally confirmed through the experiences of our students, generated the idea of using a group of practitioners as information processors.

Step Two: Classifying Substantiating Evidence

Since an information system was being developed, a standardized process for recording/classifying the data had to be created. The form we used asked for, among other things, a description of the agency, types of clients, problems, and therapists involved, an identification of the nature (theoretical or empirical) of the information, and a delineation of the major results/conclusions. The outcome was a collection of over 50 articles, books, and dissertations on dropouts from parent-child, marital, and various forms of family therapy.

Step Three: Forming Summary Generalizations

Summary generalizations attempt to express consensus in the information and at the same time identify any limiting conditions (e.g., the majority of the studies were conducted in family service agencies or child guidance clinics). Also, because contradictory findings are not uncommon, one must accept what the preponderance of evidence indicates. The purpose of this effort is heuristic, that is, to provide a basis for developing working hypotheses about the dropout problem. Some of the generalization developed from this author's review included:

1. demographic characteristic (e.g., age, sex, race) are not very helpful in understanding (explaining/predicting) family therapy dropout
2. congruence of parental views, motivation for treatment, and expectations of a favorable outcome are associated with families who tend to remain in therapy
3. parent-therapist congruence on problem and focus of treatment, participation of the father in treatment, and the use of a family rather than individual members focus increase the likelihood of a family continuing in therapy

Step Four: Deducing Practice Guidelines

Obviously, these summary generalizations do not answer the question of what one should do in practice to increase the probability of a family staying in treatment. Although practice guidelines may be implicit in the summary generalizations, it is important to articulate specifically what they are. This is also the stage at which the individual practitioner needs to be creative; filling in the gaps between theoretical/research knowledge and practice application is at times a small jump and at other times a major leap. Examples of practice guidelines derived from the above-stated summary generalizations included:

1. I should be cognizant of my preconceptions about types of families and the likelihood they will drop out, for it may be these preconceptions and not the family characteristics themselves that contribute to premature termination
2. I need to convey to the parents an appreciation of their interest in obtaining help and support them in their willingness to be involved (e.g., schedule appointments at a convenient time)
3. a tentative agreement should be reached by the end of the initial session regarding what the purpose and focus of treatment will be
4. special efforts should be made to understand and work with the

family as a unit and to encourage and support the involvement and participation of the father

Step Five: Developing an Evaluation/Feedback Plan

The final step requires an articulation of the procedures to be used for evaluating the application of the practice guideline. The consequence of this process is the refinement of the guideline and/or the specification of its limitations. Examples of methods that could be used during this stage include: focused supervision, client self-reports, therapist assessments, and single-subject designs. Particularly apropos would be the use of videotapes, since many family therapists typically rely on this medium for feedback purposes.

In closing, it should be reiterated that just as our theoretical knowledge is incomplete, so is our research knowledge. Therefore, family therapists will also have to rely on personal experience and practice wisdom as sources of information. It is important to keep in mind that there are numerous sources of information that vary in their utility at different points of time. Reliance on only one or two sources may seriously jeopardize our ability to be effective family therapists.

COMPUTERS AND THE KNOWLEDGE UTILIZATION PROCESS

The complexity and intrinsic problems associated with the knowledge utilization process surfaced early on. Given the absence of secondary reviews, the amount of materials that had to be examined and synthesized seemed to reduce the feasibility of the individual practitioner engaging in such a process. For this reason, the project team decided to explore the possibility of using computer technology. The microcomputer had not been introduced at that time, so our initial effort focused on using a mainframe computer which could be accessed via several hardcopy and video display terminals (VDT). Our strategy was to develop a list of primary and secondary articles that could be cross-referenced by subject area. However, this cataloging of clinical material still left the process of reviewing and synthesizing information up to the individual student interns in our program. This effort was only marginally helpful, to say the least.

A second strategy we pursued was the use of existing data bases that provide annotated summaries of the contents of articles. Specifically, we looked at *Psychological Abstracts* and the *Social Science Citation Index*. Unfortunately, it soon became evident that these information retrieval resources would not satisfy our needs. For example, we used the dropout problem to test the usefulness of the data base. A subject search, as opposed to an author search, was the logical choice. However, by limiting the search to key words appearing in the titles of articles, we were unable to identify many resources already known to us. There were numerous articles that discussed the continuance-discontinuance problem but which did not necessarily use any of our key terms in their titles. Yet another problem involved the access to mainframe computers. In particular, even if we could find a way to computerize clinical information, how many agencies could afford terminals and the access charges for using them?

About the time we began to experience some reservations about individual practitioner or agency involvement and the usefulness of computer technology in this process, two independent developments occurred. First, the experiences of our student interns, who were using different sources of information and developing practice guidelines in their field practicums (Mullen, Bostwick, & Ryg, 1981), highlighted the exchange of information that takes place in the field and suggested that part of the process could be a group effort. At least the collection, synthesis and development of practice guidelines could be shared by all if this part of the process was applied uniformly by each individual. A check of student practice guidelines, using the same data base, indicated great similarity in the guidelines generated. The second development was the introduction of affordable microcomputers. In short, we did not need to rely on large mainframe computers for storing information and we saw this as an opportunity to make the knowledge utilization process appear more relevant because of our increased control of the data base within each setting, i.e., it could be tailored to the agency's needs.

COMPUTERIZED DECISION SUPPORT SYSTEMS (KNOWLEDGE UTILIZATION) IN FAMILY THERAPY

A corollary of these early research efforts and advances in computer technology was the development of a project proposing to determine the feasibility of involving a small group of therapists in the knowledge utilization process and the use of a microcomputer for information management. Fortunately, the director of a local family service agency had purchased an IBM-PC for personal and business use. When we brought up the subject of creating a system that would help family therapists make decisions about intervention strategies, she expressed an interest in hosting such a project. She felt the project would not only provide useful information but also would be helpful in other ways as well. First, it would familiarize staff with computer hardware (terminology) and second, it would help desensitize staff apprehensions (computerphobia). Subsequently, the full potential of microcomputer technology could be realized because most of the pre-existing barriers would be addressed.

We are currently in the first phase of this project. It calls for each of the three agency practitioners, who are involved in conducting family therapy, to select two family therapy-oriented journals to review monthly (or quarterly) for materials on convening and engaging families in treatment. These materials are being used to guide the therapists through the five steps of the knowledge utilization process and determine inter-therapist reliability in formulating practice guidelines. We believe that this training is essential because the validity of the data base and, subsequently, therapist confidence in that information will dictate system utility. System analysts always stress the need to carefully plan the pre-computerization stages of system development. Failure to institute valid and reliable information collection and conversion procedures will only increase the likelihood of the old maxim coming true, "Garbage In, Garbage Out" (Hicks, 1984; Keen & Morton, 1978; Kupfer, Levine, & Nelson, 1976).

This phase of the project also involves the identification, testing, and selection of software (i.e., a data base management package). At first it was thought that a management information system (MIS) would best meet the project's needs. However, most MIS's are not designed for handling qualitative types of information and are structured for management types of decision-making. Consequently, an alternative type of information system was needed—one that was more relevant to the type of decision-making done by clinicians. A review of the literature led us to the idea of using a decision support system (DSS) (Briggs, 1982; Boyd, Pruger, Chase, Clark, & Miller, 1982; Brower, Hankins, Mutschler, & Nurius, 1983; Keen & Morton, 1978). A DSS can be thought of as a management information system designed to support non-routine decision-making. However, there are several characteristics that serve to differentiate DSS's and MIS's. A DSS attempts to develop a flexible and conversational data base that recognizes the language of the person using the system. Also, unlike MIS's that often *replace* management decision-making, the DSS is intended to do nothing more than *support* that process (Hicks, 1984; Schoech, 1979, 1982; Schoech & Schkade, 1980).

For our purposes, such a system required a program that not only utilizes key words and phrases typically used by family therapists, but one which was also interactive and conversational. "Interactive" means the program responds to questions proposed by the user, and "conversational" indicates that the program also asks questions of the user. For this to occur, the program must include explanations concerning system content and use, as well as personalized dialogue. Ideally, one would need an interactive, time-sharing computer and VDT's for all the therapists in order to make the plethora of clinical information available to everyone without lengthy delays. Yet, on the one hand, it is too early to advocate for the development of an elaborate DSS to complement clinical decision-making. If, on the other hand, this project is successful in demonstrating the feasibility of such a DSS, then the next step would be to expand the data base and computer hardware.

Once a decision was made to use a DSS, the next step was to examine existing software. Several programs for the IBM-PC were assessed (e.g., DECISION, DECISION-ANALYST, and EXPERT-EASE an artificial intelligence program), but, as is often the case in the human service field, nothing seemed to meet our needs. With the exception of psychiatric diagnosis, the use of computers in therapy decision making has largely been ignored. Only recently have attempts been made to explore more clinical applications of computer technology (Schwartz, 1984). Therefore, the extensive modification of existing software or custom programming was indicated. Given limited funds the author was fortunate enough to locate a student who, prior to enrolling in graduate school, had worked with micro computers and was conversant in several programming languages. She agreed to help develop the custom software required as part of a course project.

Since we knew that the psychiatric diagnostic packages are a form of a DSS we looked at several programs to see how they were structured. There are two general strategies used in constructing decision making programs (Miller, 1984). The first employs a logical decision tree model which is based on a series of questions, the answers in turn determine which branch of the tree the computer will follow. The second approach relies on statistical calculations (i.e., discriminate analysis and Bayesian Probability). For our purposes the logical decision tree design seemed to be the best choice.

Although the development of a DSS is still in the beginning stages, a BASIC data management program has been written for the Convening and Engaging Families in Treatment data base. The following conversation should illustrate how the DSS operates using both general and specific practice guidelines developed by the therapists. This family therapist is concerned about convening and engaging families in treatment in general and, in particular, a Mexican-American family. The therapist decides to use the Family Therapy Information Consultant (FTIC) for practice guideline suggestions. She turns on the computer, accesses the program diskette, and the following sequence of events takes place:

FTIC: Welcome. You are using the Family Therapy Information Consultant (FTIC). The FTIC was developed to help family therapists identify, select, and develop practice guidelines when intervening with families. Practice guidelines are prescriptive statements that suggest therapist activities. The treatment process has been broken down into four artificially discrete phases. You have two options at this point. First, you can obtain information on existing guidelines for any one of the four phases. Second, you can select one of the treatment phases and add information to the practice guidelines data base. The four treatment phases are:

A. Convening and Engaging Families in Treatment
B. Assessment of Family Structure and Communication Patterns
C. Intervention in the Family System
D. Termination of Family Therapy and Maintenance of Change

Please enter your name.

Therapist: Anne

FTIC: Anne, if you have any questions about the requests made, just hit the F1 key (which you will find on the upper left-hand side of the keyboard) and an explanation will appear.
Do you wish to add or obtain information? Please press A for add or O for obtain.

Anne: O

FTIC: Please press the letter of the treatment phase in which you are interested.

Anne: A

FTIC: Anne, you have selected Convening and Engaging Families in Treatment. However, before we can proceed you will need to boot the Convening and Engaging Families in Treatment data diskette. I'll wait. (Anne places the appropriate diskette in the unused disk drive and the conversation continues). Thank you. Since there are various practice guidelines associated with convening and engagement, they have been categorized as Generic and Situational. Generic guidelines are those that are applicable to most family therapy cases. The Situational guidelines are specific to a type of problem or family. Would you like to see the Generic or Situational guidelines? Press G for Generic or S for Situational.

Anne: G

FTIC: Based on the literature, the following guidelines are suggested for convening-engaging families in treatment:

(1) The use of reminder letters or telephone calls three days before the initial session will increase the likelihood that the family will attend.

(2) It is important to reach a tentative agreement on the problem to be worked by the end of the first session.

(3) Avoid focusing on any one individual for an extended period of time—try and maintain a *family* focus.

(Obviously this listing is incomplete; however, it should give the reader an idea of the type of information that is provided.)

FTIC: Anne, this is a complete listing of the existing data base. Would you like to see what your colleagues' experiences have been? Press Y for Yes or N for No.

Anne: Y

FTIC: Three of your colleagues found that letters did not improve attendance all that much, but that telephone calls did help. One therapist did not find either procedure helpful. Anne, do you want to look at the Situational guidelines? Press Y or N.

Anne: Y

FTIC: Before the Situational guidelines can be displayed, some additional information is needed. Please answer the following questions:
Type of presenting problem?
(1) child or spouse abuse/neglect
(2) drug abuse (legal or illegal drugs)
(3) school problems
(4) delinquency
(5) marital problems
Press the *number* that applies.

Anne: 2

FTIC: What is the family's ethnicity?
(1) Black
(2) Mexican-American
(3) Puerto Rican
(4) Asian
(5) Causasian
(6) American Indian
Press the *number* that applies.

Anne: 2

FTIC: What is the family's life cycle stage?
(1) newly formed couple
(2) family with preschool children
(3) family with school/age children
(4) family with adolescent/young adult
(5) aging family
Press the *number* that applies.

Anne: 4

FTIC: Is the family member identified as having the problem a
_____?
(1) child
(2) adolescent
(3) adult
(4) no *one* family member identified as having the problem
Press the *number* that applies

Anne: 2

FTIC: For Mexican-American families with adolescents/young adults experiencing drug problems, the following practice guidelines are recommended for convening-engaging the family in treatment:
(1) Mexican-American families may need to personalize the helping relationship in order to develop a sense of trust; some sharing of personal information is indicated
(2) You should consider the concurrent use of individual sessions with the adolescent and conjoint family interviews
(3) You should recruit family members; do not leave it up to the symptomatic adolescent
(4) It is better to approach the marital relationship by exploring parental functions

Hopefully, this example helps the reader understand how the DSS works and illustrates its potential usefulness in family therapy. This example also makes it quite clear that the data base is the crucial component of the system. The utility of the system is a function of the data base's comprehensiveness, i.e., inclusion of information from the theoretical and research literature as well as feedback from system users (practice experience and wisdom). In addition, direct practitioner input should enhance both the perceived and actual relevance of the system. It is imperative that therapists understand the collaborative nature of data base development. Moreover, they must keep in mind that a DSS is not a replacement for staff/case conferences or a substitute for human decision-making.

In closing, it is important to note several other issues germane to this project. First, because of the project's experimental nature and funding restrictions, the scope is somewhat limited. Only a small part of the existing information on family therapy (convening and engagement) is being computerized and this will obviously influence practitioner satisfaction with the system. Consequently, staff expectations need to be realistic and the evolutionary aspects of the system need to be stressed. Second, although the modular development of information systems is recommended (i.e., specialized software designed to use an integrated data base) as a way to avoid duplication of data, a decision was made to use an incremental approach instead. Specifically, an interactive-conversational program and data base is being developed for each of the four treatment phases (convening-engagement, assessment, intervention, and termination).

SUMMARY

Most family therapists probably feel overwhelmed by the amount of information they are confronted with on a day to day basis. A way of handling this information overload can be found in the use of a knowledge utilization strategy that provides a framework (method) for synthesizing family therapy materials, deriving practice guidelines, and incorporating feedback from personal experience. Such a process is extremely complex and fraught with many problems stemming from the management of large amounts of data. However, the computerized decision support system holds great potential for resolving these problems since it uses the language of the family therapist, is both interactive and conversational, and can be easily updated.

REFERENCES

Bostwick, G. J., Jr. (1981). *Factors associated with continuance-discontinuance in family therapy: A multi-variate, multi-component analysis.* Unpublished doctoral dissertation, University of Chicago.

Boyd, L., Jr., Pruger, R., Chase, M. D., Clark, M., & Miller, L. S. (1982). A decision support system to increase equity. *Administration in Social Work, 5*(3/4), 83-96.

Briggs, W. G. (1982). An evaluation of DSS packages. *Computer World, 16*(9), 31.

Brower, A. M., Hankins, J. L., Mutschler, E., & Nurius, P. S. (1983). *Computer utilization for practice based decision making: Contemporary social work training methods.* Unpublished paper, University of Michigan.

Gurman, A. S., & Kniskern, D. P. (1978). Research on marital and family therapy: Progress, perspective, and prospect. In S. L. Garfield & A. E. Bergin (eds.), *Handbook of psychotherapy and behavior change: An empirical analysis* (2nd ed.). New York: John Wiley & Sons.

Hicks, J. O. (1984). *Management information systems: A users perspective.* St. Paul, MN: West Publishing Co.

Keen, P. G., & Morton, M. S. (1978). *Decision support systems: An organizational perspective.* Reading, MA: Addison-Wesley.

Kiesler, D. J. (1971). Experimental designs in psychotherapy research. In A. E. Bergin & S. L. Garfield (Eds.), *Handbook of psychotherapy and behavior change: An empirical analysis.* New York: John Wiley & Sons, Inc.

Kupfer, D. J., Levine, M. S., & Nelson, J. A. (1976). *Mental health information systems: Design and implementation.* New York: Marcel Dekker, Inc.

Miller, M. J. (1984). Computerized models of psychiatric diagnosis. In M. D. Schwartz (Ed.), *Using computers in clinical practice: Psychotherapy and mental health applications.* New York: The Haworth Press.

Mullen, E. J. (1978). The construction of personal models for effective practice: A method for utilizing research findings to guide social interventions. *Journal of Social Service Research, 2,* 45-63.

Mullen, E. J. (1981). Development of personal intervention models. In R. J. Grinnell, Jr. (Ed.), *Social work research and evaluation.* Itasca, IL: F. E. Peacock Publishers, Inc.

Mullen, E. J. (1983). Personal practice models. In A. Rosenblatt & D. Waldfogel (Eds.), *Handbook of clinical social work.* San Francisco: Jossey-Bass Publishers.

Mullen, E. J., Bostwick, G. J., Jr., & Ryg, B. (1980). Toward an integration of research and practice in the social work curriculum: A description and evaluation of a one-quarter course. In A. Rubin & R. Weinbach (Eds.), *Teaching social work research: Alternative programs and strategies.* New York: Council on Social Work Education.

Schoech, D. (1979). A microcomputer based human service information system. *Administration in Social Work, 3*(4), 423-439.

Schoech, D. (1982). *Computer use in human services: A guide to information management.* New York: Human Science Press.

Schoech, D., & Schkade, L. L. (1980). Computers helping caseworkers: Decision support systems. *Child Welfare, 59*(9), 566-575.

Schwartz, M. D. (1984). *Using computers in clinical practice: Psychotherapy and mental health applications.* New York: The Haworth Press.

The Application
of Computer Technology
to Behavioral Marital Therapy

Nicholas S. Aradi

ABSTRACT. The usefulness of the computer as a tool for the behavioral marital therapist is explored. A rationale for its use is presented, followed by its application to three major components of behavioral marital therapy: the initial interview, assessment, and treatment. Potential advantages and disadvantages of computerizing each component are examined. Implications for research and ethical considerations of the use of computers as part of the therapy process are discussed.

The computer is touted as the indispensable tool of serious-minded professionals. No longer is it promoted exclusively for accountants, stockbrokers, and scientists, but farmers, physicians, and now mental health professionals are looking to the computer to improve their service delivery and productivity. While it is clear that the computer is designed for data-based professions, it remains unclear whether it is suited for more people-oriented fields. Although there is an abundance of literature extolling the application of computers to the mental health field (Castellan, 1981; Space, 1981), little is written about its usefulness for the practitioner. Moreover, a survey of the literature reveals that a vast majority of the articles are oriented toward the fields of psychiatry and psychology. There is a paucity of literature which examines the practical application of computer technology to the marital therapy field. This paper represents such an examination.

This paper will explore the application of computer technology to a specific approach to marital therapy, behavioral marital therapy (BMT). In doing so, several areas will be examined. First, a rationale for such an application will be presented. Second, the application of computer technology to three fundamental components of behavioral marital therapy will be examined. The components include the initial interview, assessment, and treatment. Potential advantages and disadvantages of com-

Nicholas S. Aradi, EdS, MEd, is a doctoral student in the Marriage and Family Therapy Program, Department of Child Development and Family Studies, Purdue University, West Lafayette, IN 47907.

puterization will be explored for each component. Third, other clinical applications will be explored. Fourth, the ethical implications of the use of computers in behavioral marital therapy will be examined.

RATIONALE

Behavioral marital therapy is an empirically-based approach to treating distressed married couples. The approach is founded on principles of Social Exchange Theory and experimental psychology (Skinner, 1953; Thibaut & Kelley, 1959). The goal of BMT is to conduct a functional analysis of couples' presenting problems through extensive data collection and analysis (Jacobson & Margolin, 1979). The functional analysis is used to guide the intervention and evaluate its effectiveness. From a careful analysis of the relationship between the behavior and the environment, hypotheses are developed about antecedent stimuli and consequences which control the behavior in question. Hypotheses lead to the development of intervention strategies designed to alter problematic behavior. Behavior is continually monitored to evaluate treatment effectiveness. Consistent with principles of the scientific method, BMT is a structured, quantitative, and data-based approach to therapy.

This emphasis on data collection and analysis makes reliance on the computer both appropriate and advantageous. It is appropriate since both domains are involved in processing large amounts of data. It is advantageous since data processing is performed more efficiently using a computer. Because of this complementarity, the computer has the potential to become the behavioral marital therapist's most valuable tool.

Computer technology may be applied to three specific components of the BMT process: the initial interview, assessment, and treatment. The following section will examine specific applications of computer technology to each component.

COMPUTERIZATION OF BEHAVIORAL MARITAL THERAPY

Initial Interview

The initial interview represents the first stage of BMT. According to Jacobson and Margolin (1979), the overall purpose of the initial interview is to engender hope, generate positive expectation, and induce interactions between spouses. The initial interview consists of several specific components which, in addition to engendering hope, are designed to accomplish two basic goals: set the tone for therapy, and elicit pertinent information about the couple and their problem(s).

Computer technology can facilitate the acquisition of such data in three basic ways. First, computer programs can be written which will structure the interview according to therapist's specifications. That is, a computer can be programmed to ask specific questions, in a specific sequence, to a specific interviewee. In addition, the computer can perform follow-up questioning based on key individual or couple responses. This method, known as logical interrogatory branching, provides a flexibility not afforded by a fixed linear series interview method. By using a logical interview program, the therapist is assured of obtaining a well-structured yet flexible interview which maximizes data collection by eliminating therapist error (e.g., forgetting to ask a question, asking inappropriate questions).

Second, computer interviewing methods can facilitate the disclosure of highly sensitive personal data. Studies have shown that clients are more likely to disclose personal information to a computer interviewer than to a human interviewer (Greist, Klein, VanCura, & Erdman, 1973). For example, Lucas, Mullin, Luna, and McInroy (1977) found that people told a computer that they consumed 30 percent more alcohol than they told a human interviewer.

Using computer interview methods has additional benefits. In broaching potentially sensitive areas, therapists often sense client's discomfort and act in collusion with them to avoid discussion emotionally charged issues. Moreover, therapists may collude with one spouse against another as a result of emotionally charged or value-laden disclosures. Furthermore, the likelihood of such collusion is increased when couples are seen separately to discuss sensitive issues. Using computer interviews to obtain emotionally charged information would obviate these hazards. Personal information would be disclosed more freely and openly since clients are interacting with a machine rather than a human being. Client-computer interaction would also prevent emotionally volatile confrontations between spouses. Consequently, therapist's efforts to engender hope are facilitated, while the potential for counter-transference is minimized.

Lastly, computer technology can serve to record, organize, and store data generated during the initial interview. Regardless of how the data are obtained, a computer can be used to record and process the data into useable form. If information is obtained through paper and pencil measures, the data can be transformed, read, and stored by a computer. If information is gathered by therapist-client interview, the data must be audio or video taped in order to be computerized. If data are gathered through computer-client interview, the data are recorded, stored, and analyzed directly and automatically.

Advantages of applying computer technology to the initial interview in BMT are similar to those of general computer use in the mental health professions. The fundamental advantage lies in its ability to record, store, compute, and analyze data efficiently. A secondary advantage is gained by freeing the therapist to concentrate on other aspects of his/her work. Specific advantages for this stage of therapy relate to the computer's ability to obtain emotionally-charged information in a way which facilitates therapist's efforts at engendering hope.

There are several potential disadvantages in applying computer technology to the initial stage of BMT. One disadvantage relates to overuse. Because of their efficiency and ability to handle large amounts of data, inexperienced therapists may be unselective in their use of computers. Some routine aspects of the initial interview, such as taking a developmental history, may be appropriate to computerize. While others, such as fostering positive expectancies or explaining the format of therapy with enthusiasm and confidence, are best left to the therapist. Before converting any component of the initial interview from a therapist-focused to computer-focused format, the therapist should assess human, as well as monetary costs and benefits. An efficient computerized intake interview may be cost-effective in the short-run, but if it leaves clients feeling mistreated, its long-term benefits are tenuous at best.

A final contraindication of computer-based initial interviews concerns computer-phobic or computer-prejudiced clients. Before interacting with computer, the therapist must assess the client's receptivity to computers. Instructing fearful or prejudiced clients to interact with a computer will not only yield invalid data, but may also jeopardize positive therapy outcome, and have deleterious effects on the client.

Assessment

Computers have been used for assessment purposes by mental health professionals for over twenty years (Space, 1981). Assessment functions of computers have ranged from nonprojective testing and behavioral observation assessment to diagnosis and report writing (Fowler, 1980; Greist, Klein, & Erdman, 1976; Markman & Poltrock, 1982). Two applications particularly relevant to BMT are examined. Nonprojective testing has received most of the attention of computer-oriented behavioral scientists. As early as 1960, Elwood began work on the automation of the Wechsler Adult Intelligence Test (WAIS). In 1972, Elwood and Griffen compared the automated version of the WAIS with traditional face-to-face administration and found the automated version to be more efficient and reliable. Since Elwood's pioneering work, others have automated nonprojective tests with similar results (e.g., Dunn, Lushene, & O'Neil, 1972; Gilbertstadt, Lushene & Buegel, 1976; Hedl, O'Neil, & Hansen, 1973).

In addition to scoring and interpreting paper and pencil instruments, computer programs have been developed more recently to record and analyze observational data (Markman & Poltrock, 1982; Smith & Begeman, 1980). Both objective-observer and self-observer automated coding systems are available today which provide practical and ecologically valid behavioral assessment. So, while practical applications of computer technology for assessment purposes exist, its use in BMT to date has been limited. This is especially surprising when one realizes the integral part assessment plays in the BMT process.

Assessment is the mainstay of BMT. Assessment provides the necessary information to (1) describe problems in a relationship, (2) identify variables which control the problems, (3) select intervention strategies, and (4) evaluate the effectiveness of intervention (Jacobson & Margolin, 1979).

BMT relies on a plethora of instruments and methods to assess marital functioning. The instruments may be categorized on five dimensions: observational target, observational source, timing, observational method, and setting. Moreover, each dimension includes three or more subdimensions. Given all possible combinations of dimensions, the clinician is faced with the complex task of designing an individual assessment program which will produce the most reliable and valid functional analysis of the couple's problematic behavior. In achieving this end, the therapist must be guided by considerations for couple's receptivity to assessment, efficiency, and practicality. Computer technology can assist the therapist in designing such assessment programs.

Computers can be utilized to categorize and store all available assessment instruments on the basis of these dimensions or on the basis of other dimensions the therapist deems significant. Such categorization and storage would improve the therapist's ability to select the most appropriate instrument for a given situation. With experience, the therapist will become familiar with the strengths and limitations of the instruments, as well as the most effective order of their administration. As the therapist acquires this information, he/she will be able to have computer programs developed which will generate specialized assessment programs based on couples' current level of functioning. These programs would be dynamic and self-correcting. As results of each assessment are obtained, they are instantly fed back into the computer, which in turn makes the necessary changes in terms of subsequent assessment or intervention.

On a more basic level, behavioral therapists can utilize computer technology in assessment by automating their instruments and methods. For example, the Locke-Wallace Marital Adjustment Scale, Areas of Change Questionnaire, Marital Status Inventory, and the Marital Pre-Counseling Inventory can all be converted to computer administration, scoring, and analysis. Similarly, the lengthy and labor-intensive Spouse Observation Checklist (SOC) (Weiss, 1975), Behavior Coding System (Patterson, Ray, Shaw, & Cobb, 1969), Anger Checklist (Margolin,

Olkin, & Baum, 1977), and Marital Interaction Coding System (Hops, Wills, Patterson, & Weiss, 1972) can be made more useful through automation. Checklist instruments such as the SOC and Anger Checklist can be made more efficient by having clients record their responses on an audio tape. Information from the tape may be transmitted daily by telephone to the therapist's computer. The computer would decode, analyze, and store the data. Such a system would enable the therapist to have current self-report data on the couple's marital functioning, thereby enabling him/her to plan more effectively for future sessions. A similar system has been developed for couples' self-observation methods. Markman, Jamieson, and Floyd (in press) have developed a "communication box" procedure which enables couples to measure the intent and impact of their communication using automated devices.

Many of the advantages and disadvantages of computerization of the initial interview also apply for the assessment component of BMT. Advantages of computerization unique to assessment include reduced time for administering, scoring, and analyzing tests, increase efficiency in gathering, transmitting, and analyzing observational data, increased therapist's repertoire of assessment instruments, improved ability to develop structured, yet flexible, assessment programs, and increased sensitivity and efficiency in monitoring couple's interactions. Disadvantages include the following: (1) The computer cannot detect when the client is having difficulty expressing a thought or an emotion. A clinician, in contrast, can adapt to the client's needs to stimulate, inhibit, or vary the flow of diagnostic information. (2) The computer cannot discriminate between normal error and pathological response. (3) One of the values of a psychological test is the behavioral observations that give rise to clinical inferences. Computerized assessment cannot be programmed to record these. (4) The problem of invasion of privacy, culturally unfair interpretation of test results, and the confidentiality of testing, inherent in all psychological testing, are magnified when done by a machine.

Treatment

Automated methods for providing psychological treatment have been in existence for nearly two decades. Colby, Watt, and Gilbert (1966) were the first to write a computer program which could conduct psychotherapeutic dialogue. Fourteen years later, Colby (1980) made public his latest computer psychotherapist. While verbally and cognitively more developed than its predecessor, Colby concluded that this model is still too limited to be of therapeutic value to nonmentally deficient individuals. Jennings (1978) used a computer in a counseling session (with a human being listening to the client and controlling the computer's responses) to compare with a human counselor. Results showed that the human counselor rated higher on listening, understanding, acceptance of client views, and interest and respect for the client. These studies indicate that technology is not, as yet, sufficiently advanced to produce machines capable of conducting traditional psychotherapy. However, computers have been built which effectively treat problems generally thought to be treatable only by psychotherapists. Lang (1969) used an automated desensitization device and found it as effective as a live therapist in reducing phobic behavior. Pope and Gersten (1977) successfully automated biofeedback devices for use in treating migraine headaches. Lang (1980) successfully used a CRT as a feedback mechanism in biofeedback training; he is currently involved in developing assertiveness training via a computer. Cuthbert (1976) used a computer to conduct relaxation training. These studies indicate that certain skills which can be broken down into discrete, observable units can be taught by a computer.

Many theoretical perspectives on marital discord identify communication deficits between spouses as an underlying cause or current manifestation of interpersonal conflict. Consequently, many marital therapists identify improved communication skills as one of the primary goals of therapy. Behavioral marital therapists are no exception. However, the content of the skills taught and the procedures used in training distinguish BMT from many other communication-focused therapies.

Behavioral approaches to communication training are distinguished by the systematic nature of skill building. Training consists of three major components: (1) Feedback, where couples are provided with information about their current communication patterns, (2) Instruction, where the therapist provides alternative communication patterns for the couple, and (3) Behavioral Rehearsal, couples practice communication patterns provided by the therapist.

Presently, feedback in communication training is based on a live communication exercise, conducted by the couple, in the therapy room, in the presence of a therapist (Jacobson & Margolin, 1979). This procedure is appropriate during the early stages of therapy. It gives the therapist a sense of the couple's communication style, allows for the identification of strengths and deficits, and enables the therapist to give immediate feedback. However, due to social desirability effects, the validity of observing and assessing a couple's communication skills in a therapy session is limited. A more ecologically valid approach entails unobtrusively observing/recording the couple interacting in their home. This can be accomplished by installing sound-activated electronic monitoring devices in the couple's home. The monitoring device could be programmed to begin recording at the sound of a spouse's voice. In addition, the device could be programmed to give continuous feedback. For example, while the couple's communication remains "error-free," a continuous pleasant sound would emanate from the device. However, if previously identified undesirable behaviors are exhibited (as defined by frequency or decibel level), feedback, in the form of a noxious sound, would be delivered. This procedure would not only provide the therapist with a more natural sample of the couple's communication pattern, but it would also give the couple more immediate and continuous feedback about their communication.

Once the therapist identifies the couple's skill deficits, the coaching and modeling components of training are begun. Like the feedback stage, this state of treatment can be enhanced through the use of electronic devices. Desirable behavior can be demonstrated by the therapist modeling in vivo or on video tape. Initially, it is advantageous for the therapist to model in vivo. By modeling in the session, the therapist demonstrates the realness and feasibility of the new behavior. In addition, if the therapist is credible, the couple will be more motivated to practice and learn the skills. However, with complex behaviors and with couples requiring extensive instruction, the use of video tape instruction is invaluable. Through the use of video taping, complex behaviors can be taught more effectively by neatly breaking down the behavior into discrete, easily repeatable steps. Moreover, for couples having difficulty learning new behaviors, individualized training tapes could be made for extended practice at home.

Application of computer technology to the behavioral rehearsal stage of skill training is well underway. Several behavioral scientists have developed electronic devices which enable couples to record and shape their own and their partner's behavior (Gottman, Notarius, Gonso, & Markman, 1976; Markman & Poltrock, 1982). Basically, the devices enable couples to spontaneously define and signal the "helpfulness" of their partner's communication. That is, if a spouse perceives their partner's communication as positive, he/she signals this by pushing a button which sets off a pleasant tone. An aversive tone is paired with "unhelpful" communication. These devices are not only useful in shaping desirable behavior, they also help couples identify mutually helpful communication.

The unique advantages of computers in behavioral skill training include increased quality, quantity, and immediacy of feedback, and improved ecological validity in monitoring couples' skill level. Disadvantages include cost of electronic monitoring devices, availability of shaping devices, and invasion of privacy issues associated with home monitoring devices.

OTHER CLINICAL APPLICATIONS

Behavioral marital therapy represents a scientist-practitioner model of marital therapy. As such, many behavioral marital therapists hold a strong commitment to research, as well as to practice. By conducting clinical practice as a scientist, the behavioral therapist not only allows for more object evaluation of his/her own clinical effectiveness, but may also contribute to the advancement of marital therapy. Through adherence to the empirical approach, the practitioner can isolate the active components of his/her treatment procedures, and separate them from whatever placebo effects or demand characteristics which may be contributing to treatment efficacy. This approach not only serves to enhance the rigors of one's clinical practice, but at the same time guarantees responsibility and assures accountability to the consumer.

The application of computers to BMT clearly enhances the researcher function of the therapist. Since computers make it easier to gather, store, and analyze data, the clinician is better equipped to perform reliable and valid functional analyses of clients' behavior. In addition, computers enable clinicians to gather more meaningful measures of behavior (sequences, observations in natural settings) which are capable of being analyzed more efficiently and meaningfully (sequential analysis, time series analysis). Moreover, the increased availability of canned statistical programs (BMDP, SPSS, SAS) make it feasible for more and more practitioners to investigate clinical questions which were previously addressed solely by researchers. The end result of this application is a real integration which contributes rigor and growth to the field.

ETHICAL CONSIDERATIONS

Behavioral marital therapists maintain that they shall provide the highest quality care possible to clients. This requires the application of the most up-to-date assessment and treatment methods by well trained professionals at a reasonable cost. Given equal performance in these regards, the choice between a human or a computer program would logically be left to the client. When computer programs surpass humans in these areas, ethics would dictate the use of computers.

Some clients might find a computer de-humanizing or anxiety producing for dealing with major life issues. For others, it is equally debilitating to divulge the intimate details of their lives to strangers. If it is unethical to make the first type of client use computer therapists, is it not equally unethical to deny the second type of client access to the same computer therapists? Ultimately, the client's decision to participate in computerized therapy must be made on the basis of informed consent.

Regarding confidentiality, problems are present independent of whether computer procedures are used. Individuals can misuse confidential information whether it is stored in conventional record form or stored by computer. Effective methods exist for limiting and preventing access to computerized information. Passwords, identification codes, and garbling of sensitive information can all protect data stored in central machines.

SUMMARY

Once the domain of experimental psychologists and research-oriented therapists, the application of computer technology to the practice of psychotherapy is beginning to have practical significance for a growing number of mental health professionals. Computer use is seen as especially appropriate and advantageous for behavioral therapists. Affordable technology now exists which allow therapists to conduct interviews, provide ongoing, comprehensive assessment, and plan and monitor treatment in an efficient and reliable manner. What is needed, however, is more information describing the application of technology to the practice of psychotherapy and the effects of such application on the therapeutic process.

REFERENCES

Castellan, N. J. (1981). On-line computers in psychology: The last 10 years, the next 10 years—the challenge and the promise. *Behavior Research Methods and Instrumentation, 13,* 91-96.

Colby, K. M. (1980). Computer psychotherapists. In J. B. Sidowski, J. H. Johnson, & T. A. Williams (Eds.), *Technology in mental health care delivery systems.* Norwood, NJ: Ablex.

Colby, K. M., Watt, J. B., & Gilbert, J. P. (1966). A computer method of psychotherapy: Preliminary communication. *Journal of Nervous and Mental Diseases, 142,* 148-152.

Cuthbert, B. N. (1976). *Voluntary slowing of heart rate: A survey of various techniques.* Unpublished doctoral dissertation, University of Wisconsin.

Dunn, T. G., Lushene, R. E., & O'Neil, H. H. (1972). The automation of the MMPI and a study of its response latencies. *Journal of Consulting and Clinical Psychology, 39,* 381-387.

Elwood, D. L., & Griffin, R. H. (1972). Individual intelligence testing without the examiner: Reliability of an automated test. *Journal of Consulting and Clinical Psychology, 39,* 311-318.

Fowler, R. D. (1980). The automated MMPI. In J. B. Sidowski, J. H. Johnson & T. A. Williams (Eds.), *Technology and mental health care delivery systems.* Norwood, NJ: Ablex.

Gilbertstadt, H., Lushene, R., & Buegel, B. (1976). Automated assessment of intelligence: The PACAC test battery and computerized report writing. *Perceptual and Motor Skills, 43,* 627-635.

Gottman, J., Notarious, C., Gonso, J., & Markman, H. (1976). *A couples guide to communication.* Champaign: Research Press.

Greist, J. H., & Erdman, H. P (1976). Routine on-line psychiatric diagnosis by computer. *American Journal of Psychiatry, 133,* 1405-1408.

Greist, J. H., Klein, M. H., & VanCura, L. J. (1973). A computer interview for psychiatric patient target symptoms. *Archives of General Psychiatry, 29,* 247-253.

Hedl, J. J., O'Neil, H. F., & Hanson, D. H. (1973). Affective reactions toward computer-based intelligence testing. *Journal of Consulting and Clinical Psychology, 40,* 217-222.

Hops, H., Wills, T. A., Patterson, G. R., & Weiss, R. L. (1972). *Marital interaction coding system.* Unpublished manuscript, University of Oregon and Oregon Research Institute.

Jacobson, N. S., & Margolin, G. (1979). *Marital therapy.* New York: Brunner/Mazel.

Jennings, J. (1978). *A test of the effectiveness of a computer-client inter-face in a counseling setting.* Unpublished doctoral dissertation, University of Mississippi.

Lang, P. J. (1980). Behavioral treatment and bio-behavioral assessment: Computer applications. In J. B. Sidowski, J. H. Johnson, & T. A. Williams (Eds.), *Technology in mental health care delivery systems.* Norwood, NJ: Ablex.

Lucas, R. W., Mullin, P. J. Luna, C. D., & McInroy, D. D. (1977). Psychiatrists and computers as interrogators or patients with alcohol related illness: A comparison. *British Journal of Psychiatry, 131,* 160-167.

Margolin, G., Olkin, R., & Baum, M. (1977). *The anger checklist.* Unpublished inventory, University of California, Santa Barbara.

Markman, H., Jamieson, K., & FLoyd, F. (in press). The assessment and modification of premarital relationships: Implications for the etiology and prevention of marital distress. In J. Vincent (Ed.), *Advances in family interaction assessment and theory* (Vol. 3). Greenwich, CT: JAI.

Markman, H. J., & Poltrock, S. E. (1982). A computerized system for recording and analysis of self-observations of couples' interaction. *Behavior Research Methods & Instrumentation, 14,* 186-190.

Patterson, G. R., Ray, R. S., Shaw, D. A., & Cobb., J. A. (1969). *Manual for coding family interactions.* Oregon Research Institute.

Pope, A. T., & Gersten, C. D. (1977). Computer automation of biofeedback training. *Behavior Research Methods & Instrumentation, 9,* 164-168.

Skinner, B. S. (1953). *Science in human behavior.* New York: MacMillan.

Smith, E. O., & Begeman, M. L. (1980). BORES: Behavior observation recording and editing systems. *Behavior Research Methods & Instrumentation, 12,* 1-7.

Space, L. G. (1981). The computer as psychometrician. *Behavior Research Methods & Instrumentation, 13,* 595-606.

Thibaut, J. W., & Kelley, H. H. (1959). *Social psychology of most groups.* New York: Wiley.

Weiss, R. L. (1975). *Marital interaction coding system—revised.* Unpublished manuscript, University of Oregon.

Teaching Systems Psychotherapy[1]
With Micro-Computers:
A Creative Approach

Randy Gerson

ABSTRACT. Micro-computers can be a valuable tool in the teaching of systems psychotherapy. The paper begins with a theoretical discussion of the uses of the micro-computer in teaching systems psychotherapy. This discussion includes the limitation of the computer as well as its disadvantages. Next some applications are demonstrated on the micro-computer that have been developed specifically for systems psychotherapists. Finally, the latter section speculates on the future potential of the micro-computer. Overall it is argued that the micro-computer can extend the therapist's ability to understand and creatively teach about systems and the family.

THE DUMB COMPUTER

Micro-computers are not very bright. They do only one thing and do it well: they follow instructions to manipulate and process information. The computer author or programmer gives the micro-computer a series of commands that are part of the micro-computer's repertoire and those commands are carried out step by step. The micro-computer has no autonomous judgement or creativity; it does not consider the advisability of what it is told to do; it simply does it.

Although, the micro-computer lacks intelligence in itself, what it does can be guided by the intelligence and creativity of the computer author that instructs it. In some ways, this is no different than the relationship between an author and his book. No one would ever claim that the book itself is "smart" or "creative," but what is said in the book may be very creative and intelligent indeed and guide and inform people in many different areas. Similarly, the outcome of a computer program may seem creative, intelligent and useful, but it is the computer author, not the program itself, that is "smart" or "creative."

There has been great effort over the last twenty years to make com-

Randy Gerson received his PhD in clinical psychology from Clark University and is currently on the faculty of the Family Institute of Westchester (Mt. Vernon, NY) and a consultant to Applied Innovations, Inc., for computer applications in mental health.

Inquiries about obtaining software programs should be directed to Dr. Gerson at the Family Institute of Westchester, Mt. Vernon, 147 Archer Avenue, Mt. Vernon, NY 10550 (914-699-4300) or by calling Applied Innovations (Wakefield, RI) at 800-272-2250.

179

puters truly "smart," to give them what is called "artificial intelligence." Though this subject is beyond the scope of this paper, suffice it to say, that true progress in this area has been minimal primarily due to the difficulties in designing a "creative" computer and micro-computers have inherited very little "artificial intelligence" from their larger counterparts. We need not fear that computers will replace therapists in the near or distant future. I would even argue that a focus on artificial intelligence detracts from the more profitable use of computer power: as an extension of the human creative process.

THE ADVANTAGES OF THE MICRO-COMPUTER

There are at least two advantages that the computer author has over the book author. First of all, the computer is interactional. By this is meant that what the computer author tells the computer to do can interact with and be informed by the audience, i.e., the user or student. For example, suppose a teacher wants to demonstrate a particular procedure or process. In a book, the author would be limited to a few instances determined by the author that illustrated the procedure or process. With a computer program that could demonstrate the same procedure or process, the teacher could have the student enter the relevant information with instances that are of particular interest to the student.

Similarly, and related to the interactional nature of the computer, is its ability to display material in a non-linear form. The book author is stuck with the linear nature of the written word. One paragraph must follow another paragraph in every copy of the book. In a computer program, the flow of material may branch out in many directions according to conditions determined by the computer author. Here is where the interactional nature of the computer is so important: the varied directions the material can take can be influenced or determined by the input of the user. For example, the computer author can ask the user for gender and then tailor the material presented to that particular sex. As we shall see, more complex examples involve simulations where the actions of the participants determine the flow of the narrative.

It is the interactional, non-linear nature of computer use that provides such exciting new opportunities for the teacher and creator. There is a creative explosion going on currently with micro-computers. Not only business applications and games, but educational software is being produced at an accelerating rate and by people who five years earlier would have nothing to do with computers. Due to the widespread availability of micro-computers, people are coming to realize the creative potential of a medium that is interactional and non-linear. Micro-computers are not more advanced or sophisticated than larger computers that have been around for years. Nevertheless, it has been micro-computers, not the larger "smarter" computers, that have recently begun to tap the creative efforts of so many professionals and educators in many different fields. It is not the power of the main-frame computer, but the creative efforts of so many knowledgeable, non-computer enthusiasts that have made the difference.

THE SYSTEMS PSYCHOTHERAPIST AND THE COMPUTER

I would argue that the systems psychotherapist should be particularly responsive to the unique qualities of computer-base educational material. For the systems psychotherapist is specifically concerned with the interactional and non-linear flow of information that occurs in the family system and how the therapist can change the structure of this flow, i.e., how the family learns new ways to adapt to a changing informational environment. In fact, the development of the computer and the field of systems psychotherapy has much in common. Over the last 30 years with the development of the systemic view of the family, we have come to see families as organisms regulated by the complex flow of information between its members. Just as cybernetic, systems and information theory has led to the development of complex information systems, e.g., the computer, these theories have also led to a view of the family as a complex interactional system and information processor. Thus, systems psychotherapy and computers have common roots in history and theory.

In the following, I will describe some of the educational applications of the micro-computer that I have developed that may prove useful to systems psychotherapy.

COMPUTER-GENERATED GENOGRAMS

A major tool used by systems psychotherapists to understand and teach about family structure and transgenerational patterns in families is the *genogram*. A genogram is a multi-generational diagram that gives both the therapist and the family a visual gestalt of family structure and pattern and relevant demographic and relational information. Its use comes primarily out of the work of Murray Bowen and his efforts to discern multi-generational patterns in families (Bowen, 1978).

I use many genograms both for teaching and in my practice. One day, I was working on a particularly complex genogram in which I was making some additions which would require either cramping a lot of information in a small space or completely redrawing the genogram when I thought to myself how nice it would be if the computer could take the tedious work out of producing genograms. The result was a program that generates genograms with the computer. I call the entire system THE FAMILY DATA-BASE MANAGER.

Before the computer can draw genograms, the information on a family must first be organized in a way that can be used by the computer. The computer is an information organizer par excellence. Its whole purpose in life is to manage and manipulate information in ways determined by the program author.

I decided to organize family information in files: each family member would have a file with basic information on that person. However, each file would have to be cross-referenced with other files so the computer would know how to hierarchically relate family members with one another on the genogram. A typical family member's file looks like this:

NAME:	TOM SMITH (1)
1. SEX:	M
2. D.O.B.:	1/9/51 (32 Y.O.)
3. D.D.D.:	—
4. OCCUPATION:	BIOLOGIST
5. LOCATION:	CHICAGO
6. PROBLEM:	MARRIAGE
7. MOTHER:	EVE SMITH (2)
8. FATHER:	JOHN SMITH (3)
9. # OF SPOUSE:	1
10. SPOUSE #1:	SUE SMITH (4)
11. MARRIAGE DATE:	4/5/75 (AGE 24)
12. # OF CHILDREN:	2
13. CHILD #1:	BEN SMITH (5)
14. CHILD #2:	CARLA SMITH (6)
15. SEP OR DIVORCE:	—
16. COMMENT:	9/69 (AGE 18)
	EVENT: WENT TO COLLEGE

The number in parentheses next to each name is the file number of that person. The user determines what categories are to be included in each file. Sex, dates of birth and death, and relational information are necessary items in all files. Thus, in the above file, OCCUPATION, LOCATION, and PROBLEM are the optional categories chosen by the user. Other categories such as EDUCATIONAL LEVEL and ETHNIC GROUP could have been chosen as well.

Once the information has been entered into the family files, i.e., what computer people call a data-base, the information can be retrieved and processed in order to generate genograms. The genogram is graphically displayed on the computer monitor and can be printed out onto paper. (Figure 1 is an example of a computer-generated genogram.)

ALICE JONES'S FAMILY GENOGRAM

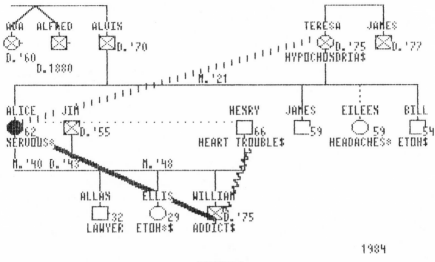

FIGURE 1

The computer eliminates the usual design problems of creating a neat, well-spaced, readable genogram. In addition, when new information is obtained that would change the genogram, the program does it for the therapist automatically. The therapist can draw three-generational genograms from the perspective of any family member that highlight different types of family information.

Note that on the genogram illustrated in Figure 1, standard relational lines used in genograms are also present on the computerized genogram. The displayed triangle shows a fused relationship (thick solid line), a conflictual relationship (jagged line), and a distant relationship (dotted line). The program allows the therapist to define relationships between family members on a relational spreadsheet, and those definitions then appear on the genogram.

The therapist is also often interested in a chronological listing of important family events. THE FAMILY DATA-BASE MANAGER can also generate a family chronology:

1/5/1918	HENRY JONES WAS BORN (CURRENT AGE: 64)
7/12/1922	ALICE JONES WAS BORN (CURRENT AGE: 60)
2/6/1940	ALICE JONES (AGE 17) AND JIM KENT MARRY
9/16/1943	ALICE JONES (AGE 21) AND JIM KENT DIVORCED
4/5/1948	HENRY JONES (AGE 30) AND ALICE JONES (AGE 25) MARRY

2/4/1952	ALLAN JONES WAS BORN (CURRENT AGE: 30)
7/9/1955	ELLIS JONES WAS BORN (CURRENT AGE: 27)
11/13/1955	SUE JONES WAS BORN (CURRENT AGE: 27)
2/28/1957	WILLIAM JONES WAS BORN
3/18/1975	ALLAN JONES (AGE 23) AND SUE JONES (AGE 19) MARRY
6/15/1975	WILLIAM JONES (AGE 18) DIED. CAUSE OF DEATH: DRUGS

The chronology puts critical family events in historical order and indicates the temporal connections and coincidences that occur in the life of a family.

I believe THE FAMILY DATA-BASE MANAGER is the first step in the evolution of computerized family information systems that will be of great use to the clinician. The software has already begun to be tested at different clinical sites to evaluate the clinical utility of the program and to provide the necessary clinical feedback to further develop a practical family system assessment and educational tool.

Its educational potential is obvious. One can imagine at a case conference (or with a family) immediately generating a genogram to make a particular point. A genogram can be produced from the perspective of any family member and it will show the family at any particular time period in its history. For example, suppose you have a family that still seems to be dealing with a loss of a family member a number of years ago. One could date the genogram to show the family before the loss and with the aid of the visual prompt of the revised genogram have the family reconsider the earlier period. Since the computer changes all the ages to correspond to the set date and shows only relevant information as of that date, it helps both the therapist and the family visualize that past time in the family. Similarly, the family chronology can be produced to demonstrate and convince family members that historical events in the family are interconnected and related and not just random events.

There are at least two advantages to the computer-aided method of displaying family information in teaching systems concepts. First of all, because THE FAMILY DATA-BASE MANAGER is interactional and therefore uses the therapist's input to immediately process and display many different types of information (both to the therapist and the family), it allows the therapist to reveal family structure and pattern in a dynamic, live, often dramatic, way that emphasizes the interactional and circular nature of family functioning. Secondly, THE FAMILY DATA-BASE MANAGER provides a multi-perspective view of the family. That is, one can look at the family from perspective of different family members and different time periods, and thus obtain larger systemic view of the family than any static monocular view could provide.

The information manipulating ability of the computer will, I believe, become an increasingly valuable tool to the systems psychotherapist and other mental health professionals. It will be useful not only in teaching about systems but in the assessment and research of systems. In order to help families with its problems, the systems psychotherapist needs to cope with the vast amounts of information presented by the family and try to make sense of the often puzzling patterns in that information. I already see the day when we will be able to enter family information into the computer and manipulate that information in numerous ways until we are better able to make more sense of it and thus more able to help and educate the family.

THERAPY SIMULATION—A TRAINING TOOL

The simulation of family interactions on the computer offers the possibility of interactive training tools for teaching systems psychotherapists and other professionals. A beginning therapist can face a simulated family and learn about the possible likely reactions a family may have to his or her different therapeutic choices.

For example, I have already developed simulation software depicting a therapy scenario that exposes the student/therapist to some of the critical decisions and considerations made in the initial session with a family. The scenario begins as follows:

SESSION I:

A NEW FAMILY WALKS INTO THE ROOM. THEY INTRODUCE THEMSELVES AS THE PARKS. THERE ARE MR. AND MRS. PARK, IN THEIR LATE 30'S, PETE, AGE 10, AND MARY, AGE 16. THE TWO ADULTS SIT ON OPPOSITE SIDES OF THE ROOM WITH MARY IN-BETWEEN.

PETE IMMEDIATELY GOES AND SITS IN YOUR SEAT.

WHAT DO YOU DO?

1. "PETE WOULD YOU MIND SITTING OVER HERE?"
2. "PETE, THIS IS MY SEAT. I WANT YOU TO SIT OVER HERE."
3. YOU LOOK AT THE PARENTS, EXPECTING THEM TO GET THEIR CHILD OUT OF YOUR SEAT.
4. YOU MOVE TO ANOTHER SEAT.

In this opening of the scenario, the therapist must respond with one of four choices. Each choice leads to the next scene which poses a new set of choices and so on. The therapist's choices effect how the family reacts both to the therapist and each other. At the end of the simulation, the therapist gets feedback on how well he or she has done and what is the probability that the family will return for a second session.

The therapist/student is presented with prototypical family therapy situations in which the therapist must use sound therapeutic principles in order to effectively work with the simulated family. The effects of the therapist's interventions are not always immediately apparent and may influence the family's interactions and cooperation throughout the session. The simulation allows the student to test his or her skills and understanding of families in a non-threatening situation in preparation for working with real families.

In order to evaluate the therapist's choices and determine the flow of the simulation, I had to have a set of underlying variables which would be influenced by the therapist's choices. These variables were based on a particular theoretical model which I will not be able to elaborate on in the short space of this chapter except to mention that the simulation is loosely based on the structural-strategic approach (Minuchin, 1974; Haley, 1976). I am now in the process of developing with the help of well-known family therapists a whole series of similar simulation scenarios which will teach about a variety of theoretical models and therapy situations.

Again, what makes computer simulations so exciting is the interactional, non-linear nature of computer information processing. What could be a better medium for demonstrating the interactive and circular complexities of doing systems psychotherapy than computer simulations which display the same interactive, dynamic, non-linear characteristics in its educational format.

Of course, there are also limitations in the simulation approach. First of all, the simulation will only be as good as the author who creates it. Only to the degree it is well designed and thought out and follows the principles of its underlying theoretical model will the simulation have something to teach the student. This is of course true of all educational material, but when the material is presented on the computer, there is the danger that the student or instructor will be overawed by the "supposed" intelligence of the machine and forego his or her usual critical evaluation of what is being taught or learned. Therefore, it is important to demystify the computer and explain the authoring process behind the creation of a simulation.

Secondly, there are inherent limits in the ability to truly simulate a clinical situation. In any clinical situation, there are practically an infinite set of choices or interventions that may be effective with a client or family. In a simulation, the author is forced to define a finite and relatively short list of alternatives for the student to choose from at any one point in the simulation. A common reaction to the choices provided by the simulation I wrote is that the reader would not do any of the alternatives I provided but would do something entirely different instead. Nevertheless, the reader is restricted to the choices given. Similarly, there is a wide range of possible responses of the family to what the student does, but only a limited number of reactions can be shown on the computer. Even if the simulation is based on actual case material, only a few of the pathways of the simulation will follow the actual case, whereas the author will have to decide in most cases what the family would have done if the therapist had chosen many of the interventions not actually tried. Thus, it is important for the student to recognize that a simulation is necessarily a simplification of the therapeutic process for the purposes of teaching.

Related to the above point, there is a possible danger of the student seeing the simulation as providing a cookbook-style recipe for doing therapy. They may think that when faced with a situation similar to that portrayed in the simulation, you necessarily do that which had the best result in the situation. In fact, a well-written simulation should demonstrate that many possible interventions can lead to a positive outcome. Nevertheless, the student may miss this point and instead be looking for concrete "how to's" in the choices provided by the simulation.

Despite the above limitations, I believe the therapy simulation can still be a powerful educational tool in the hands of a knowledgeable instructor. It is important that the process of creating simulations is explained and their limitations pointed out. Simulations should be seen and explained not as a cookbook for doing therapy but as a means of raising some of the typical issues and dilemmas in the therapeutic process. I have found it particularly useful to use the simulation in a group setting where the choices both given by the computer and originating out of the group can be evaluated and discussed.

SPECULATIONS ON THE FUTURE

This section will be more speculative than the earlier sections which discussed applications already developed. Rather, I will describe what I see as some of the potential uses of the micro-computer in systems psychotherapy.

The same creative potential that can be used to teach systems professionals about systems and doing psychotherapy can also be used to educate families about themselves. Many systems psychotherapists already have families construct their own genograms as an exercise in learning about how their family system is structured and operates. Some therapists display large genograms on paper or blackboard each time they work with the family as a reminder of the information of the family system as a whole. There is no reason that this same information cannot be displayed to the family by the computer on a large video monitor. The family members might even enter the information into the computer themselves. What would be needed is a version of THE FAMILY DATA-BASE MANAGER so simple to use that any family member could easily enter the information with prompts from the computer. (I am currently working on such an intake program as an adjunct to THE FAMILY DATA-BASE MANAGER. This will also decrease the work of the clinician who will then not have to enter into the computer all the family information.)

Once the information has been entered, the therapist can use the computer to display and highlight the information in a variety of ways in order to make specific points to the family. For example, the therapist can show the family from the perspective of different family members and at different times in the family's history. The therapist can also highlight particular relationships, patterns, or types of information in order to make a therapeutic point. In fact, as the graphic manipulations that one can make on the computer become more sophisticated, the therapist as well as the family may find startling new patterns revealed in new displays of family information.

As regards family simulations, there is no reason why family members cannot learn from family simulations as well. Often family members will become stuck in their own perspective and not recognize the viewpoints of other family members well enough to make the necessary compromises in family life. We have already seen that a computerized therapy simulation allows the reader to enter the family from a particular perspective: that of the therapist. There is no reason that a simulation could not let a family member enter a simulated family as a family member or as a number of different family members. Taking the perspective of different family roles (mother, father, child, etc.) in a simulated family might help family members recognize and understand the particular demands and responsibilities of similar roles in their own family.

I am currently working on a family simulation that will describe the day in the life of a family under stress. It is Thanksgiving Day and a family prepares for Thanksgiving dinner. A number of crises are evident in the family: a daughter coming home from college and reluctant to be with the family, a son receiving bad conduct marks at school, and parents in disagreement over in-laws. The user will choose one of four different family members to be and will go through the day as that family member. What happens during the day and how the crises are resolved will be affected both by the user's choices and the previous choices of previous users who took a different role in the family. Each family member will be able to learn about how this simulated family operates from the perspective of different family members.

The goal of having a family participate in a family simulation would be the development of what I call "interactional intelligence." Interactional intelligence is developed when the user starts to view a family system from a number of different perspectives and can observe the independent, reciprocal nature of family interactions.

Teaching Interactional Intelligence

I believe that ultimately one of the greatest values of using microcomputers as an educational tool is its ability to teach interactional intelligence. Systems psychotherapists have found that to really understand how families work and to overcome certain family problems, one has to learn how to think in a different way than we normally think. The usual terms for this way of thinking are "circular" or "systems" thinking, but I have coined the phrase "interactional intelligence" to communicate to general audiences this important concept.

Normally, we think in a straight line: this caused this, this one is responsible, this person is to blame. We see one causal connection at a time. Interactional intelligence is the ability to see many connections at once, how everyone interacts with everyone else, how one person's actions are conditioned by another person's actions whose actions are conditioned by the first person's actions, and so on. There is a complex web of interactions that go in a family and it is usually difficult to say where responsibility begins or ends. Systems psychotherapists are trained to see patterns in this complexity, and to develop interactional intelligence. Family members who are able to get this larger perspective are better able to understand one another and work out their mutual problems.

The interactional nature of a computer simulation is the perfect tool for getting across the principles of interactional intelligence. As explained earlier, unlike a book which is linear, a computer simulation can branch off in many directions, conditioned by the responses of the user, and is capable of showing multiple perspectives almost simultaneously. In fact, in order to write a family simulation on the computer, one needs a good deal of interactional intelligence in order to display the complex flow of interactional events and interplay that goes on in a family.

CONCLUSIONS

The micro-computer allows the clinician to present information in an interaction, non-linear form. Whether this is information in the genogram or a series of events in a family simulation, the result is that the clinician, student, or family is able to access information in non-linear, more interactive and systemic way. I believe that is is what the computer offers beyond the normal written medium.

I have discussed in some detail two applications of the micro-computer that I have already developed. One is a data-base system for collecting family information and creating genograms, a graphic display of family information. The other is a therapy simulation that gives the user a simulated experience of actually doing systems psychotherapy with a family. I also discussed some of the potential developments of these applications.

I believe that we have only started to tap the potential uses of the micro-computer in the mental health professions. Ours is a service profession where information is one of the major mediums of exchange. It is the computer that can store, organize, and manipulate information. Once the systems psychotherapist recognizes the creative potential of micro-computers, a whole new medium and method for educating both the professional community and families themselves opens up on the computer screen.

REFERENCE NOTE

1. This term is preferred over the usual term "family therapy" because it does not imply that the whole family is seen or that the only relevant social system is the family. Many so-called "family therapists," including the author, will often see an individual alone but use a systems psychotherapy model in helping that individual.

REFERENCES

Bowen, M. (1978). *Family therapy in clinical practice.* New York: Jason Aronson, Inc.
Haley, J. (1976). *Problem-solving therapy.* San Francisco: Jossey-Bass Publishers.
Minuchin, S. (1974). *Families and family therapy.* Cambridge, MA: Harvard University Press.

Computers and Family Therapy: An Epilogue

John A. Constantine

The papers in this collection focus on computer utilization that exists or is in development. Just ten years ago any such utilization by clinicians would have been considered out of the question other than for those affiliated with a large institution that could afford a computer. Even if an institutional computer was available however, it would not be used for working with clinical clients. The microcomputer changed all this. Clinicians have discovered that the microcomputer is an especially powerful tool for working with families. It is our belief that microcomputer applications are only beginning; that they will soon be integrated into the family therapy practice. This will be possible due to the reduced cost of computers and, more significantly, the introduction of low-cost multi-user machines which allows for more than one person to use the machine at the same time. The introduction of multi-user machines is a significant development if the machines are to be used by family therapists. Previously for a family therapist to give a family a battery of instruments on a computer the family therapist would either have to have two to six machines or give the instruments serially to one family member at a time on one machine. The time involved with giving instruments serially was frequently prohibitive.

This epilogue will note new possibilities for computers and family therapy and focus primarily on the usages that directly relate to therapy practice.

THE FUTURE

When discussing the future usage of computer technology in any field, the discussion involves the melding of two technologies. The first is the hardware. This is the physical equipment and its capabilities. This is the amount of memory in the machine, the type of equipment that it can use such as a voice synthesizer, number of terminals that can be attached to the machine, printers, modems and/or the speed of the machine.

John A. Constantine, PhD, is Assistant Professor, Department of Child Development and Family Studies, Purdue University, West Lafayette, IN 47906.

The second is the software. The software is the instructions to the machine. These are written in a variety of different languages such as FORTRAN, BASIC, MUMPS, LISP, assembler language, etc. The different languages have different capabilities and are better suited for different types of projects. For example, FORTRAN is widely known for its capabilities in number crunching, whereas LISP (*List P*rocessing) was developed for artificial intelligent projects. Artificial intelligence programs are programs that attempt to mimic the process of human decision making.

The potential developments to be discussed are not beyond the capabilities of the current hardware and software available and in some cases they are being utilized in other fields. One impediment to the implementation of this technology in family therapy is the lack of detail in the treatment protocol and the theory of treatment.

Integration of Video and Computer

Saba (1984) has suggested that the availability of the video tape was a boon to the early development of the family therapy field. He goes on to suggest that the computer may do the same for the field. If this is the case, the integration of the two technologies presents the potential of providing a quantum leap forward. The technology for the integration of the video and computer exists at both the hardware level (Jarvis, 1984) and the software level (Daynes and Holder, 1984).

The reader has only to go into a video arcade and play one of the games where a video disc is integrated into the game. In this type of game the player must make a decision based on the scene on the video screen. For example, in one arcade game the player is facing a door and is asked whether to open the door or to continue walking down the hall. Based on the player's decision, the game presents a segment of the video which is a scene of either continuing down the hall or the door opening and the player entering the room.

This technology has the potential for the development of new types of family assessment instruments which explore perceived parenting styles. In addition, the instrument would be able to test what the parents' response would be if their first response was not met with success. For example, the video may show a scene of a four year old child who is in a store throwing a temper tantrum. The parents are asked what they would do to handle the problem. The choices could be: (1) give in to what the child wants; (2) leave the store; (3) talk to the child; (4) spank the child. Based on their response the video would show a new scene. The video game/assessment could be programmed to repeat the scene to test what the parents' limits are and whether the parents change their strategies for dealing with the child when s/he does not respond to their first intervention. This type of instrument would also allow the investigator to look for differences in parenting styles based on the age of the child by repeating similar scenes but varying the age of the child.

A similar technique could be used to provide training for therapists. In this case the video image would be one of a family and the therapist would have to choose what intervention technique he would use at a particular point in the therapy. Based on the technique he used, the video would show the family's response to the intervention and the session would continue. Various levels of difficulty could be built into the program based on the experience level of the therapist.

One scene may first show a couple who are arguing. The therapist is given a choice to reframe the argument as passion or give an empathic response such as "You are both really angry." Based on the therapist's decision, the video would show differences in the responses a couple would make to the different interventions. For example, one possible response would be for the couple to agree to the reframe and begin to talk about the passion that they have for each other in different aspects of their lives.

This response would be at the simplest level of the program with the couple being an easy case for a beginning level therapist. For the most skilled therapist the video might give a response to reframing the argument as passion such as, "How can you call this passion—he has a mean streak in him a mile wide." At this point the therapist is asked to make another decision about the case, e.g., to refute the wife, side with her or give a new reframe.

This is the point at which the technology has the greatest potential for increasing the knowledge bases of the process of therapy. This type of project demands a rethinking of the way therapy is presented. It demands a specificity in the thinking of the therapist who is describing his/her therapy in much the same manner as books on chess describe the possible moves and countermoves in a chess game. One therapist who is currently thinking about his work in this manner is Pinsof (1984). He lists the behavior of the couple, the intervention he uses, what the possible reactions of the family are, and, based on the family's response, what is his next intervention.

Computer as Therapist

Since the development of ELIZA, a program which simulates a nondirective therapist, the issue has arisen whether the computer can act as a therapist, and if it can, whether it should. The initial reaction of the therapist is that it cannot be possible for a computer to manage the complexity or the "art" of therapy. One of the original developers of ELIZA does not believe the computer can do therapy. His reason for this is the computer's inability to be empathetic and to show that it can understand a person's problems (Weizenbaum, 1976). Since this paper is based on the computer technology that is *currently* available, the author would agree that this is accurate.

There are factors beyond the computer technology that prevent the computer from acting as a therapist. In order for the computer to act as a therapist, it would have to be programmed as an *expert system*. The expert systems that have been currently developed in other fields have the following characteristics. The first is that the possible solutions to the problem have to be narrowly defined. Secondly, there has to be a limited number of specified rules for making the decision. And finally, the amount of data necessary to make the decision has to be manageable. From an interactional view of family therapy, this would first entail specifying which interactional segments are important to change, extracting the meaning from the interaction and then acting on the meaning of the interactions in a manner to produce change. For example, the computer would first have to recognize a repeating pattern such as the parent consistently correcting a child in a coercive manner. Secondly, the computer would have to be able to recognize when this is being done correctly or incorrectly by the parent. Then, finally, it would have to intervene in a manner that would benefit both the parent and the child in the future. The knowledge base of family therapy is currently not at this level of theoretical development to become this specific.

Computers Teaching/Training

Even though the computer may not be able to be a therapist, this does not mean that the computer does not have a place in the therapeutic practice. As was suggested earlier in this volume by Olsen, Mead et al. and Constantine, the potential for its use in the development of a new class of diagnostic tools is tremendous. The potential to use the computer as a therapeutic aid has just begun to be explored, as described by Bostwick in this volume. Another example of this is Reitman's (1984) self-help program for men who are impotent. This program's goals are to change the clients cognitive set and to provide information to the clients that they may not have. The program goes on to suggest techniques that the clients may try to relieve the impotence.

As most therapists are aware, not all cases of male impotence can be solved by just giving information to the male of the couple without exploring the relationship aspects between the man and the woman. This is the task of the therapist, and correcting those aspects of the relationship that interfere with the sexuality of the couple is the therapist's role. In addition, for a therapist to use this program s/he must assume the client will not be resistant to viewing sexually oriented material. If the client is resistant to dealing with sexual matters, the therapist would have to first deal with the resistance to the task of using the program. Combined with a skilled therapist, this program can be a powerful tool in therapy.

Children

The computer is also useful as a tool with children. Two methods of using the computer with children have been described by Allen (1984) and Clarke and Schoech (1984). Allen has described the use of computer games as a safe method for children to bring affect to the surface that they may be unable to deal with directly. And Clarke and Schoech describe a game in which impulse control and attitudes were imbedded in the game.

The potential for the computer to be the focal point when developing social skills has been utilized by the author when working with siblings. The goal was to encourage cooperative behavior between the latency age siblings in a family where competition was the norm between the siblings in a family. The computer was used as a reinforcer around which they had to learn increasingly more complex modes of cooperative behavior in order for the machine to play a game. The author was the one who instructed the children in the specific skills they needed to exhibit in order to play on the machine, and the machine also provided reinforcement to the kids by congratulating them if the report from the parents was positive each week.

This required the author to write a short program each week in which the computer would applaud their progress based on the successful completion of tasks they had that week. They would then play a game which was chosen because it encouraged cooperation. If the task was not done, the machine gave a different message. The message would be that the machine was disappointed that they did not do the task. Because of this the computer would not be able to play with them and hopes that it would be able to on their next visit. The author felt, although he has no solid evidence to support this, that the kids became more concerned with the machine's response to their progress than the therapist's or the parents'. The children also appeared to not want to disappoint the machine and prevent it from being able to play with them.

FINAL NOTE

The power of the computer for a therapeutic practice is great because of the wide variety of tasks that it can perform. The machine can be a ledger to help manage office practice, it can interface with the outside world to rapidly share data and information, it can be a toy, etc. The computer's potential will in the future allow therapists to develop new tasks and apply them to the families that they see in their practices.

This will initially mean using the machine in a manner similar to what is currently being done. For example, simply translating paper and pencil tests to be given and scoring them on the computer makes it an expensive paper and pencil test. But as more machines are utilized by therapists, creative new usages for the computer will emerge. New usages will be developed to take advantage of the power of the machine. These usages may not mimic how therapy is currently practiced. Just as the transportation industry does not use legs for movement. Having either the computer or the therapist mimic current therapy practice prevents them both from enhancing the treatment of the client.

REFERENCES

Allen, D. H. (1984). The use of computer fantasy games in child therapy. In M. D. Schwartz (Ed.), *Using computers in clinical practice: Psychotherapy and mental health applications* (pp. 329-334). New York: The Haworth Press.

Clarke, B. and Schoech, D. (1984). A computer-assisted therapeutic game for adolescents: Initial development and comments. In M. D. Schwartz (Ed.), *Using computers in clinical practice: Psychotherapy and mental health applications* (pp. 335-354). New York: The Haworth Press.

Daynes, R. and Holder, S. (1984). Controlling videodiscs with micros. *Byte, 9,* 207-228.

DeMuth, P. (1984). Eliza and her offspring. In M. D. Schwartz (Ed.), *Using computers in clinical practice: Psychotherapy and mental health applications* (pp. 321-327). New York: The Haworth Press.

Jarvis, S. (1984). Videodiscs and computer. *Byte, 9,* 187-206.

Pinsoff, W. (1984). Integrated problem centered family therapy. Workshop presented at Indiana Assoc. of Marriage and Family Therapy, Indianapolis, IN.

Saba, G. (1984). Computers and family therapy: If you can't beat 'em. *Family Therapy News, 15,* 3, 7.

Reitman, R. (1984). The use of small computers in self-help sex therapy. In M. D. Schwartz (Ed.), *Using computers in clinical practice: Psychotherapy and mental health applications* (pp. 363-380). New York: The Haworth Press.

Weizenbaum, J. (1976). *Computer power and human reason,* San Francisco: W. H. Freeman.

Glossary

The language of computers is alien to most of us, including clinicians. At least a general understanding of the basic concepts is critical to your reading this collection. The following concepts are the most important:

ACCESS TIME is the time needed for the computer to locate certain data in the memory (either inside the computer or within a tape which stores the data).

ACOUSTIC COUPLER is a type of MODEM which uses a phone hand set, defined below.

ADDRESS is the identification (number or name) of a particular location in the memory.

ANALOG is a continuously variable value (e.g., voltage).

ALGORITHM is a set of steps for managing data or problems within a program.

ASSEMBLER LANGUAGE is a programming language specific to the microprocessor of the computer.

BASIC (*B*eginner's *A*ll-purpose *S*ymbolic *I*nstruction *C*ode) is the most commonly distributed microcomputer language.

BAUD RATE is the speed at which data are sent from one point to another (e.g., from one computer to another).

BENCHMARK is a computer program which allows the comparison of computing speeds on computers.

BINARY SYSTEM is a two-based number system, thus limited to two digits or symbols (most often 1 and 0).

BIT (*BI*nary digi*T*) is the basic unit of computer memory and has a value of either 1 or 0.

BOOT is to access and activate the software program.

BUBBLE MEMORY is a means of carrying data via tiny magnetized "bubbles."

BUFFER is a temporary, limited-capacity memory storage area/device which holds data in the process of being transferred between two areas/devices within the computer system.

BUG is a problem or error in computer hardware or software.

BYTE is a memory location which can store eight bits; a "word" in 8-bit computers.

CARTRIDGE is one or more memory chips contained in a case that is inserted into the computer.

CASSETTE DRIVE is data or software stored on audio cassette tape and fed into a computer by a audio cassette recorder.

CENTRAL PROCESSING UNIT (CPU) is key system of the computer which controls all primary functions; the "brains" of the computer.

CHIP is a microscopic piece of semiconductor component containing precisely designed electronic circuits.

COMMAND is a word or character that initiates some computer action.

COMPILER is a program which translates commands of various languages (e.g., BASIC) into the machine language used by the computer.

COMPUTER is a device that processes information. While analog computers process approximate information, digital computers process exact information.

197

CONCATENATION is the process of linking two things together (e.g., two software programs) compatible structures to make a larger one.

CONDITIONAL is a program instruction that specifies an action, such as a branch to another part of the program if a specified condition is reached (e.g., if the light is red then stop).

CP/M (Control Program for Microprocessors) is a trademark for a popular operating systems for microcomputers.

CPS is an abbreviation for characters per second.

CRT TERMINAL is a packaged or linked keyboard and cathode ray tube for input and output on a computer.

CURSOR is an indicator on a video screen where the next character or number will appear.

DAISY WHEEL PRINTER is a printer which utilizes a small, daisy flower-like wheel containing all the characters around its circumference. This is frequently referred to as a letter quality type of printer.

DATA are all types of information.

DATA BASE is an organized set of data amenable to quick sorting, searching, and analyzing.

DATA PROCESSING is the activities of the computer when it processes information (e.g., rearranges, manipulates, sorts, statistical analysis).

DBMS (Data Base Management System) is a program designed to manipulate the information sorted in a data base.

DEBUG is an effort to find and correct any programming error.

DECIMAL SYSTEM (in contrast to a binary system) is the most commonly used numbering system and is based on both the number and power of ten.

DECODE is the process by which the computer's CPU reads instructions stored in its memory.

DEFAULT is a value (e.g., a particular option or command in a program) which is chosen automatically in the absence of other instructions.

DISK like a cassette tape, is a circular plastic or metal magnetic surface which stores data and feeds data into the computer using a disk drive.

DISK DRIVE is a device which reads the data stored on the disk and feeds it into the computer.

DISK OPERATING SYSTEM (DOS) is a particular computer program that controls the disk drive(s).

DOCUMENTATION is the instruction manual for the computer or program.

DOT MATRIX PRINTER a printing machine that forms characters and numbers from patterns of tiny dots.

DUMB TERMINAL is a video display and keyboard which must depend on a computer to perform most operations; see SMART TERMINAL.

ELECTRONIC MAIL is a system of sending and receiving letters or messages between one computer and another via telephone lines.

FILE is a collection of information/data/messages under a designated name and stored on a disk or tape for future use.

FIRMWARE is software program used exclusively with one or more integrated circuits (IC) or ROMs (Read Only Memory), meaning the computer can only read (detect and follow commands) but cannot write (modify) to them.

FLOPPY DISK is a flexible plastic disk (in contrast to a hard disk); see DISK.

FLOWCHART is used to design computer program by charting a map of the course followed by the data through various steps in the program.

FORTRAN is derived from FORmula TRANslation and is a high level language used by computers.

FRICTION FEED is a method of feeding paper into a printer, similar to a typewriter.

FUNCTION KEY is one which issues particular instructions to the computer (e.g., underline, bold type), in contrast to the conventional keys which generate a single alphanumeric character.

GARBAGE is a slang term for bad, incorrect, or the wrong data.

GLICH is an unwanted/undesirable electrical pulse, caused by either a programming error or some environmental interference (e.g., via power lines), inside a digital computer causing program errors.

GRAPHICS is a computer-generated pictorial display on either the printer or the video monitor.

HARD COPY is the printed material generated by a computer program.

HARD DISK (in contrast to a floppy disk) is a means of storing a great deal of data, with faster access.

HARDWARE in contrast to software, are the physical components, the equipment of the computer.

HEXADECIMAL (in contrast to a binary and decimal system) is a number system with a base of 16 with digits 0-9 and A-F.

HIGH LEVEL LANGUAGE is a computer language which is composed of words, symbols and syntaxes more easily understood by people (e.g., FORTRAN, BASIC).

I/O is a data input-output component used to load information into a computer and to read information from the computer.

INPUT PERIPHERAL is any device (e.g., keyboards, joysticks) designed to transfer information into a computer.

INTELLIGENT TERMINAL (i.e., smart terminal) is a terminal which is generally self-contained with the necessary internal software to operate most programs.

INTERFACE is a component which enables two other components in a computing system to operate together.

JOYSTICK is often used in video games to move various animated figures around the video screen.

K (kilo-) is an indication of a computer's information memory capability which equals 1024 bytes of information (i.e., 8K = 8192 storable pieces of information).

LIGHT PEN is a pen-like device held to a computer video screen which can create graphics and transfer it into the computer for analysis and recreation.

LOOP is a sequence of computer programming instructions that are executed repeatedly until one or more specified conditions have been met (e.g., statistical analysis).

LOW-LEVEL LANGUAGE is the language the computer understands (e.g., binary coding).

MACHINE LANGUAGE is the *particular* pattern of binary coding required for a particular device (e.g., printer).

MENU is a list of user choices displayed from a computer program.

MICROCOMPUTER is a small computer system using semiconductor chip technology in which the CPU is a microprocessor which includes only one or two chips.

MODEM (MOdulator DEModulator) is a component which serves as an interface between one computer and another through a telephone and/or telephone line.

OPERATING SYSTEM is set of software programs (e.g., PC-DOS) to enable the computer to operate.

OUTPUT PERIPHERAL is a device (e.g., video monitors, printers) designed to receive signals from a computer.

PARITY is a mathematical verification of accurate transmission of data.

PASCAL is a powerful and sophisticated language designed for business and general purposes.

PERSONAL COMPUTER (PC) or home computer is a basic, low-cost microcomputer.

PLOTTER is a device that produces an inked drawing of graphic patterns or text.

PROCESSOR is a digital computer.

PROGRAM is a coded set of instructions which tells the computer to do specific tasks.

PROMPT is a message to the user about an error (e.g., "program not available") or instruction (e.g., insert diskette).

RANDOM-ACCESS MEMORY (RAM) is the memory contained within the computer for read and write operations.

READ-ONLY MEMORY (ROM) is a form of RAM which programs the computer for specific operations and cannot be changed.

RF MODULATOR is an electronic circuit that enables the use of a television set to serve as a computer video monitor.

SMART TERMINAL. See INTELLIGENT TERMINAL.

SOFTWARE are programs and their documentation.

STRING is a sequence of data set items (e.g., addresses).

SUBROUTINE is one or more sequential instructions in a computer program.

TABLE is an index of values or variables within a program.

TERMINAL is a component which includes a keyboard, printer, and video display and can enter and access data.

TEXT EDITOR is a program which permits access to the contents of the computer's memory.

VOICE SYNTHESIZER is an electronic circuit that simulates the human voice.

WORD PROCESSOR is a program for writing texts (e.g., letters, manuscripts) and permits easy editing.